Learning Network Programming with Java

Harness the hidden power of Java to build
network-enabled applications with lower network
traffic and faster processes

Richard M Reese

[PACKT] open source✱
PUBLISHING   community experience distilled

BIRMINGHAM - MUMBAI

Learning Network Programming with Java

Copyright © 2015 Packt Publishing

First published: December 2015

Production reference: 1141215

Published by Packt Publishing Ltd.
Livery Place
35 Livery Street
Birmingham B3 2PB, UK.
ISBN 978-1-78588-547-1

www.packtpub.com

Credits

Author
Richard M Reese

Reviewer
Daniel MÜHLBACHLER

Commissioning Editor
Veena Pagare

Acquisition Editors
Vivek Anantharaman

Rahul Nair

Content Development Editor
Arshiya Ayaz Umer

Technical Editor
Humera Shaikh

Copy Editor
Priyanka Ravi

Project Coordinator
Shipra Chawhan

Proofreader
Safis Editing

Indexer
Monica Ajmera Mehta

Production Coordinator
Nilesh Mohite

Cover Work
Nilesh Mohite

About the Author

Richard M Reese has worked in both industry and academia. For 17 years, he worked in the telephone and aerospace industries, serving in several capacities, including research and development, software development, supervision, and training. He currently teaches at Tarleton State University, where he has the opportunity to apply his years of industry experience to enhance his teaching.

Richard has written several Java books and a C Pointer book. He uses a concise and easy-to-follow approach to topics at hand. His Java books have addressed EJB 3.1, updates to Java 7 and 8, certification, functional programming, jMonkeyEngine, and natural language processing.

I would like to thank my daughter, Jennifer, for her numerous reviews and contributions; my wife, Karla, for her continued support; and to the staff of Packt for their work in making this a better book.

About the Reviewer

Daniel MÜHLBACHLER got interested in computer science shortly after entering high school, where he later developed web applications as part of a scholarship system for outstanding pupils.

He has a profound knowledge of web development (PHP, HTML, CSS/LESS, and AngularJS), and has worked with a variety of other programming languages and systems, such as Java/Groovy, Grails, Objective-C and Swift, Matlab, C (with Cilk), Node.js, and Linux servers.

Furthermore, he works with some database management systems based on SQL, and also some NoSQL systems, such as MongoDB, and SOLR. This is also reflected in several projects that he is currently involved in at Catalysts GmbH.

After studying abroad as an exchange student in the United Kingdom, he completed his bachelor's degree at Johannes Kepler University in Linz, Austria, with a thesis on aerosol satellite data processing for mobile visualization. This is where he also became familiar with processing large amounts of data.

Daniel enjoys solving challenging problems and is always keen on working with new technologies, especially related to the fields of big data, functional programming, optimization, and NoSQL databases.

More detailed information about his experience, as well as his contact details, can be found at www.muehlbachler.org and www.linkedin.com/in/danielmuehlbachler.

www.PacktPub.com

Support files, eBooks, discount offers, and more

For support files and downloads related to your book, please visit www.PacktPub.com.

Did you know that Packt offers eBook versions of every book published, with PDF and ePub files available? You can upgrade to the eBook version at www.PacktPub.com and as a print book customer, you are entitled to a discount on the eBook copy. Get in touch with us at service@packtpub.com for more details.

At www.PacktPub.com, you can also read a collection of free technical articles, sign up for a range of free newsletters and receive exclusive discounts and offers on Packt books and eBooks.

https://www2.packtpub.com/books/subscription/packtlib

Do you need instant solutions to your IT questions? PacktLib is Packt's online digital book library. Here, you can search, access, and read Packt's entire library of books.

Why subscribe?

- Fully searchable across every book published by Packt
- Copy and paste, print, and bookmark content
- On demand and accessible via a web browser

Free access for Packt account holders

If you have an account with Packt at www.PacktPub.com, you can use this to access PacktLib today and view 9 entirely free books. Simply use your login credentials for immediate access.

Table of Contents

Preface

The world is becoming interconnected on an unprecedented scale with more services being provided on the Internet. Applications ranging from business transactions to embedded applications, such as those found in refrigerators, are connecting to the Internet. With isolated applications no longer being the norm, it is becoming increasingly important for applications to be network enabled.

The goal of this book is to provide the reader with the necessary skills to develop Java applications that connect and work with other applications and services across a network. You will be introduced to a wide range of networking options that are available using Java, which will enable you to develop applications using the appropriate technology for the task at hand.

What this book covers

Chapter 1, Getting Started with Network Programming, introduces the essential network terminology and concepts. The networking support that Java provides is illustrated with brief examples. A simple client/server application is presented along with a threaded version of the server.

Chapter 2, Network Addressing, explains how nodes on a network use addresses. How Java represents these addresses is introduced along with support for IPv4 and IPv6. This chapter also covers how Java can configure various network properties.

Chapter 3, NIO Support for Networking, explains how the NIO package provides support for communication using buffers and channels. These techniques are illustrated with a client/server application. The support that NIO provides for asynchronous communication is also demonstrated.

Chapter 4, Client/Server Development, covers how HTTP is an important and widely-used protocol. Java provides support for this protocol in a variety of ways. These techniques are illustrated along with a demonstration of how cookies are handled in Java.

Chapter 5, Peer-to-Peer Networks, discusses how peer-to-peer networks provide a flexible alternative to the traditional client/server architecture. The basic peer-to-peer concepts are introduced along with demonstrations of how Java supports this architecture. FreePastry is used to illustrate one open source peer-to-peer solution framework.

Chapter 6, UDP and Multicasting, explains how UDP is an alternative to TCP. It provides a less reliable but more efficient way for applications to communicate across the Internet. Java's extensive support for this protocol is demonstrated, including NIO support, and how UDP can support streaming media.

Chapter 7, Network Scalability, explains how, as more demands are placed on a server, systems need to scale to address these demands. Several threading techniques supporting this need are demonstrated, including thread pools, futures, and the NIO's selector.

Chapter 8, Network Security, discusses how applications need to protect against a variety of threats. This is supported in Java using encryption and secure hashing techniques. Symmetric and asymmetric encryption techniques are illustrated. In addition, the use of TLS/SSL is demonstrated.

Chapter 9, Network Interoperability, covers how Java applications may need to exchange information with other applications that are written in different languages. The issues that impact an application's interoperability are examined, including byte order. Communication between different implementations is demonstrated using sockets and middleware.

What you need for this book

Java SDK 1.8 is needed for the network programming examples that are encountered in the book. An IDE, such as NetBeans or Eclipse, is recommended. NetBeans IDE 8.0.2 EE edition is used to illustrate the development of a web service.

Who this book is for

This book is for developers who are already proficient in Java and want to learn how to develop network-enabled Java applications. Familiarity with basic Java and object-oriented programming concepts is all that is needed. You will learn the basics of network programming and how to use a multitude of different sockets to create secure and scalable applications.

Conventions

In this book, you will find a number of text styles that distinguish between different kinds of information. Here are some examples of these styles and an explanation of their meaning.

Code words in text, database table names, folder names, filenames, file extensions, pathnames, dummy URLs, user input, and Twitter handles are shown as follows: "The SSLSocketFactory class' getDefault returns an SSLSocketFactory instance whose createSocket creates a socket that is connected to the secure echo server."

A block of code is set as follows:

```
public class ThreadedEchoServer implements Runnable {
    private static Socket clientSocket;

    public ThreadedEchoServer(Socket clientSocket) {
        this.clientSocket = clientSocket;
    }
    ...
}
```

Any command-line input or output is written as follows:

```
Enter keystore password:
Re-enter new password:
What is your first and last name?
  [Unknown]:  First Last
What is the name of your organizational unit?
  [Unknown]:  packt
What is the name of your organization?
  [Unknown]:  publishing
What is the name of your City or Locality?
  [Unknown]:  home
```

```
What is the name of your State or Province?
   [Unknown]:  calm
What is the two-letter country code for this unit?
   [Unknown]:  me
Is CN=First Last, OU=packt, O=publishing, L=home, ST=calm, C=me correct?
   [no]:  y


Enter key password for <mykey>
        (RETURN if same as keystore password):
```

New terms and **important words** are shown in bold. Words that you see on the screen, for example, in menus or dialog boxes, appear in the text like this: "Once NetBeans has been installed, start it and then create a new project from the **File | New Project...** menu item."

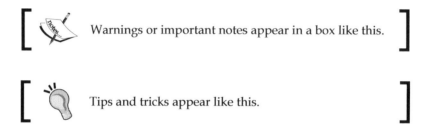

Warnings or important notes appear in a box like this.

Tips and tricks appear like this.

Reader feedback

Feedback from our readers is always welcome. Let us know what you think about this book—what you liked or disliked. Reader feedback is important for us as it helps us develop titles that you will really get the most out of.

To send us general feedback, simply e-mail feedback@packtpub.com, and mention the book's title in the subject of your message.

If there is a topic that you have expertise in and you are interested in either writing or contributing to a book, see our author guide at www.packtpub.com/authors.

Customer support

Now that you are the proud owner of a Packt book, we have a number of things to help you to get the most from your purchase.

Downloading the example code

You can download the example code files from your account at `http://www.packtpub.com` for all the Packt Publishing books you have purchased. If you purchased this book elsewhere, you can visit `http://www.packtpub.com/support` and register to have the files e-mailed directly to you.

Downloading the color images of this book

We also provide you with a PDF file that has color images of the screenshots/diagrams used in this book. The color images will help you better understand the changes in the output. You can download this file from: `https://www.packtpub.com/sites/default/files/downloads/LearningNetworkProgrammingwithJava_Graphics.pdf`.

Errata

Although we have taken every care to ensure the accuracy of our content, mistakes do happen. If you find a mistake in one of our books—maybe a mistake in the text or the code—we would be grateful if you could report this to us. By doing so, you can save other readers from frustration and help us improve subsequent versions of this book. If you find any errata, please report them by visiting `http://www.packtpub.com/submit-errata`, selecting your book, clicking on the **Errata Submission Form** link, and entering the details of your errata. Once your errata are verified, your submission will be accepted and the errata will be uploaded to our website or added to any list of existing errata under the Errata section of that title.

To view the previously submitted errata, go to `https://www.packtpub.com/books/content/support` and enter the name of the book in the search field. The required information will appear under the **Errata** section.

Piracy

Piracy of copyrighted material on the Internet is an ongoing problem across all media. At Packt, we take the protection of our copyright and licenses very seriously. If you come across any illegal copies of our works in any form on the Internet, please provide us with the location address or website name immediately so that we can pursue a remedy.

Please contact us at copyright@packtpub.com with a link to the suspected pirated material.

We appreciate your help in protecting our authors and our ability to bring you valuable content.

Questions

If you have a problem with any aspect of this book, you can contact us at questions@packtpub.com, and we will do our best to address the problem.

1
Getting Started with Network Programming

Access to networks (the Internet in particular) is becoming an important and often necessary feature of applications. Applications frequently need to access and provide services. As the **Internet of Things (IoT)** connects more and more devices, understanding how to access networks becomes crucial.

The important factors that have been the driving forces for more network applications include the availability of faster networks with greater bandwidth. This has made it possible to transmit wider ranges of data, such as video streams. In recent years, we have seen an increase in connectivity, whether it has been for new services, more extensive social interactions, or games. Knowing how to develop network applications is an important development skill.

In this chapter, we will cover the basics of Network programming:

- Why networking is important
- The support that Java provides
- Simple programs to address basic network operations
- Basic networking terminology
- A simple server/client application
- Using a thread to support a server

Throughout this book, you will be exposed to many network concepts, ideas, patterns, and implementation strategies using both older and newer Java technologies. Network connections occur at a low level using sockets, and at a much higher level using a multitude of protocols. Communications can be synchronous requiring careful coordination of requests and responses, or they can be asynchronous where other activities are performed until the response has been submitted.

These and other concepts are addressed through a series of chapters, each focusing on a specific topic. The chapters complement each other by elaborating on concepts that were previously introduced, whenever possible. Numerous code examples are used whenever possible to further your understanding of the topic.

Central to accessing a service is knowing or discovering its address. This address may be human readable, such as www.packtpub.com, or in the form of an **IP** address such as 83.166.169.231. **Internet Protocol (IP)** is a low-level addressing scheme that is used to access information on the Internet. Addressing has long used IPv4 to access resources. However, these addresses are all but gone. The newer IPv6 is available to provide a larger range of addresses. The basics of network addressing and how they can be managed in Java is the focus of *Chapter 2, Network Addressing*.

The intent of network communication is to transfer information to and from other applications. This is facilitated using buffers and channels. Buffers hold information temporarily until it can be processed by an application. Channels are an abstraction that simplifies communications between applications. The NIO and NIO.2 packages provide much of the support for buffers and channels. We will explore these techniques along with other techniques, such as blocking and non-blocking IO, in *Chapter 3, NIO Support for Networking*.

Services are provided by servers. An example of this is the simple echo server, which retransmits what it was sent. More sophisticated servers, such as HTTP servers, can support extensive services to meet a wide range of needs. The client/server model and its Java support are covered in *Chapter 3, NIO Support for Networking*.

Another service model is the **peer-to-peer (P2P)** model. In this architecture, there is no central server, but rather a network of applications that communicate to provide a service. This model is represented by applications, such as BitTorrent, Skype, and BBC's iPlayer. While much of the support that is required for the development of these types of applications is beyond the scope of this book, *Chapter 4, Client/Server Development*, explores P2P issues and the support provided by Java and JXTA.

IP is used at a low level to send and receive packets of information across a network. We will also demonstrate the use of **User Datagram Protocol (UDP)** and **Transmission Control Protocol (TCP)** communication protocols. These protocols are layered on top of IP. UDP is used to broadcast short packets or messages with no guarantee of reliable delivery. TCP is used more commonly and provides a higher level of service than that of UDP. We will cover the use of these related technologies in *Chapter 5, Peer-to-Peer Networks*.

A service will often be faced with varying levels of demand placed on it due to a number of factors. Its load may vary by the time of the day. As it becomes more popular, its overall demand will also increase. The server will need to scale to meet increases and decreases in its load. Threads and thread pools have been used to support this effort. These and other technologies are the focus of *Chapter 6, UDP and Multicasting*.

Increasingly, applications need to be secure against attacks by hackers. When it is connected to a network, this threat increases. In *Chapter 7, Network Scalability*, we will explore many of the techniques available to support secure Java applications. Among these is the **Secure Socket Level (SSL)**, and how Java supports it.

Applications rarely work in isolation. Hence, they need to use networks to access other applications. However, not all applications are written in Java. Networking with these applications can pose special problems ranging from how the bytes of a data type are organized to the interface supported by the application. It is common to work with specialized protocols, such as HTTP, and WSDL. The last chapter of this book examines these issues from a Java perspective.

We will demonstrate both older and newer Java technologies. Understanding the older technologies may be necessary in order to maintain older code, and it can provide insight into why the newer technologies were developed. We will also complement our examples using many of the Java 8 functional programming techniques. Using Java 8 examples along with pre-Java 8 implementations, we can learn how to use Java 8 and be better informed as to when it can and should be used.

It is not the intent to fully explain the newer Java 8 technologies, such as lambda expressions, and streams. However, the use of Java 8 examples will provide an insight into how they can be used to support networked applications.

The remainder of this chapter touches on many of the network technologies that are explored in this book. You will be introduced to the basics of these techniques, and you should find them easy to understand. However, there are a few places where time does not permit us to fully explore and explain these concepts. These issues will be addressed in subsequent chapters. So, let's begin our exploration with network addressing.

Network addressing using the InetAddress class

An IP address is represented by the `InetAddress` class. Addresses can be either unicast where it identifies a specific address, or it can be multicast, where a message is sent to more than one address.

The `InetAddress` class has no public constructors. To get an instance, use one of the several static get type methods. For example, the `getByName` method takes a string representing the address as shown next. The string in this case is a **Uniform Resource Locator (URL)**:

```
InetAddress address =
    InetAddress.getByName("www.packtpub.com");
System.out.println(address);
```

Downloading the example code

You can download the example code files for all Packt books you have purchased from your account at `http://www.packtpub.com`. If you purchased this book elsewhere, you can visit `http://www.packtpub.com/support` and register to have the files e-mailed directly to you.

This will display the following results:

www.packtpub.com/83.166.169.231

The number attached to the end of the name is the IP address. This address uniquely identifies an entity on the Internet.

If we need other information about the address, we can use one of several methods, as illustrated here:

```
System.out.println("CanonicalHostName: "
    + address.getCanonicalHostName());
System.out.println("HostAddress: " +
    address.getHostAddress());
System.out.println("HostName: " + address.getHostName());
```

This produces the following output when executed:

CanonicalHostName: 83.166.169.231

HostAddress: 83.166.169.231

HostName: www.packtpub.com

To test to see whether this address is reachable, use the `isReachable` method as shown next. Its argument specifies how long to wait before deciding that the address cannot be reached. The argument is the number of milliseconds to wait:

```
address.isReachable(10000);
```

There are also the `Inet4Address` and `Inet6Address` classes that support IPv4 and IPv6 addresses, respectively. We will explain their use in *Chapter 2, Network Addressing*.

Once we have obtained an address, we can use it to support network access, such as with servers. Before we demonstrate its use in this context, let's examine how we can obtain and process data from a connection.

NIO support

The `java.io`, `java.nio`, and `java.nio` subpackages provide most of the Java support for IO processing. We will examine the support that these packages provide for network access in *Chapter 3, NIO Support for Networking*. Here, we will focus on the basic aspects of the `java.nio` package.

There are three key concepts used in the NIO package:

- **Channel**: This represents a stream of data between applications
- **Buffer**: This works with a channel to process data
- **Selector**: This is a technology that allows a single thread to handle multiple channels

A channel and a buffer are typically associated with each other. Data may be transferred from a channel to a buffer or from a buffer to a channel. The buffer, as its name implies, is a temporary repository for information. The selector is useful in supporting application scalability, and this will be discussed in *Chapter 7, Network Scalability*.

There are four primary channels:

- `FileChannel`: This works with a file
- `DatagramChannel`: This supports UDP communications
- `SocketChannel`: This is used with a TCP client
- `ServerSocketChannel`: This is used with a TCP server

There are several buffer classes that support primitive data types, such as character, integer, and float.

Using the URLConnection class

A simple way of accessing a server is to use the `URLConnection` class. This class represents a connection between an application and a `URL` instance. A `URL` instance represents a resource on the Internet.

In the next example, a URL instance is created for the Google website. Using the URL class' openConnection method, a URLConnection instance is created. A BufferedReader instance is used to read lines from the connection that is then displayed:

```
try {
    URL url = new URL("http://www.google.com");
    URLConnection urlConnection = url.openConnection();
    BufferedReader br = new BufferedReader(
            new InputStreamReader(
                urlConnection.getInputStream()));
    String line;
    while ((line = br.readLine()) != null) {
        System.out.println(line);
    }
    br.close();
} catch (IOException ex) {
    // Handle exceptions
}
```

The output is rather lengthy, so only part of the first line is shown here:

<!doctype html><html itemscope="" itemtype="http://schema.org/WebPage" ...

The URLConnection class hides some of the complexity of accessing HTTP servers.

Using the URLConnection class with buffers and channels

We can rework the previous example to illustrate the use of channels and buffers. The URLConnection instance is created as before. We will create a ReadableByteChannel instance and then a ByteBuffer instance, as illustrated in the next example. The ReadableByteChannel instance allows us to read from the site using its read method. A ByteBuffer instance receives data from the channel and is used as the argument of the read method. The buffer created holds 64 bytes at a time.

The read method returns the number of bytes read. The ByteBuffer class' array method returns an array of bytes, which is used as the argument of the String class' constructor. This is used to display the data read. The clear method is used to reset the buffer so that it can be used again:

```
try {
    URL url = new URL("http://www.google.com");
    URLConnection urlConnection = url.openConnection();
```

```
        InputStream inputStream = urlConnection.getInputStream();
        ReadableByteChannel channel =
            Channels.newChannel(inputStream);
        ByteBuffer buffer = ByteBuffer.allocate(64);
        String line = null;
        while (channel.read(buffer) > 0) {
            System.out.println(new String(buffer.array()));
            buffer.clear();
        }
        channel.close();
    } catch (IOException ex) {
        // Handle exceptions
    }
```

The first line of output is shown next. This produces the same output as before, but it is restricted to displaying 64 bytes at a time:

<!doctype html><html itemscope="" itemtype="http://schema.org/We

The `Channel` class and its derived classes provide an improved technique to access data found on a network than data provided by older technologies. We will be seeing more of this class.

The client/server architecture

There are several ways of creating servers using Java. We will illustrate a couple of simple approaches and postpone a detailed discussion of these techniques until *Chapter 4, Client/Server Development*. Both a client and a server will be created.

A server is installed on a machine with an IP address. It is possible for more than one server to be running on a machine at any given time. When the operating system receives a request for a service on a machine, it will also receive a port number. The port number will identify the server to where the request should be forwarded. A server is, thus, identified by its combination of IP address and port number.

Typically, a client will issue a request to a server. The server will receive the request and send back a response. The nature of the request/response and the protocol used for communication is dependent on the client/server. Sometimes a well-documented protocol, such as the **Hypertext Transfer Protocol (HTTP)**, is used. For simpler architectures, a series of text messages are sent back and forth.

For the server to communicate with an application making a request, specialized software is used to send and receive messages. This software is called a socket. One socket is found on the client side, and the other socket is located on the server side. When they connect, communication is possible. There are several different types of sockets. These include datagram sockets; stream sockets, which frequently use TCP; and raw sockets, which normally work at the IP level. We will focus on TCP sockets for our client/server application.

Specifically, we will create a simple echo server. This server will receive a text message from a client and will immediately send it back to that client. The simplicity of this server allows us to focus on the client-server basics.

Creating a simple echo server

We will start with the definition of the SimpleEchoServer class as shown next. In the main method, an initial server message will be displayed:

```
public class SimpleEchoServer {
    public static void main(String[] args) {
        System.out.println("Simple Echo Server");
        ...
    }
}
```

The remainder of the method's body consists of a series of try blocks to handle exceptions. In the first try block, a ServerSocket instance is created using 6000 as its parameter. The ServerSocket class is a specialized socket that is used by a server to listen for client requests. Its argument is its port number. The IP of the machine on which the server is located is not necessarily of interest to the server, but the client will ultimately need to know this IP address.

In the next code sequence, an instance of the ServerSocket class is created and its accept method is called. The ServerSocket will block this call until it receives a request from a client. Blocking means that the program is suspended until the method returns. When a request is received, the accept method will return a Socket class instance, which represents the connection between that client and the server. They can now send and receive messages:

```
try (ServerSocket serverSocket = new ServerSocket(6000)){
    System.out.println("Waiting for connection.....");
    Socket clientSocket = serverSocket.accept();
    System.out.println("Connected to client");
    ...
```

```
    } catch (IOException ex) {
        // Handle exceptions
    }
```

After this client socket has been created, we can process the message sent to the server. As we are dealing with text, we will use a `BufferedReader` instance to read the message from the client. This is created using the client socket's `getInputStream` method. We will use a `PrintWriter` instance to reply to the client. This is created using the client socket's `getOutputStream` method, shown as follows:

```
    try (BufferedReader br = new BufferedReader(
            new InputStreamReader(
            clientSocket.getInputStream()));
        PrintWriter out = new PrintWriter(
            clientSocket.getOutputStream(), true)) {

        ...
        }
    }
```

The second argument to the `PrintWriter` constructor is set to `true`. This means that text sent using the `out` object will automatically be flushed after each use.

When text is written to a socket, it will sit in a buffer until either the buffer is full or a flush method is called. Performing automatic flushing saves us from having to remember to flush the buffer, but it can result in excessive flushing, whereas a single flush issued after the last write is performed, will also do.

The next code segment completes the server. The `readLine` method reads a line at a time from the client. This text is displayed and then sent back to the client using the `out` object:

```
    String inputLine;
    while ((inputLine = br.readLine()) != null) {
        System.out.println("Server: " + inputLine);
        out.println(inputLine);
    }
```

Before we demonstrate the server in action, we need to create a client application to use with it.

Creating a simple echo client

We start with the declaration of a `SimpleEchoClient` class where in the `main` method, a message is displayed indicating the application's start that is shown as follows:

```
public class SimpleEchoClient {
    public static void main(String args[]) {
        System.out.println("Simple Echo Client");
        ...
    }
}
```

A `Socket` instance needs to be created to connect to the server. In the following example, it is assumed that the server and the client are running on the same machine. The `InetAddress` class' static `getLocalHost` method returns this address, which is then used in the `Socket` class's constructor along with port `6000`. If they are located on different machines, then the server's address needs to be used instead. As with the server, an instance of the `PrintWriter` and `BufferedReader` classes are created to allow text to be sent to and from the server:

```
try {
    System.out.println("Waiting for connection.....");
    InetAddress localAddress = InetAddress.getLocalHost();

    try (Socket clientSocket = new Socket(localAddress, 6000);
                PrintWriter out = new PrintWriter(
                    clientSocket.getOutputStream(), true);
                BufferedReader br = new BufferedReader(
                    new InputStreamReader(
                    clientSocket.getInputStream())))) {
        ...
    }
} catch (IOException ex) {
    // Handle exceptions
}
```

Localhost refers to the current machine. This has a specific IP address: `127.0.0.1`. While a machine may be associated with an additional IP address, every machine can reach itself using this localhost address.

The user is then prompted to enter text. If the text is the quit command, then the infinite loop is terminated, and the application shuts down. Otherwise, the text is sent to the server using the out object. When the reply is returned, it is displayed as shown next:

```
System.out.println("Connected to server");
Scanner scanner = new Scanner(System.in);
while (true) {
    System.out.print("Enter text: ");
    String inputLine = scanner.nextLine();
    if ("quit".equalsIgnoreCase(inputLine)) {
        break;
    }
    out.println(inputLine);
    String response = br.readLine();
    System.out.println("Server response: " + response);
}
```

These programs can be implemented as two separate projects or within a single project. Either way, start the server first and then start the client. When the server starts, you will see the following displayed:

Simple Echo Server

Waiting for connection.....

When the client starts, you will see the following:

Simple Echo Client

Waiting for connection.....

Connected to server

Enter text:

Enter a message, and watch how the client and the server interact. The following is one possible series of input from the client's perspective:

Enter text: Hello server

Server response: Hello server

Enter text: Echo this!

Server response: Echo this!

Enter text: quit

The server's output is shown here after the client has entered the `quit` command:

Simple Echo Server

Waiting for connection.....

Connected to client

Client request: Hello server

Client request: Echo this!

This is one approach to implement the client and server. We will enhance this implementation in later chapters.

Using Java 8 to support the echo server and client

We will be providing examples of using many of the newer Java 8 features throughout this book. Here, we will show you alternative implementations of the previous echo server and client applications.

The server uses a while loop to process a client's request as duplicated here:

```
String inputLine;
while ((inputLine = br.readLine()) != null) {
    System.out.println("Client request: " + inputLine);
    out.println(inputLine);
}
```

We can use the `Supplier` interface in conjunction with a `Stream` object to perform the same operation. The next statement uses a lambda expression to return a string from the client:

```
Supplier<String> socketInput = () -> {
    try {
        return br.readLine();
    } catch (IOException ex) {
        return null;
    }
};
```

An infinite stream is generated from the `Supplier` instance. The following `map` method gets input from the user and then sends it to the server. When `quit` is entered, the stream will terminate. The `allMatch` method is a short-circuit method, and when its argument evaluates to `false`, the stream is terminated:

```
Stream<String> stream = Stream.generate(socketInput);
stream
        .map(s -> {
            System.out.println("Client request: " + s);
            out.println(s);
            return s;
        })
        .allMatch(s -> s != null);
```

While this implementation is lengthier than the traditional implementation, it can provide more succinct and simple solutions to more complex problems.

On the client side, we can replace the while loop as duplicated here with a functional implementation:

```
while (true) {
    System.out.print("Enter text: ");
    String inputLine = scanner.nextLine();
    if ("quit".equalsIgnoreCase(inputLine)) {
        break;
    }
    out.println(inputLine);

    String response = br.readLine();
    System.out.println("Server response: " + response);
}
```

The functional solution also uses a `Supplier` instance to capture console input as shown here:

```
Supplier<String> scannerInput = () -> scanner.next();
```

An infinite stream is generated, as shown next, with a `map` method providing the equivalent functionality:

```
System.out.print("Enter text: ");
Stream.generate(scannerInput)
    .map(s -> {
        out.println(s);
        System.out.println("Server response: " + s);
        System.out.print("Enter text: ");
```

```
        return s;
    })
    .allMatch(s -> !"quit".equalsIgnoreCase(s));
```

A functional approach is often a better solution to many problems.

Note that an additional prompt, **Enter text:**, was displayed on the client side after the `quit` command was entered. This is easily corrected by not displaying the prompt if the `quit` command was entered. This correction is left as an exercise for the reader.

UDP and multicasting

Multicasting is a useful technique to use if you need to send messages to a group on a periodic basis. It uses a UDP server and one or more UDP clients. To illustrate this capability, we will create a simple time server. The server will send a date and time string to clients every second.

Multicasting will send an identical message to every member of a group. A group is identified by a multicast address. A multicast address must use the following IP address range: `224.0.0.0` through `239.255.255.255`. The server will send a message mark with this address. Clients must join the group before they can receive any multicast messages.

Creating a multicast server

A `MulticastServer` class is declared next, where a `DatagramSocket` instance is created. The try-catch blocks will handle exceptions as they occur:

```
public class MulticastServer {
    public static void main(String args[]) {
        System.out.println("Multicast  Time Server");
        DatagramSocket serverSocket = null;
        try {
            serverSocket = new DatagramSocket();
            ...
            }
        } catch (SocketException ex) {
            // Handle exception
        } catch (IOException ex) {
            // Handle exception
        }
    }
}
```

The body of the try block uses an infinite loop to create an array of bytes to hold the current date and time. Next, an `InetAddress` instance representing the multicast group is created. Using the array and the group address, a `DatagramPacket` is instantiated and used as an argument to the `DatagramSocket` class' `send` method. The data and time sent is then displayed. The server then pauses for one second:

```
while (true) {
    String dateText = new Date().toString();
    byte[] buffer = new byte[256];
    buffer = dateText.getBytes();

    InetAddress group = InetAddress.getByName("224.0.0.0");
    DatagramPacket packet;
    packet = new DatagramPacket(buffer, buffer.length,
        group, 8888);
    serverSocket.send(packet);
    System.out.println("Time sent: " + dateText);

    try {
        Thread.sleep(1000);
    } catch (InterruptedException ex) {
        // Handle exception
    }
}
```

This server only broadcasts messages. It never receives messages from a client.

Creating the multicast client

The client is created using the following `MulticastClient` class. In order to receive a message, the client must use the same group address and port number. Before it can receive messages, it must join the group using the `joinGroup` method. In this implementation, it receives 5 date and time messages, displays them, and then terminates. The `trim` method removes leading and trailing white space, from a string. Otherwise, all 256 bytes of the message will be displayed:

```
public class MulticastClient {
    public static void main(String args[]) {
        System.out.println("Multicast  Time Client");
        try (MulticastSocket socket = new MulticastSocket(8888)) {
            InetAddress group =
                InetAddress.getByName("224.0.0.0");
            socket.joinGroup(group);
            System.out.println("Multicast  Group Joined");
```

```
        byte[] buffer = new byte[256];
        DatagramPacket packet =
            new DatagramPacket(buffer, buffer.length);

        for (int i = 0; i < 5; i++) {
            socket.receive(packet);
            String received = new String(packet.getData());
            System.out.println(received.trim());
        }

        socket.leaveGroup(group);
    } catch (IOException ex) {
        // Handle exception
    }
    System.out.println("Multicast  Time Client Terminated");
    }
}
```

When the server is started, the messages sent are displayed as shown here:

Multicast Time Server

Time sent: Thu Jul 09 13:19:49 CDT 2015

Time sent: Thu Jul 09 13:19:50 CDT 2015

Time sent: Thu Jul 09 13:19:51 CDT 2015

Time sent: Thu Jul 09 13:19:52 CDT 2015

Time sent: Thu Jul 09 13:19:53 CDT 2015

Time sent: Thu Jul 09 13:19:54 CDT 2015

Time sent: Thu Jul 09 13:19:55 CDT 2015

...

The client output will look similar to the following:

Multicast Time Client

Multicast Group Joined

Thu Jul 09 13:19:50 CDT 2015

Thu Jul 09 13:19:51 CDT 2015

Thu Jul 09 13:19:52 CDT 2015

Thu Jul 09 13:19:53 CDT 2015

Thu Jul 09 13:19:54 CDT 2015

Multicast Time Client Terminated

 If the example is executed on a Mac, you may receive an exception indicating that it cannot assign the requested address. This can be fixed by using the JVM option `-Djava.net.preferIPv4Stack=true`.

There are numerous other multicast capabilities, which will be explored in *Chapter 6, UDP and Multicasting*.

Scalability

When the demand on a server increases and decreases, it is desirable to change the resources dedicated to the server. The options available range from the use of manual threads to allow concurrent behavior to those embedded in specialized classes to handle thread pools and NIO channels.

Creating a threaded server

In this section, we will use threads to augment our simple echo server. The definition of the `ThreadedEchoServer` class is as follows. It implements the `Runnable` interface to create a new thread for each connection. The private `Socket` variable will hold the client socket for a specific thread:

```
public class ThreadedEchoServer implements Runnable {
    private static Socket clientSocket;

    public ThreadedEchoServer(Socket clientSocket) {
        this.clientSocket = clientSocket;
    }
    ...
}
```

A thread is a block of code that executes concurrently with other blocks of code in an application. The Thread class supports threads in Java. While there are several ways of creating threads, one way is to pass an object that implements the Runnable interface to its constructor. When the Thread class' start method is invoked, the thread is created and the Runnable interface's run method executes. When the run method terminates, so does the thread.

Another way of adding the thread is to use a separate class for the thread. This can be declared separate from the ThreadedEchoServer class or as an inner class of the ThreadedEchoServer class. Using a separate class, better splits the functionality of the application.

The main method creates the server socket as before, but when a client socket is created, the client socket is used to create a thread, as shown here:

```
public static void main(String[] args) {
    System.out.println("Threaded Echo Server");
    try (ServerSocket serverSocket = new ServerSocket(6000)) {
        while (true) {
            System.out.println("Waiting for connection.....");
            clientSocket = serverSocket.accept();
            ThreadedEchoServer tes =
                new ThreadedEchoServer(clientSocket);
            new Thread(tes).start();
        }

    } catch (IOException ex) {
        // Handle exceptions
    }
    System.out.println("Threaded Echo Server Terminating");
}
```

The actual work is performed in the run method as shown next. It is essentially the same implementation as the original echo server, except that the current thread is displayed to clarify which threads are being used:

```
@Override
public void run() {
    System.out.println("Connected to client using ["
        + Thread.currentThread() + "]");
    try (BufferedReader br = new BufferedReader(
            new InputStreamReader(
```

```
            clientSocket.getInputStream())); 
        PrintWriter out = new PrintWriter(
            clientSocket.getOutputStream(), true)) {
    String inputLine;
    while ((inputLine = br.readLine()) != null) {
        System.out.println("Client request ["
            + Thread.currentThread() + "]: " + inputLine);
        out.println(inputLine);
    }
    System.out.println("Client [" + Thread.currentThread()
        + " connection terminated");
} catch (IOException ex) {
    // Handle exceptions
}
}
```

Using the threaded server

The following output shows the interaction between the server and two clients. The original echo client was started twice. As you can see, each client interaction is performed with a different thread:

Threaded Echo Server

Waiting for connection.....

Waiting for connection.....

Connected to client using [Thread[Thread-0,5,main]]

Client request [Thread[Thread-0,5,main]]: Hello from client 1

Client request [Thread[Thread-0,5,main]]: Its good on this side

Waiting for connection.....

Connected to client using [Thread[Thread-1,5,main]]

Client request [Thread[Thread-1,5,main]]: Hello from client 2

Client request [Thread[Thread-1,5,main]]: Good day!

Client request [Thread[Thread-1,5,main]]: quit

Client [Thread[Thread-1,5,main] connection terminated

Client request [Thread[Thread-0,5,main]]: So long

Client request [Thread[Thread-0,5,main]]: quit

The following interaction is from the first client's perspective:

Simple Echo Client

Waiting for connection.....

Connected to server

Enter text: Hello from client 1

Server response: Hello from client 1

Enter text: Its good on this side

Server response: Its good on this side

Enter text: So long

Server response: So long

Enter text: quit

Server response: quit

The following interaction is from the second client's perspective:

Simple Echo Client

Waiting for connection.....

Connected to server

Enter text: Hello from client 2

Server response: Hello from client 2

Enter text: Good day!

Server response: Good day!

Enter text: quit

Server response: quit

This implementation permits multiple clients to be handled at a time. Clients are not blocked because another client is using the server. However, it also allows a large number of threads to be created. If there are too many threads in existence, then server performance can degrade. We will address these issues in *Chapter 7, Network Scalability*.

Security

Security is a complex topic. In this section, we will demonstrate a few simple aspects of this topic, as it relates to networks. Specifically, we will create a secure echo server. Creating a secure echo server is not that much different from the non-secure echo server that we developed earlier. However, there is a lot going on behind the scenes to make it work. We can ignore many of these details for now, but we will delve more deeply into it in *Chapter 8, Network Security*.

We will be using the SSLServerSocketFactory class to instantiate secure server sockets. In addition, it is necessary to create keys that the underlying SSL mechanism can use to encrypt the communications.

Creating a SSL server

An SSLServerSocket class is declared in the following example to serve as the echo server. As it is similar to the previous echo server, we will not explain its implementation, except for its relation to the use of the SSLServerSocketFactory class. Its static getDefault method returns an instance of ServerSocketFactory. Its createServerSocket method returns an instance of a ServerSocket bound to port 8000 that is capable of supporting secure communications. Otherwise, it is organized and functions similarly to the previous echo server:

```
public class SSLServerSocket {

    public static void main(String[] args) {
        try {
            SSLServerSocketFactory ssf =  (SSLServerSocketFactory)
                SSLServerSocketFactory.getDefault();
            ServerSocket serverSocket =
                ssf.createServerSocket(8000);
            System.out.println("SSLServerSocket Started");
            try (Socket socket = serverSocket.accept();
                    PrintWriter out = new PrintWriter(
                            socket.getOutputStream(), true);
                    BufferedReader br = new BufferedReader(
                        new InputStreamReader(
                        socket.getInputStream())))) {
            System.out.println("Client socket created");
            String line = null;
            while (((line = br.readLine()) != null)) {
                System.out.println(line);
                out.println(line);
            }
        }
```

```
                    br.close();
                    System.out.println("SSLServerSocket Terminated");
                } catch (IOException ex) {
                    // Handle exceptions
                }
            } catch (IOException ex) {
                // Handle exceptions
            }
        }
    }
```

Creating an SSL client

The secure echo client is also similar to the previous non-secure echo client. The
SSLSocketFactory class' getDefault returns an SSLSocketFactory instance whose
createSocket creates a socket that is connected to the secure echo server. The
application is as follows:

```java
public class SSLClientSocket {

    public static void main(String[] args) throws Exception {
        System.out.println("SSLClientSocket Started");
        SSLSocketFactory sf =
            (SSLSocketFactory) SSLSocketFactory.getDefault();
        try (Socket socket = sf.createSocket("localhost", 8000);
                PrintWriter out = new PrintWriter(
                        socket.getOutputStream(), true);
                BufferedReader br = new BufferedReader(
                    new InputStreamReader(
                    socket.getInputStream())))) {
            Scanner scanner = new Scanner(System.in);
            while (true) {
                System.out.print("Enter text: ");
                String inputLine = scanner.nextLine();
                if ("quit".equalsIgnoreCase(inputLine)) {
                    break;
                }
                out.println(inputLine);
                System.out.println("Server response: " +
                    br.readLine());
            }
            System.out.println("SSLServerSocket Terminated");
        }
    }
}
```

If we executed this server followed by the client, they will abort with a connection error. This is because we have not provided a set of keys that the applications can share and use to protect the data passed between them.

Generating secure keys

To provide the necessary keys, we need to create a keystore to hold the keys. When the applications execute, the keystore must be available to the applications. First, we will demonstrate how to create a keystore, and then we will show you which runtime parameters must be supplied.

Within the Java SE SDK's bin directory is a program titled keytool. This is a command-level program that will generate the necessary keys and store them in a key file. In Windows, you will need to bring up a command window and navigate to the root directory of your source files. This directory will contain the directory holding your application's package.

On a Mac, you may have problems generating a key pair. More information about using this tool on a Mac is found at https://developer.apple.com/library/mac/documentation/Darwin/Reference/ManPages/man1/keytool.1.html.

You will also need to set the path to the bin directory using a command that is similar to the following one. This command is needed to find and execute the keytool application:

```
set path= C:\Program Files\Java\jdk1.8.0_25\bin;%path%
```

Next, enter the keytool command. You will be prompted for a password and other information that is used to create the keys. This process is shown here, where a password of 123456 is used although it is not displayed as it is entered:

```
Enter keystore password:
Re-enter new password:
What is your first and last name?
  [Unknown]:  First Last
What is the name of your organizational unit?
  [Unknown]:  packt
What is the name of your organization?
  [Unknown]:  publishing
What is the name of your City or Locality?
```

```
  [Unknown]:  home
What is the name of your State or Province?
  [Unknown]:  calm
What is the two-letter country code for this unit?
  [Unknown]:  me
Is CN=First Last, OU=packt, O=publishing, L=home, ST=calm, C=me correct?
  [no]:  y


Enter key password for <mykey>
        (RETURN if same as keystore password):
```

With the keystore created, you can run the server and client applications. How these applications are started depends on how your projects have been created. You may be able to execute it from an IDE, or you may need to start them from a command window.

Next are the commands that can be used from a command window. The two arguments to the java command are the location of the keystore and a password. They need to be executed from the root directory of your package's directory:

```
java -Djavax.net.ssl.keyStore=keystore.jks -
  Djavax.net.ssl.keyStorePassword=123456 packt.SSLServerSocket
java -Djavax.net.ssl.trustStore=keystore.jks -
  Djavax.net.ssl.trustStorePassword=123456 packt.SSLClientSocket
```

If you want to use an IDE, then use the equivalent settings for your runtime command arguments. The following one illustrates one possible interchange between the client and the server. The output of the server window is shown first, followed by that of the client:

SSLServerSocket Started

Client socket created

Hello echo server

Safe and secure

SSLServerSocket Terminated

SSLClientSocket Started

Enter text: Hello echo server

Server response: Hello echo server

Enter text: Safe and secure

Server response: Safe and secure

Enter text: quit

SSLServerSocket Terminated

There is more to learn about SSL than what is shown here. However, this provides an overview of the process with more details presented in *Chapter 8, Network Security*.

Summary

Network enabled applications fulfill an increasingly important role in our society today. With more and more devices being connected to the Internet, it is important to understand how to build applications that can communicate with other applications.

We briefly identified and explained several of the technologies that Java uses to connect to a network. We illustrated how the InetAddress class can represent an IP address, and we used this class for several examples. The basic elements of the client/server architecture were demonstrated using UDP, TCP, and SSL technologies. They provide different types of support. UDP is fast but not as reliable or as capable as TCP. TCP is a reliable and convenient way of communicating, but is not secure unless used with SSL.

The NIO support for buffers and channels was illustrated. These techniques can result in more efficient communications. The scalability of an application is critical for many applications, specifically the client/server model. We also saw how threads can support scalability.

Each of these topics will be addressed in more detail in later chapters. This includes the support NIO provides for scalability, how P2P applications work, and the myriad of interoperability technologies that are available for use with Java.

We'll start with a detailed examination of networks, and network addressing, in particular, in the next chapter.

2
Network Addressing

For a program to communicate with another program, it must have an address. In this chapter, the use of addresses, including Internet addresses, will be examined. We will introduce many of the basic concepts in the first part of this chapter. This includes the architecture of networks and the protocols that are used to communicate between the nodes.

We will address several topics, including:

- **Network basics**: This is where essential concepts and terms are introduced
- **Using the NetworkInterface class**: This provides access to system devices
- **URL/UII/URN**: We will discuss how these terms relate to each other
- **The Inet4Address and Inet6Address classes**: We will discuss how these are used
- **Network properties**: We will consider the properties that are configurable in Java

This will provide you with the foundation to pursue networking in more depth.

Networking basics

Networking is a broad and complex topic. In particular, a subtopic, such as addressing, is quite involved. We will introduce the terms and concepts that are commonly encountered and useful from a Java perspective.

Most of this discussion will focus on Java support for the Internet. A **Uniform Resource Locator (URL)** is recognized by most Internet users. However, the terms **Uniform Resource Identifier (URI)** and **Uniform Resource Name (URN)** are not recognized or understood as well as URL. We will differentiate between these terms and examine the Java supporting classes.

A browser user would normally enter a URL for the site that they would like to visit. This URL needs to be mapped to an IP address. The IP address is a unique number identifying the site. The URL is mapped to an IP address using a **Domain Name System (DNS)** server. This avoids a user having to remember a number for each site. Java uses the InetAddress class to access IP addresses and resources.

UDP and TCP are used by many applications. IP supports both of these protocols. The IP protocol transfers packets of information between nodes on a network. Java supports both the IPv4 and IPv6 protocol versions.

Both UDP and TCP are layered on top of IP. Several other protocols are layered on top of TCP, such as HTTP. These relationships are shown in this following figure:

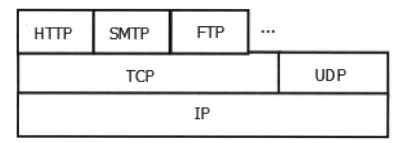

When communications occur between different networks using different machines and operating systems, problems can occur due to differences at the hardware or software level. One of these issues is the characters used in URLs. The URLEncoder and URLDecoder classes can help address this problem, and they are discussed in *Chapter 9, Network Interoperability*.

The IP address assigned to a device may be either **static** or **dynamic**. If it is static, it will not change each time the device is rebooted. With dynamic addresses, the address may change each time the device is rebooted or when a network connection is reset.

Static addresses are normally manually assigned by an administrator. Dynamic addresses are frequently assigned using the **Dynamic Host Configuration Protocol (DHCP)** running from a DHCP server. With IPv6, DHCP is not as useful due to the large IPv6 address space. However, DHCP is useful for tasks, such as supporting the generation of random addresses, which introduce more privacy within a network when viewed from outside of the network.

The **Internet Assigned Numbers Authority (IANA)** is responsible for the allocation of IP address space allocations. Five **Regional Internet Registries (RIRs)** allocate IP address blocks to local Internet entities that are commonly referred to as **Internet Service Providers (ISP)**.

There are several publications that detail the IP protocol:

- **RFC 790 — assigned numbers**: This specification addresses the format of network numbers. For example, the IPv4 A, B, and C classes are defined in this specification (`https://tools.ietf.org/html/rfc790`).

- **RFC 1918 — address allocation for private internets**: This specification is concerned with how private addresses are assigned. This allows multiple private addresses to be associated with a single public address (`https://tools.ietf.org/html/rfc1918`).

- **RFC 2365 — administratively scoped IP multicast**: This specification defines the multicast address space and how it can be implemented. The mapping between IPv4 and IPv6 multicast address spaces is defined (`https://tools.ietf.org/html/rfc2365`).

- **RFC 2373 — IPv6 addressing architecture**: This specification examines the IPv6 protocol, its format, and the various address types that are supported by IPv6 (`http://www.ietf.org/rfc/rfc2373.txt`).

Many of the concepts introduced here will be illustrated with Java code whenever possible. So let's start with understanding networks.

Understanding network basics

A network consists of nodes and links that are combined to create network architecture. A device connected to the Internet is called a **node**. A computer node is called a **host**. Communication between nodes is conducted along these links using protocols, such as HTTP, or UDP.

Links can either be wired, such as coaxial cable, twisted pairs, and fiber optics, or wireless, such as microwave, cellular, Wi-Fi, or satellite communications. These various links support different bandwidth and throughput to address particular communication needs.

Nodes include devices, such as **Network Interface Controllers** (**NIC**), bridges, switches, hubs, and routers. They are all involved with transmitting various forms of data between computers.

The NIC has an IP address and is part of a computer. Bridges connect two network segments allowing a larger network to be broken down into smaller ones. Repeaters and hubs are used primarily to retransmit a signal boosting its strength.

Hubs, switches, and routers are similar to each other but differ in their complexity. A hub handles multiple ports and simply forwards the data to all connected ports. A switch will learn where to send data based on its traffic. A router can be programmed to manipulate and route messages. Routers are more useful in many networks, and most home networks use a router.

When a message is sent across the Internet from a home computer, there are several things going on. The computer's address is not globally unique. This requires that any messages sent to and from the computer be handled by a **Network Address Translation** (**NAT**) device that changes the address to one that can be used on the Internet. It allows a single IP address to be used for multiple devices on a network, such as a home LAN.

The computer may also use a proxy server, which acts as a gateway to other networks. Java provides support for proxies using the `Proxy` and `ProxySelector` classes. We will examine their use in *Chapter 9*, *Network Interoperability*.

Messages are often routed through a firewall. The firewall protects the computer from malicious intent.

Network architectures and protocols

Common network architectures include bus, star, and tree-type networks. These physical networks are often used to support an overlay network, which is a virtual network. Such a network abstracts the underlying network to create a network architecture supporting applications, such as peer-to-peer applications.

When two computers communicate, they use a protocol. There are many different protocols used at various layers of a network. We will mainly focus on HTTP, TCP, UDP, and IP.

There are several models depicting how networks can be layered to support different tasks and protocols. One common model is the **Open Systems Interconnection** (**OSI**) model, which defines seven layers. Each layer of a network model can support one or more protocols. The relationships of various protocols are depicted in the following table:

Layer	Example protocols	Purpose
Application	HTTP, FTP, SNMP	High-level protocols supporting specialized operations
Presentation	Transport layer security	Support delivery and processing of data for the application layer
Session	Network file system	Managing sessions

Layer	Example protocols	Purpose
Transport	TCP, UDP	Manages packets of data
Network	IP	Transfer packets
Data link	Ethernet, frame relay	Transfers data between network segments
Physical	DSL, Bluetooth	Handles raw data

A more complete list of protocols for the OSI layers can be found at `https://en.wikipedia.org/wiki/List_of_network_protocols_(OSI_model)`. We are not able address all of these protocols and will focus on the more important ones that are supported by the Java SDK.

Consider the transfer of a web page from a server to a client. As it is sent to a client, the data will be encapsulated in an HTTP message, which is further encapsulated in TCP, IP, and link-level protocol messages, each frequently containing a header and footer. This encapsulated set of headers is sent across the Internet to the destination client, where the data is extracted for each encapsulating header until the original HTML file is displayed.

Fortunately, we do not need to be familiar with the details of this process. Many of the classes hide how this occurs, allowing us to focus on the data.

The protocols of the transport layer that we are interested in are TCP and UDP. TCP provides a more reliable communication protocol than UDP. However, UDP is better suited for short messages when delivery does not need to be robust. Streaming data often uses UDP.

The differences between UDP and TCP are outlined in the following table:

Characteristic	TCP	UDP
Connection	Connection-oriented	Connectionless
Reliability	Higher	Lower
Order of packets	Order restored	Order potentially lost
Data boundaries	Packets are merged	Packets are distinct
Transmission time	Slower than UDP	Faster than TCP
Error checking	Yes	Yes, but no recovery options
Acknowledgement	Yes	No
Weight	Heavy weight requiring more support	Light weight requiring less support

TCP is used for a number of protocols, such as HTTP, **Simple Mail Transfer Protocol (SMTP)**, and **File Transfer Protocol (FTP)**. UDP is used by DNS to stream media, such as movies, and for **Voice Over IP (VOIP)**.

Using the NetworkInterface class

The NetworkInterface class provides a means of accessing the devices that act as nodes on a network. This class also provides a means to get low-level device addresses. Many systems are connected to multiple networks at the same time. These may be wired, such as a network card, or wireless, such as for a wireless LAN or Bluetooth connection.

The NetworkInterface class represents an IP address and provides information about this IP address. A **network interface** is the point of connection between a computer and a network. This frequently uses an NIC of some type. It does not have to have a physical manifestation, but it can be performed in software as done with the loopback connection (127.0.0.1 for IPv4 and ::1 for IPv6).

The NetworkInterface class does not have any public constructors. Three static methods are provided to return an instance of the NetworkInterface class:

- getByInetAddress: This is used if the IP address is known

- getByName: This is used if the interface name is known

- getNetworkInterfaces: This provides an enumeration of available interfaces

The following code illustrates how to use the getNetworkInterfaces method to obtain and display an enumeration of the network interfaces for the current computer:

```
try {
    Enumeration<NetworkInterface> interfaceEnum =
        NetworkInterface.getNetworkInterfaces();
    System.out.printf("Name      Display name\n");
    for(NetworkInterface element :
            Collections.list(interfaceEnum)) {
        System.out.printf("%-8s  %-32s\n",
                element.getName(), element.getDisplayName());
} catch (SocketException ex) {
    // Handle exceptions
}
```

One possible output is as follows, but it has been truncated to save space:

Name   Display name

lo   Software Loopback Interface 1

eth0   Microsoft Kernel Debug Network Adapter

eth1   Realtek PCIe FE Family Controller

wlan0   Realtek RTL8188EE 802.11 b/g/n Wi-Fi Adapter

wlan1   Microsoft Wi-Fi Direct Virtual Adapter

net0   Microsoft 6to4 Adapter

net1   Teredo Tunneling Pseudo-Interface

...

A getSubInterfaces method will return an enumeration of subinterfaces if any exist, as shown next. A subinterface occurs when a single physical network interface is divided into logical interfaces for routing purposes:

```
Enumeration<NetworkInterface> interfaceEnumeration =
    element.getSubInterfaces();
```

Each network interface will have one or more IP addresses associated with it. The getInetAddresses method will return an Enumeration of these addresses. As shown next, the initial list of network interfaces has been augmented to display the IP addresses associated with them:

```
Enumeration<NetworkInterface> interfaceEnum =
    NetworkInterface.getNetworkInterfaces();
System.out.printf("Name      Display name\n");
for (NetworkInterface element :
        Collections.list(interfaceEnum)) {
    System.out.printf("%-8s  %-32s\n",
            element.getName(), element.getDisplayName());
    Enumeration<InetAddress> addresses =
        element.getInetAddresses();
    for (InetAddress inetAddress :
            Collections.list(addresses)) {
        System.out.printf("    InetAddress: %s\n",
            inetAddress);
    }
```

One possible output is as follows:

Name   Display name

lo   Software Loopback Interface 1

   InetAddress: /127.0.0.1

   InetAddress: /0:0:0:0:0:0:0:1

eth0   Microsoft Kernel Debug Network Adapter

eth1   Realtek PCIe FE Family Controller

   InetAddress: /fe80:0:0:0:91d0:8e19:31f1:cb2d%eth1

wlan0   Realtek RTL8188EE 802.11 b/g/n Wi-Fi Adapter

   InetAddress: /192.168.1.5

   InetAddress: /2002:6028:2252:0:0:0:0:1000

   InetAddress: /fe80:0:0:0:9cdb:371f:d3e9:4e2e%wlan0

wlan1   Microsoft Wi-Fi Direct Virtual Adapter

   InetAddress: /fe80:0:0:0:f8f6:9c75:d86d:8a22%wlan1

net0   Microsoft 6to4 Adapter

net1   Teredo Tunneling Pseudo-Interface

   InetAddress: /2001:0:9d38:6abd:6a:37:3f57:fefa

   ...

We can also use the following Java 8 technique. A stream and a lambda expression are used to display the IP addresses to generate the same output:

```
addresses = element.getInetAddresses();
Collections
        .list(addresses)
        .stream()
        .forEach((inetAddress) -> {
            System.out.printf("    InetAddress: %s\n",
                inetAddress);
        });
```

There are numerous `InetworkAddress` methods, which reveal more details about the network connection. They will be discussed as we encounter them.

Getting a MAC address

A **Media Access Control (MAC)** address is used to identify an NIC. MAC addresses are usually assigned by the manufacturer of an NIC and are a part of its hardware. Each NIC on a node must have a unique MAC address. Theoretically, all NICs, regardless of their location, will have a unique MAC address. A MAC address consists of 48 bits that are usually written in groups of six pairs of hexadecimal digits. These groups are separated by either a dash or a colon.

Getting a specific MAC address

Normally, MAC addresses are not needed by the average Java programmer. However, they can be retrieved whenever needed. The following method returns a string containing the IP address and its MAC address for a NetworkInterface instance. The getHardwareAddress method returns an array of bytes holding the number. This array is then displayed as a MAC address. Most of this code-segment logic is devoted to formatting the output, where the tertiary operator determines whether a dash should be displayed:

```java
public String getMACIdentifier(NetworkInterface network) {
    StringBuilder identifier = new StringBuilder();
    try {
        byte[] macBuffer = network.getHardwareAddress();
        if (macBuffer != null) {
            for (int i = 0; i < macBuffer.length; i++) {
                    identifier.append(
                    String.format("%02X%s",macBuffer[i],
                    (i < macBuffer.length - 1) ? "-" : ""));
            }
        } else {
            return "---";
        }
    } catch (SocketException ex) {
        ex.printStackTrace();
    }
    return identifier.toString();
}
```

The method is demonstrated in the following example where we use the localhost:

```java
InetAddress address = InetAddress.getLocalHost();
System.out.println("IP address: " + address.getHostAddress());
NetworkInterface network =
    NetworkInterface.getByInetAddress(address);
System.out.println("MAC address: " +
    getMACIdentifier(network));
```

The output will vary depending on the computer used. One possible output is as follows:

IP address: 192.168.1.5

MAC address: EC-0E-C4-37-BB-72

 The getHardwareAddress method will only allow you to access a localhost MAC address. You cannot use it to access a remote MAC address.

Getting multiple MAC addresses

Not all network interfaces will have MAC addresses. This is demonstrated here, where an enumeration is created using the getNetworkInterfaces method, and then each network interface is displayed:

```
Enumeration<NetworkInterface> interfaceEnum =
    NetworkInterface.getNetworkInterfaces();
System.out.println("Name    MAC Address");
for (NetworkInterface element :
        Collections.list(interfaceEnum)) {
    System.out.printf("%-6s  %s\n",
        element.getName(), getMACIdentifier(element));
```

One possible output is as follows. The output is truncated to save space:

Name   MAC Address

lo   ---

eth0   ---

eth1   8C-DC-D4-86-B1-05

wlan0   EC-0E-C4-37-BB-72

wlan1   EC-0E-C4-37-BB-72

net0   ---

net1   00-00-00-00-00-00-00-E0

net2   00-00-00-00-00-00-00-E0

...

Alternatively, we can use the following Java implementation. It converts the enumeration into a stream and then processes each element in the stream:

```
interfaceEnum = NetworkInterface.getNetworkInterfaces();
Collections
        .list(interfaceEnum)
        .stream()
        .forEach((inetAddress) -> {
            System.out.printf("%-6s   %s\n",
                inetAddress.getName(),
                getMACIdentifier(inetAddress));
        });
```

The power of streams comes when we need to perform additional processing, such as filtering out certain interfaces, or converting the interface into a different data type.

Network addressing concepts

There are different types of network addresses. An address serves to identify a node in a network. For example, the **Internetwork Packet Exchange (IPX)** protocol was an earlier protocol that was used to access nodes on a network. The X.25 is a protocol suite for **Wide Area Network (WAN)** packet switching. A MAC address provides a unique identifier for network interfaces at the physical network level. However, our primary interests are IP addresses.

URL/URI/URN

These terms are used to refer to the name and location of an Internet resource. A URI identifies the name of a resource, such as a website, or a file on the Internet. It may contain the name of a resource and its location.

A URL specifies where a resource is located, and how to retrieve it. A protocol forms the first part of the URL, and specifies how data is retrieved. URLs always contain protocol, such as HTTP, or FTP. For example, the following two URLs use different protocols. The first one uses the HTTPS protocol, and the second one uses the FTP protocol:

https://www.packtpub.com/

ftp://speedtest.tele2.net/

Java provides classes to support URIs and URLs. The discussion of these classes begins in the next section. Here, we will discuss URNs in more depth.

A URN identifies the resource but not its location. A URN is like a city's name, while a URL is similar to a city's latitude and longitude. When a resource, such as web page, or file, is moved, the URL for the resource is no longer correct. The URL will need to be updated wherever it is used. A URN specifies the name of a resource but not its location. Some other entity, when supplied with a URN, will return its location. URNs are not used that extensively.

The syntax of a URN is shown next. The `<NID>` element is a namespace identifier and `<NSS>` is a namespace-specific string:

<URN> ::= "urn:" <NID> ":" <NSS>

For example, the following is a URN specifying as part of a SOAP message to qualify its namespace:

```
<?xml version='1.0'?>
<SOAP:Envelope
  xmlns:SOAP='urn:schemas-xmlsoap-org:soap.v1'>
 <SOAP:Body>
  ...
    xmlns:i='urn:gargantuan-com:IShop'>
  ...
 </SOAP:Body>
</SOAP:Envelope>
```

It is used in other places, such as to identify books using their ISBN. Entering the following URL in a browser will bring up a reference to an EJB book:

https://books.google.com/books?isbn=9781849682381

The syntax of a URN depends on the namespace. The IANA is responsible for the allocation of many Internet resources, including URN namespaces. URNs are still an active area of research. URLs and URNs are both URIs.

Using the URI class

The general syntax of a URI consists of a scheme and a scheme-specific-part:

[scheme:] scheme-specific-part

There are many schemes that are used with a URI, including:

- **file**: This is used for files systems
- **FTP**: This is File Transfer Protocol
- **HTTP**: This is commonly used for websites
- **mailto**: This is used as part of a mail service
- **urn**: This is used to identify a resource by name

The scheme-specific-part varies by the scheme that is used. URIs can be categorized as absolute or relative, or as opaque or hierarchical. These distinctions are not of immediate interest to us here, though Java provides methods to determine whether a URI falls into one of these categories.

Creating URI instances

A URI can be created for different schemes using several constructor variations. The simplest way of creating a URI is to use a string argument specifying the URI, as shown here:

```
URI uri = new
    URI("https://www.packtpub.com/books/content/support");
```

The next URI uses a fragment to access a subsection of the Wikipedia article dealing with the normalization of a URL:

```
uri = new URI("https://en.wikipedia.org/wiki/"
    + "URL_normalization#Normalization_process");
```

We can also use the following version of the constructor to specify the scheme, host, path, and fragment of the URI:

```
uri = new
    URI("https","en.wikipedia.org","/wiki/URL_normalization",
    "Normalization_process");
```

These latter two URIs are identical.

Splitting apart a URI

Java uses the URI class to represent a URI, and it possesses several methods to extract parts of a URI. The more useful methods are listed in the following table:

Method	Purpose
getAuthority	This is the entity responsible for resolving the URI
getScheme	The scheme used
getSchemeSpecificPart	The scheme specific part of the URI
getHost	The host
getPath	The URI path
getQuery	The query, if any
getFragment	The sub-element being accessed, if used
getUserInfo	User information, if available
normalize	Removes unnecessary "." and ".." from the path

There are also several "raw" methods, such as getRawPath, or getRawFragment, which return versions of a path or fragment, respectively. This includes special characters, such as the question mark, or character sequences beginning with an asterisk. There are several character categories defining these characters and their use, as documented at http://docs.oracle.com/javase/8/docs/api/java/net/URI.html.

We have developed the following helper method that is used to display URI characteristics:

```
private static void displayURI(URI uri) {
    System.out.println("getAuthority: " + uri.getAuthority());
    System.out.println("getScheme: " + uri.getScheme());
    System.out.println("getSchemeSpecificPart: "
        + uri.getSchemeSpecificPart());
    System.out.println("getHost: " + uri.getHost());
    System.out.println("getPath: " + uri.getPath());
    System.out.println("getQuery: " + uri.getQuery());
    System.out.println("getFragment: " + uri.getFragment());
    System.out.println("getUserInfo: " + uri.getUserInfo());
    System.out.println("normalize: " + uri.normalize());
}
```

The next code sequence creates a URI instance for the Packtpub website and then calls the displayURI method:

```
try {
    URI uri = new
        URI("https://www.packtpub.com/books/content/support");
    displayURI(uri);
} catch (URISyntaxException ex) {
    // Handle exceptions
}
```

The output of this sequence is as follows:

getAuthority: www.packtpub.com

getScheme: https

getSchemeSpecificPart: //www.packtpub.com/books/content/support

getHost: www.packtpub.com

getPath: /books/content/support

getQuery: null

getFragment: null

getUserInfo: null

normalize: https://www.packtpub.com/books/content/support

http://www.packtpub.com

More often, these methods are used to extract relevant information for additional processing.

Using the URL class

One of the easiest ways to connect to a site and retrieve data is through the URL class. All that you need to provide is the URL for the site and the details of the protocol. An instance of the InetAddress class will hold an IP address and possibly the hostname for the address.

The URLConnection class was introduced in *Chapter 1, Getting Started with Network Programming*. It can also be used to provide access to an Internet resource represented by a URL. We will discuss this class and its use in *Chapter 4, Client/Server Development*.

Creating URL instances

There are several ways of creating a URL instance. The easiest is to simply provide the URL of the site as the argument of the class' constructor. This is illustrated here where a URL instance for the Packtpub website is created:

```
URL url = new URL("http://www.packtpub.com");
```

A URL requires a protocol to be specified. For example, the following attempt to create a URL will result in a **java.net.MalformedURLException: no protocol: www.packtpub.com** error message:

```
url = new URL("www.packtpub.com");
```

There are several constructor variations. The following two variations will create the same URL. The second one uses parameters for the protocol, host, port number, and file:

```
url = new URL("http://pluto.jhuapl.edu/");
url = new URL("http", "pluto.jhuapl.edu", 80,
    "News-Center/index.php");
```

Splitting apart a URL

It can be useful to know more about a URL. We may not even know what URL we are using if the user entered one that we need to process. There are several methods that support splitting a URL into its components, as summarized in the following table:

Method	Purpose
getProtocol	This is the name of the protocol.
getHost	This is the host name.
getPort	This is the port number.
getDefaultPort	This is the default port number for the protocol.
getFile	This returns the result of getPath concatenated with the results of getQuery.
getPath	This retrieves the path, if any, for the URL.
getRef	This is the return name of the URL's reference.
getQuery	This returns the query part of the URL if present.
getUserInfo	This returns any user information associated with the URL.
getAuthority	The authority usually consists of the server host name or IP address. It may include the port number.

We will use the following method to illustrate the methods in the preceding table:

```
private static void displayURL(URL url) {
    System.out.println("URL: " + url);
    System.out.printf("  Protocol: %-32s  Host: %-32s\n",
        url.getProtocol(),url.getHost());
    System.out.printf("      Port: %-32d  Path: %-32s\n",
        url.getPort(),url.getPath());
    System.out.printf(" Reference: %-32s  File: %-32s\n",
        url.getRef(),url.getFile());
    System.out.printf(" Authority: %-32s Query: %-32s\n",
        url.getAuthority(),url.getQuery());
    System.out.println(" User Info: " + url.getUserInfo());
}
```

The following output demonstrates the output when several URL are used as arguments to this method.

```
URL: http://www.packtpub.com

   Protocol: http                         Host: www.packtpub.com

       Port: -1                           Path:

  Reference: null                         File:

  Authority: www.packtpub.com            Query: null

  User Info: null


URL: http://pluto.jhuapl.edu/

   Protocol: http                         Host: pluto.jhuapl.edu

       Port: -1                           Path: /

  Reference: null                         File: /

  Authority: pluto.jhuapl.edu            Query: null

  User Info: null


URL: http://pluto.jhuapl.edu:80News-Center/index.php

   Protocol: http                         Host: pluto.jhuapl.edu
```

```
        Port: 80                          Path: News-Center/
index.php
   Reference: null                        File: News-Center/
index.php
   Authority: pluto.jhuapl.edu:80         Query: null
   User Info: null


URL: https://en.wikipedia.org/wiki/Uniform_resource_
locator#Syntax
     Protocol: https                      Host: en.wikipedia.org
        Port: -1                          Path: /wiki/Uniform_
resource_locator
   Reference: Syntax                      File: /wiki/Uniform_
resource_locator
   Authority: en.wikipedia.org            Query: null
   User Info: null


URL: https://www.google.com/webhp?sourceid=chrome-
instant&ion=1&espv=2&ie=UTF-8#q=url+syntax
     Protocol: https                      Host: www.google.com
        Port: -1                          Path: /webhp
   Reference: q=url+syntax                File: /
webhp?sourceid=chrome-instant&ion=1&espv=2&ie=UTF-8
   Authority: www.google.com              Query: sourceid=chrome-
instant&ion=1&espv=2&ie=UTF-8
   User Info: null


URL: https://www.packtpub.com/books/content/support
     Protocol: https                      Host: www.packtpub.com
        Port: -1                          Path: /books/content/
support
   Reference: null                        File: /books/content/
support
   Authority: www.packtpub.com            Query: null
   User Info: null
```

The URL class also supports opening connections and IO streams. We demonstrated the openConnection method in *Chapter 1, Getting Started with Network Programming*. The getContent method returns the data referenced by the URL. For example, the following applies the method against the Packtpub URL:

```
url = new URL("http://www.packtpub.com");
System.out.println("getContent: " + url.getContent());
```

The output is as follows:

sun.net.www.protocol.http.HttpURLConnection$HttpInputStream@5c647e05

This suggests that we need to use an input stream to process the resource. The type of data depends on the URL. This topic is explored with the URLConnection class that is discussed in *Chapter 4, Client/Server Development*.

IP addresses and the InetAddress class

An IP address is a numerical value that is used to identify a node, such as a computer, printer, scanner, or a similar device. It is used for network interface addressing, and location addressing. The address, unique in its context, identifies the device. At the same time it constitutes a location in the network. A name designates an entity, such as www.packtpub.com. Its address, 83.166.169.231, tells us where it is located. If we want to send or receive a message from a site, the message is unusually routed though one or more nodes.

Obtaining information about an address

The InetAddress class represents an IP address. The IP protocol is a low-level protocol used by the UDP and TCP protocols. An IP address is either a 32-bit or a 128-bit unsigned number that is assigned to a device.

IP addresses have a long history and use two major versions: IPv4 and IPv6. The number 5 was assigned to the **Internet Stream Protocol**. This was an experimental protocol, but it was never actually referred to as version IPv5 and was not intended for general use.

The InetAddress class' getAllByName method will return the IP address for a given URL. In the following example, the addresses associated with www.google.com are displayed:

```
InetAddress names[] =
    InetAddress.getAllByName("www.google.com");
for(InetAddress element : names) {
    System.out.println(element);
}
```

One possible output is as follows. The output will vary depending on the location and time because many web sites have multiple IP addresses assigned to them. In this case, it uses both IPv4 and IPv6 addresses:

www.google.com/74.125.21.105

www.google.com/74.125.21.103

www.google.com/74.125.21.147

www.google.com/74.125.21.104

www.google.com/74.125.21.99

www.google.com/74.125.21.106

www.google.com/2607:f8b0:4002:c06:0:0:0:69

The `InetAddress` class possesses several methods to provide access to an IP address. We will introduce them as they become relevant. We start with methods to return its canonical hostname, hostname, and host address. They are used in the following helper method:

```
private static void displayInetAddressInformation(
        InetAddress address) {
    System.out.println(address);
    System.out.println("CanonicalHostName: " +
        address.getCanonicalHostName());
    System.out.println("HostName: " + address.getHostName());
    System.out.println("HostAddress: " +
        address.getHostAddress());
}
```

The canonical hostname is a **Fully Qualified Domain Name** (**FQDN**). As the term implies, it is the full name of the host, including the top-level domain. The values returned by these methods depend on several factors, including the DNS server. The system provides information regarding entities on the network.

The following sequence uses the display method for the Packtpub website:

```
InetAddress address =
    InetAddress.getByName("www.packtpub.com");
displayInetAddressInformation(address);
```

You will get an output that is similar to the following one:

www.packtpub.com/83.166.169.231

CanonicalHostName: 83.166.169.231

HostAddress: 83.166.169.231

HostName: www.packtpub.com

The `InetAddress` class' `toString` method returned the hostname, followed by the forward slash and then the host address. The `getCanonicalHostName` method, in this case, returned the host address, which is not the FQDN. The method will do its best to return the name but may not be able to depending on the machine's configuration.

Address scoping issues

The scope of an IP address refers to the uniqueness of an IP address. Within a local network, such as those used in many homes and offices, the address may be local to that network. There are three types of scopes:

- **Link-local**: This is used within a single local subnet that is not connected to the Internet. No routers are present. Allocation of link-local addresses is done automatically when the computer does not have a static IP-address and cannot find a DHCP server.
- **Site-local**: This is used when the address does not require a global prefix and is unique within a site. It cannot be reached directly from the Internet and requires a mapping service such as NAT.
- **Global**: As its name implies, the address is unique throughout the Internet.

There are also private addresses that are discussed in the *Private addresses in IPv4* and *Private addresses in IPv6* sections. The `InetAddress` class supports several methods to identify the type of address being used. Most of these methods are self-explanatory, as found in the following table where MC is an abbreviation for multicast:

Method	Scope	Description
isAnyLocalAddress	Any	This is an address that matches any local address. It is a wildcard address.
isLoopbackAddress	Loopback	This is a loopback address. For IPv4, it is `127.0.0.1`, and for IPv6, it is `0:0:0:0:0:0:0:1`.
isLinkLocalAddress	Link-local	This is a link-local address.

Method	Scope	Description
isSiteLocalAddress	Site-local	This is local to a site. They can be reached by other nodes on different networks but within the same site.
isMulticastAddress	MC	This is a multicast address.
isMCLinkLocal	MC link-local	This is a link-local multicast address.
isMCNodeLocal	MC node local	This is a node-local multicast address.
isMCSiteLocal	MC site-local	This is a site-local multicast address.
isMCOrgLocal	MC org local	This is an organization-local multicast address.
isMCGlobal	MC global	This is a global multicast address.

The addresses types and ranges used are summarized in the following table for IPv4 and IPv6:

Address type	IPv4	IPv6
Multicast	224.0.0.0 to 239.255.255.25	Begins with byte FF
MC global	224.0.1.0 to 238.255.255.255	FF0E or FF1E
Org MC	239.192.0.0/14	FF08 or FF18
MC site-local	N/A	FF05 or FF15
MC link-local	224.0.0.0	FF02 or FF12
MC node local	127.0.0.0	FF01 or FF11
Private	10.0.0.0 to 10.255.255.255 172.16.0.0 to 172.31.255.255 192.168.0.0 to 192.168.255.255	fd00::/8

Testing reachability

The InetAddress class' isReachable method will attempt to determine whether an address can be found. If it can, the method returns true. The following example demonstrates this method. The getAllByName method returns an array of an InetAddress instance available for the URL. The isReachable method uses an integer argument to specify how long to wait in milliseconds at a maximum before deciding that the address is not reachable:

```
String URLAddress = "www. packtpub.com";
InetAddress[] addresses =
    InetAddress.getAllByName(URLAddress);
for (InetAddress inetAddress : addresses) {
```

```
        try {
            if (inetAddress.isReachable(10000)) {
                System.out.println(inetAddress + " is reachable");
            } else {
                System.out.println(inetAddress +
                    " is not reachable");
            }
        } catch (IOException ex) {
            // Handle exceptions
        }
    }
```

The URL www.packtpub.com was reachable, as shown here:

www.packtpub.com/83.166.169.231 is reachable

However, www.google.com was not:

www.google.com/173.194.121.52 is not reachable

www.google.com/173.194.121.51 is not reachable

www.google.com/2607:f8b0:4004:809:0:0:0:1014 is not reachable

Your results may vary. The isReachable method will do its best to determine whether an address is reachable or not. However, its success depends on more than simply whether the address exists. Reasons for failure can include: the server may be down, network response time was too long, or a firewall may be blocking a site. The operating system and JVM settings can also impact how well the method works.

An alternative to this method is to use the RunTime class' exec method to execute a ping command against the URL. However, this is not portable and may still suffer from some of the same factors that impact the success of the isReachable method.

Introducing the Inet4Address

This address consists of 32 bits, permitting up to 4,294,967,296 (232) addresses. The human readable form of the address consists of four decimal numbers (8 bits), each ranging from 0 to 255. Some of the addresses have been reserved for private networks and multicast addresses.

Early on in the use of IPv4, the first **octet** (8 bit unit) represented a network number (also called the network prefix or network block), and the remaining bits represented a **rest** field (host identifier). Later, three classes were used to partition the addresses: A, B, and C. These system have largely fallen into disuse and have been replaced by the **Classless Inter-Domain Routing (CIDR)**. This routing approach allocates addresses on bit boundaries, providing more flexibility. This scheme is called classless in contrast to the earlier class-full systems. In IPv6, 64-bit network identifiers are used.

Private addresses in IPv4

Private networks do not necessarily need global access to the Internet. This results in a series of addresses being allocated for these private networks.

Range	Number of bits	Number of addresses
10.0.0.0 to 10.255.255.255	24-bit	16,777,216
172.16.0.0 to 172.31.255.255	20-bit	1,048,576
192.168.0.0 to 192.168.255.255	16-bit	65,536

You may recognize that the last set of addresses is used by the home network. A private network often interfaces with the Internet using NAT. This technique maps a local IP address to one accessible on the Internet. It was originally introduced to ease the IPv4 address shortage.

IPv4 address types

There are three address types that are supported in IPv4:

- **Unicast**: This address is used to identify a single node in a network
- **Multicast**: This address corresponds to a group of network interfaces. Members will join a group and a message is sent to all members of the group
- **Broadcast**: This will send a message to all network interfaces on a subnet

The Inet4Address class supports the IPv4 protocol. We will examine this class in more depth next.

The Inet4Address class

The `Inet4Address` class is derived from the `InetAddress` class. As a derived class, it does not override many of the `InetAddress` class' methods. For example, to obtain an `InetAddress` instance, we can use the `getByName` method of either class, as shown here:

```
Inet4Address address;
address = (Inet4Address)
    InetAddress.getByName("www.google.com");
address = (Inet4Address)
    Inet4Address.getByName("www.google.com");
```

In either case, the address needs to be cast because the base class method is used in either case. The `Inet4Address` class does not add any new methods above and beyond that of the `InetAddress` class.

Special IPv4 addresses

There are several special IPv4 addresses, including these two:

- **0.0.0.0**: This is called an unspecified IPv4 address (wildcard address) and is normally used when a network interface does not have a IP address and is attempting to obtain one using DHCP.

- **127.0.0.1**: This is known as the loopback address. It provides a convenient way to send oneself a message, often for testing purposes.

The `isAnyLocalAddress` method will return `true` if the address is a wildcard address. This method is demonstrated here, where it returns `true`:

```
address = (Inet4Address) Inet4Address.getByName("0.0.0.0");
System.out.println(address.isAnyLocalAddress());
```

The `isLoopbackAddress` method is shown next and will return `true`:

```
address = (Inet4Address) Inet4Address.getByName("127.0.0.1");
System.out.println(address.isLoopbackAddress());
```

We will use this frequently to test servers in subsequent chapters.

In addition to these, other special addresses include those used for protocol assignments, IPv6 to IPv4 relay, and testing purposes. More details about these and other special addresses can be found at `https://en.wikipedia.org/wiki/IPv4#Special-use_addresses`.

Introducing the Inet6Address class

IPv6 addresses use 128 bits (16 octets). This permits up to 2^{128} addresses. An IPv6 address is written as a series of eight groups, with 4 hexadecimal numbers each, separated by colons. The digits are case insensitive. For example, the IPv6 address for www.google.com is as follows:

2607:f8b0:4002:0c08:0000:0000:0000:0067

An IPv6 address can be simplified in several ways. Leading zeroes in a group can be removed. The previous example can be rewritten as:

2607:f8b0:4002:c08:0:0:0:67

Consecutive groups of zeroes can be replaced with : :, as shown here:

2607:f8b0:4002:c08::67

IPv6 supports three addressing types:

- **Unicast**: This specifies a single network interface.
- **Anycast**: This type of address is assigned to a group of interfaces. When a packet is sent to this group, only one member of the group receives the packet, often the one that is closest.
- **Multicast**: This sends a packet to all members of a group.

This protocol does not support broadcast addressing. There is much more to IPv6 than an increase in network size. It includes several improvements, such as easier administration, more efficient routing capabilities, simple header formats, and the elimination of the need for NAT.

Private addresses in IPv6

Private address space is available in IPv6. Originally, it used site-local addresses using a block with a prefix of fec0::/10. However, this has been dropped due to problems with its definition, and it was replaced with **Unique Local (UL)** addresses using the address block fc00::/7.

These addresses can be generated by anyone and do not need to be coordinated. However, they are not necessarily globally unique. Other private networks can use the same addresses. They cannot be assigned using a global DNS server and are only routable in the local address space.

The Inet6Address class

In general, using the `Inet6Address` class is not necessary unless you are developing an IPv6-only application. Most networking operations are handled transparently. The `Inet6Address` class is derived from the `InetAddress` class. The `Inet6Address` class's `getByName` method uses its base class, the `InetAddrress` class's `getAllByName` method, to return the first address that it finds, as shown next. This might not be an IPv6 address:

```
public static InetAddress getByName(String host)
    throws UnknownHostException {
    return InetAddress.getAllByName(host)[0];
}
```

 For some of these examples to work correctly, your router may need to be configured to support an IPv6 Internet connection.

The `Inet6Address` class added only one method above and beyond that of the `InetAddress` class. This is the `isIPv4CompatibleAddress` method that is discussed in the *Using IPv4-compatible IPv6 addresses* section.

Special IPv6 addresses

There is a block of addresses consisting of 64 network prefixes: `2001:0000::/29` through `2001:01f8::/29`. These are used for special needs. Three have been assigned by IANA:

- `2001::/32`: This is the teredo tunneling, which is a transition technology from IPv4
- `2001:2::/48`: This is used for benchmarking purposes
- `2001:20::/28`: This is used for cryptographic hash identifiers

Most developers will not need to work with these addresses.

Testing for the IP address type

Normally, we are not concerned with whether the IP address is IPv4 or IPv6. The differences between the two are hidden beneath the various protocol levels. When you do need to know the difference, then you can use either of the two approaches. The `getAddress` method returns a byte array. You check the size of the byte array to determine if it is IPv4 or IPv6. Or you can use the `instanceOf` method. These two approaches are shown here:

```
byte buffer[] = address.getAddress();
```

```
    if(buffer.length <= 4) {
        System.out.println("IPv4 Address");
    } else {
        System.out.println("IPv6 Address");
    }
    if(address instanceof Inet4Address) {
        System.out.println("IPv4 Address");
    } else {
        System.out.println("IPv6 Address");
    }
```

Using IPv4-compatible IPv6 addresses

The dotted quad notation is a way of expressing an IPv4 address using IPv6. The `::ffff:` prefix is placed in front of either the IPv4 address or its equivalent in hexadecimal. For example, the hexadecimal equivalent of the IPv4 address `74.125.21.105` is `4a7d1569`. Both represent a 32 bit quantity. Thus, any of the following three addresses represent the same website:

```
    address = InetAddress.getByName("74.125.21.105");
    address = InetAddress.getByName("::ffff:74.125.21.105");
    address = InetAddress.getByName("::ffff:4a7d:1569");
```

If we used these addresses with the `displayInetAddressInformation` method, the output will be identical, as shown here:

/74.125.21.105

CanonicalHostName: yv-in-f105.1e100.net

HostName: yv-in-f105.1e100.net

HostAddress: 74.125.21.105

CanonicalHostName: 83.166.169.231

These are referred to as IPv4-compatible IPv6 addresses.

The `Inet6Address` class possesses an `isIPv4CompatibleAddress` method. The method returns `true` if the address is merely an IPv4 address that is placed inside of an IPv6 address. When this happens, all but the last four bytes are zero.

The following example illustrates how this method can be used. Each address associated with `www.google.com` is tested to determine whether it is an IPv4 or IPv6 address. If it is an IPv6 address, then the method is applied to it:

```
    try {
        InetAddress names[] =
```

```
            InetAddress.getAllByName("www.google.com");
        for (InetAddress address : names) {
            if ((address instanceof Inet6Address) &&
                        ((Inet6Address) address)
                            .isIPv4CompatibleAddress()) {
                System.out.println(address
                        + " is IPv4 Compatible Address");
            } else {
                System.out.println(address
                        + " is not a IPv4 Compatible Address");
            }
        }
    } catch (UnknownHostException ex) {
        // Handle exceptions
    }
```

The output depends on the servers available. The following is one possible output:

www.google.com/173.194.46.48 is not a IPv4 Compatible Address

www.google.com/173.194.46.51 is not a IPv4 Compatible Address

www.google.com/173.194.46.49 is not a IPv4 Compatible Address

www.google.com/173.194.46.52 is not a IPv4 Compatible Address

www.google.com/173.194.46.50 is not a IPv4 Compatible Address

www.google.com/2607:f8b0:4009:80b:0:0:0:2004 is not a IPv4 Compatible Address

An alternative Java 8 solution is as follows:

```
        names = InetAddress.getAllByName("www.google.com");
        Arrays.stream(names)
                .map(address -> {
                    if ((address instanceof Inet6Address) &&
                            ((Inet6Address) address)
                                .isIPv4CompatibleAddress()) {
                        return address +
                            " is IPv4 Compatible Address";
                    } else {
                        return address +
                            " is not IPv4 Compatible Address";
                    }
                })
                .forEach(result -> System.out.println(result));
```

Controlling network properties

On many operating systems, the default behavior is to use IPv4 instead of IPv6. The following JVM options can be used when executing a Java application to control this behavior. The first setting is as follows:

```
-Djava.net.preferIPv4Stack=false
```

This is the default setting. If IPv6 is available, then the application can use either IPv4 or IPv6 hosts. If set to `true`, it will use IPv4 hosts. IPv6 hosts will not be used.

The second setting deals with the type of addresses used:

```
-Djava.net.preferIPv6Addresses=false
```

This is the default setting. If IPv6 is available, it will prefer IPv4 addresses over IPv6 addresses. This is preferred because it allows backward compatibility for IPv4 services. If set to `true`, it will use IPv6 addresses whenever possible.

Summary

This chapter provided an overview of the basic network terms and concepts. Networking is a large and complicated subject. In this chapter, we focused on those concepts that are relevant to networking in Java.

The `NetworkInterface` class was introduced. This class provides low-level access to the devices connected to a computer that support networking. We also learned how to obtain the MAC address for a device.

We focused on the support that Java provides to access the Internet. The foundation IP protocol was detailed. This protocol is supported by the `InetAddress` class. Java uses the `Inet4Address` and `Inet6Address` classes to support IPv4 and IPv6 addresses, respectively.

We also illustrated the use of the `URI` and `URL` classes. These classes possess several methods that allow us to obtain more information about specific instances. We can use these methods to split the URI or URL into parts for further processing.

We also discussed how to control some network connection properties. We will cover this topic in more detail in later chapters.

With this foundation in place, we can now move forward and address the use of the NIO packages to support networking. NIO is buffer oriented and supports nonblocking IO. In addition, it provides better performance for many IO operations.

3
NIO Support for Networking

In this chapter, we will focus on the Java **New IO (NIO)** package's `Buffer` and `Channels` classes. NIO is an alternative for the earlier Java IO API and parts of the network API. While NIO is a broad and complex topic, our interest is how it provides support for network applications.

We will explore several topics, including the following:

- The nature and relationship between buffers, channels, and selectors
- The use of NIO techniques to build a client/server
- The process of handling multiple clients
- Support for asynchronous socket channels
- Basic buffer operations

The NIO package provides extensive support to build efficient network applications.

Java NIO

Java NIO uses three core classes:

- `Buffer`: This holds information that is read or written to a channel
- `Channel`: This is a stream-like technique that supports asynchronous read/write operations to a data source/sink
- `Selector`: This is a mechanism to handle multiple channels in a single thread

Conceptually, buffers and channels work together to process data. As shown in the next figure, data can be moved in either direction between a buffer and a channel:

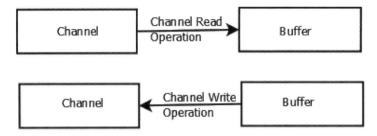

The channel is connected to some external data source, while the buffer is used internally to process the data. There are several types of channels and buffers. A few of these are listed in the following tables.

The table for channels is as follows:

Channel class	Purpose
FileChannel	This connects to a file
DatagramChannel	This supports datagram sockets
SocketChannel	This supports streaming sockets
ServerSocketChannel	This listens for socket requests
NetworkChannel	This supports a network socket
AsynchronousSocketChannel	This supports asynchronous streaming sockets

The table for buffers is as follows:

Buffer class	Data type supported
ByteBuffer	byte
CharBuffer	char
DoubleBuffer	double
FloatBuffer	float
IntBuffer	int
LongBuffer	long
ShortBuffer	short

The Selector class is useful when an application uses many low-traffic connections that can be handled using a single thread. This is more efficient than creating a thread for each connection. This is also a technique that is used to make an application more scalable, something that we will discuss in *Chapter 7, Network Scalability*.

In this chapter, we will create client/server applications to illustrate the interaction between channels and buffers. This includes a simple time server, a chat server to demonstrate variable length messages, a parts server to illustrate one technique to handle multiple clients, and an asynchronous server. We will also examine specialized buffer techniques, including bulk transfers and views.

We will begin our discussion with an overview of buffers, and how they work with channels.

Introduction to buffers

Buffers hold data temporarily because it is being moved to and from channels. When a buffer is created, it is created with a fixed size or capacity. Part or all of a buffer's memory can be used with several Buffer class fields available to manage the data in a buffer.

The Buffer class is abstract. However, it possesses the basic methods used to manipulate a buffer, including:

- capacity: This returns the number of elements in the buffer
- limit: This returns the first index of the buffer that should not be accessed
- position: This returns the index of the next element to be read or written

The element depends on the buffer type.

The mark and reset methods also control the position within a buffer. The mark method will set the buffer's mark to its position. The reset method restores the mark position to the previously marked position. The following code shows the relationships between various buffer terms:

```
0 <= mark <= position <= limit <= capacity
```

A buffer can be either **direct** or **non-direct**. A direct buffer will attempt to use the native IO methods whenever possible. The creation of a direct buffer tends to be more expensive but will perform more efficiently for larger buffers, which reside in the memory longer. The allocateDirect method is used to create a direct buffer and accepts an integer specifying the size of the buffer. The allocate method also accepts an integer size argument but creates a non-direct buffer.

A non-direct buffer will not be as efficient as a direct buffer for most operations. However, memory used by the non-direct buffer will be reclaimed by the JVM garbage collector, whereas direct memory buffers may be outside the control of the JVM. This makes the management of memory more predictable with non-direct buffers.

There are several methods that are used to transfer data between a channel and a buffer. These can be classified as either of the following:

- Absolute or relative
- Bulk transfers
- Using primitive data types
- Supporting a view
- Compacting, duplicating, and slicing a byte buffer

Many `Buffer` class's methods support invocation chaining. A put type method will transfer data to a buffer, while a get type method retrieves information from a buffer. We will be using the get and put methods extensively in our examples. These methods will transfer a single byte at a time.

These get and put methods are relative to the current location of the position within a buffer. There are also several absolute methods that use an index in the buffer to isolate a specific buffer element.

Bulk data transfers contiguous blocks of data. These get and put methods use an array of bytes as one of their arguments to hold the data. These are discussed in the *Bulk data transfer* section.

When all of the data in a `Buffer` class is of the same type, a **view** can be created permitting convenient access to the data using a specific data type such as `Float`. We will demonstrate this buffer in the *Using a view* section.

Compacting, duplicating, and slicing type operations are supported. The compacting operation will shift the contents of a buffer to eliminate data that has already been processed. Duplication will make a copy of a buffer, while slicing creates a new buffer that is based on the all or part of the original buffer. Changes to either buffer will be reflected in the other. However, the position, limit, and mark values of each buffer are independent.

Let's see a buffer in action starting with the creation of a buffer.

Using channels with a time server

The time server and client that were introduced in *Chapter 1, Getting Started with Network Programming*, will be implemented here to demonstrate the use of buffers and channels. These applications are simple, but they illustrate how buffers and channels can be used together. We will start by creating a server and then create a client that uses the server.

Creating a time server

The following code is the initial declaration of the ServerSocketChannelTimeServer
class, which will be our time server. The ServerSocketChannel class's open
method creates a ServerSocketChannel instance. The socket method retrieves the
ServerSocket instance for the channel. The bind method then associates this server
socket with port 5000. While the ServerSocketChannel class has a close method, it is
easier to use the try-with-resources block:

```
public class ServerSocketChannelTimeServer {
    public static void main(String[] args) {
        System.out.println("Time Server started");
        try {
            ServerSocketChannel serverSocketChannel =
                ServerSocketChannel.open();
            serverSocketChannel.socket().bind(
                new InetSocketAddress(5000));
            ...
        }
    } catch (IOException ex) {
        // Handle exceptions
    }
    }
}
```

The server will enter an infinite loop where the accept methods blocks until a
request is received from a client. When this happens, a SocketChannel instance
is returned:

```
while (true) {
    System.out.println("Waiting for request ...");
    SocketChannel socketChannel =
        serverSocketChannel.accept();
```

Assuming this instance is not null, a string containing the current date and time
is created:

```
if (socketChannel != null) {
    String dateAndTimeMessage = "Date: "
        + new Date(System.currentTimeMillis());
    ...

}
```

A `ByteBuffer` instance is created with a size of 64 bytes. This is more than enough for most messages. The `put` method moves the data into the buffer. This is a bulk data transfer operation. If the buffer not large enough, then a `BufferOverflowException` exception is thrown:

```
ByteBuffer buf = ByteBuffer.allocate(64);
buf.put(dateAndTimeMessage.getBytes());
```

We need to invoke the `flip` method so that we can use it with the channel's write operation. This has the effect of setting; the limit is set to the current position and the position to zero. A while loop is used to write out each byte and is terminated when there are no more bytes to write as determined by the `hasRemaining` method. The last action is to display the message that is sent to the client:

```
buf.flip();
while (buf.hasRemaining()) {
    socketChannel.write(buf);
}
System.out.println("Sent: " + dateAndTimeMessage);
```

When the server is started, it will produce an output that is similar to the following one:

Time Server started

Waiting for request ...

We are now ready to create our client.

Creating a time client

The client is implemented in the `SocketChannelTimeClient` class, as defined next. To simplify the example, the client is assumed to be on the same machine as the server. A `SocketAddress` instance is created using the IP address `127.0.0.1` and is associated with port `5000`. The `SocketChannel` class's `open` method returns a `SocketChannel` instance, which will be used to handle the response from the server within the try-with-resources block:

```
public class SocketChannelTimeClient {
    public static void main(String[] args) {
        SocketAddress address = new InetSocketAddress(
            "127.0.0.1", 5000);
        try (SocketChannel socketChannel =
                SocketChannel.open(address)) {
            ...
```

```
        } catch (IOException ex) {
            ex.printStackTrace();
        }
    }
}
```

In the body of the try block, a `ByteBuffer` instance of size 64 is created. Using a size smaller than the actual message will complicate this example. In the *Handling variable length messages* section, we will re-examine buffer sizes. The message is read from the channel and placed into the `ByteBuffer` instance using the `read` method. This buffer is then flipped to prepare it for processing. Each byte is read and then displayed:

```
ByteBuffer byteBuffer = ByteBuffer.allocate(64);
int bytesRead = socketChannel.read(byteBuffer);
while (bytesRead > 0) {
    byteBuffer.flip();
    while (byteBuffer.hasRemaining()) {
        System.out.print((char) byteBuffer.get());
    }
    System.out.println();
    bytesRead = socketChannel.read(byteBuffer);
}
```

When client is started, its output will be similar to the following:

Date: Tue Aug 18 21:36:25 CDT 2015

The server's output will now appear similar to this one:

Time Server started

Waiting for request ...

Sent: Date: Tue Aug 18 21:36:25 CDT 2015

Waiting for request ...

We are now ready to examine the details of channel and buffer interaction.

The chat server/client applications

The intent of this section is to demonstrate how buffers and channels work together in more depth. We will use client and server applications that pass messages back and forth. Specifically, we will create a simple version of a chat server.

We will perform the following actions:

- Create a server and a client that send messages back and forth
- Demonstrate how to handle variable length messages

First, we will demonstrate using a fixed size message using the `sendFixedLengthMessage` and `receiveFixedLengthMessage` methods. Then we will use the `sendMessage` and `receiveMessage` methods to handle variable length messages. Fixed length messages are easier to handle but will not work if the length of a message exceeds the size of the buffer. Variable length messages require more careful handling than what we have seen in previous examples. These methods have been placed in a class called `HelperMethods` to enable their use in multiple applications.

The chat server

Let's start with the server. The server is defined in the `ChatServer` class as defined next. A `ServerSocketChannel` instance is created and bound to port `5000`. It will be used in the body of the while loop. The `running` variable controls the lifetime of the server. Exceptions are caught as needed. As in the previous server, the server will block at the `accept` method until a client connects to the server:

```
public class ChatServer {

    public ChatServer() {
        System.out.println("Chat Server started");
        try {
            ServerSocketChannel serverSocketChannel =
                ServerSocketChannel.open();
            serverSocketChannel.socket().bind(
                new InetSocketAddress(5000));

            boolean running = true;
            while (running) {
                System.out.println("Waiting for request ...");
                SocketChannel socketChannel
                        = serverSocketChannel.accept();
                ...
            }
        } catch (IOException ex) {
            ex.printStackTrace();
        }
    }
```

```
      public static void main(String[] args) {
          new ChatServer();
      }
  }
```

In this chat/server application, communication is restricted. Once a connection is made, the server will prompt the user for a message to send to the client. The client will wait until this message is received, and then it will prompt its user for a reply. The reply is sent back to the server. This sequence is limited to simplify the interaction to focus on the channel/buffer interaction.

When a connection is made, the server displays a message to that effect and then enters a loop as shown next. The user is prompted for a message. The sendFixedLengthMessage method is invoked. If the user entered quit, then a terminating message is sent to the server, and the server terminates. Otherwise, the message is sent to the server and then the server blocks at the receiveFixedLengthMessage method waiting for the client to respond:

```
      System.out.println("Connected to Client");
      String message;
      Scanner scanner = new Scanner(System.in);
      while (true) {
          System.out.print("> ");
          message = scanner.nextLine();
          if (message.equalsIgnoreCase("quit")) {
              HelperMethods.sendFixedLengthMessage(
                      socketChannel, "Server terminating");
              running = false;
              break;
          } else {
              HelperMethods.sendFixedLengthMessage(
                  socketChannel, message);
              System.out.println(
                  "Waiting for message from client ...");
              System.out.println("Message: " + HelperMethods
                  .receiveFixedLengthMessage(socketChannel));
          }
      }
```

When the server starts, its output will appear as follows:

Chat Server started

Waiting for request ...

With the server created, let's examine the client application.

The chat client

The client application uses the ChatClient class, as defined next. Its structure is similar to the previous client application. The localhost (127.0.0.1) is used with a port of 5000. Once a connection has been established, the program enters an infinite loop and waits for the server to send it a message:

```java
public class ChatClient {

    public ChatClient() {
        SocketAddress address =
            new InetSocketAddress("127.0.0.1", 5000);
        try (SocketChannel socketChannel =
                SocketChannel.open(address)) {
            System.out.println("Connected to Chat Server");
            String message;
            Scanner scanner = new Scanner(System.in);
            while (true) {
                System.out.println(
                    "Waiting for message from the server ...");
                ...
            }
        } catch (IOException ex) {
            ex.printStackTrace();
        }
    }

    public static void main(String[] args) {
        new ChatClient();
    }
}
```

Within the loop, the program blocks at the receiveFixedLengthMessage method until the server sends it a message. The message is then displayed, and the user is prompted for a message to send back to the server. If the message is **quit**, then a terminating message is sent to the server using the sendFixedLengthMessage method, and the application terminates. Otherwise the message is sent to the server, and the program waits for another message:

```java
System.out.println("Waiting for message from the server ...");
System.out.println("Message: "
        + HelperMethods.receiveFixedLengthMessage(
                socketChannel));
System.out.print("> ");
message = scanner.nextLine();
```

```
if (message.equalsIgnoreCase("quit")) {
    HelperMethods.sendFixedLengthMessage(
        socketChannel, "Client terminating");
    break;
}
HelperMethods.sendFixedLengthMessage(socketChannel, message);
```

With the client and server created, let's take a look at how they interact.

Server/client interaction

With the server started, start the client application. The client's output will appear as follows:

Connected to Chat Server

Waiting for message from the server ...

The server output will reflect this connection:

Chat Server started

Waiting for request ...

Connected to Client

>

Enter the message Hello. You will then get the following output:

> Hello

Sent: Hello

Waiting for message from client ...

The client side will now appear as:

Message: Hello

>

Enter a reply of Hi! The client output will appear as shown here:

> Hi!

Sent: Hi!

Waiting for message from the server ...

The server will appear as:

Message: Hi!

>

We can continue this process until either side enters the `quit` command. However, entering a message that exceeds the 64 byte buffer limit will result in a `BufferOverflowException` exception being thrown. Replacing the `sendFixedLengthMessage` method with the `sendMessage` method and the `receiveFixedLengthMessage` method with the `receiveMessage` method will avoid this problem.

Let's examine how these send and receive methods work.

The HelperMethods class

The `HelperMethods` class is defined next. It possesses the send and receive methods that were used previously. These methods are declared as static to allow them to be accessed easily:

```
public class HelperMethods {
    ...
}
```

The fixed length message methods are shown next. They perform essentially the same way as the approach that was used in the *Using channels with a time server* section:

```
public static void sendFixedLengthMessage(
        SocketChannel socketChannel, String message) {
    try {
        ByteBuffer buffer = ByteBuffer.allocate(64);
        buffer.put(message.getBytes());
        buffer.flip();
        while (buffer.hasRemaining()) {
            socketChannel.write(buffer);
        }
        System.out.println("Sent: " + message);
    } catch (IOException ex) {
        ex.printStackTrace();
    }
}

public static String receiveFixedLengthMessage
        (SocketChannel socketChannel) {
    String message = "";
    try {
```

```
        ByteBuffer byteBuffer = ByteBuffer.allocate(64);
        socketChannel.read(byteBuffer);
        byteBuffer.flip();
        while (byteBuffer.hasRemaining()) {
            message += (char) byteBuffer.get();
        }
    } catch (IOException ex) {
        ex.printStackTrace();
    }
    return message;
}
```

Handling variable length messages

The technique to handle variable length messages is discussed in this section. The problem with variable length messages is that we do not know their length. We cannot assume that when a buffer is not completely filled that the end of the message has been reached. While this may be true with most messages, if the message length is the same size as the message buffer, then we may miss the end of a message.

Another approach to determining when we have reached the end of a message is to either send the length of a message prefixed to the message or append a special termination character to the end of the message. We choose the latter approach.

> This example works for ASCII characters. If Unicode characters are used instead, then a `BufferOverflowException` exception will be generated. The `CharBuffer` class is used for character data and provides similar capabilities as the `ByteBuffer` class. The `CharBuffer` class is detailed at http://docs.oracle.com/javase/8/docs/api/java/nio/CharBuffer.html.

The value of 0x00 was used to mark the end of a message. We choose this value because it is not easily entered accidently by the user because it is not printable and happens to correspond to how strings are often terminated internally in languages, such as C.

In the `sendMessage` method that follows, the `put` method adds this termination byte to the end of the message before it is sent. The buffer size is the length of the message plus one. Otherwise, the code is similar to that used to send a fixed length message:

```
public static void sendMessage(
    SocketChannel socketChannel, String message) {
    try {
        ByteBuffer buffer =
            ByteBuffer.allocate(message.length() + 1);
```

```
        buffer.put(message.getBytes());
        buffer.put((byte) 0x00);
        buffer.flip();
        while (buffer.hasRemaining()) {
            socketChannel.write(buffer);
        }
        System.out.println("Sent: " + message);
    } catch (IOException ex) {
        ex.printStackTrace();
    }
}
```

In the `receiveMessage` method, each byte received is checked to see if it is the termination byte. If it is, then the message is returned. The `clear` method is applied to the `byteBuffer` variable after we have extracted part of the message. This method is required; otherwise, the read method will return 0. The method will set the buffer's position back to 0 and the limit to capacity:

```
public static String receiveMessage(SocketChannel
    socketChannel) {
    try {
        ByteBuffer byteBuffer = ByteBuffer.allocate(16);
        String message = "";
        while (socketChannel.read(byteBuffer) > 0) {
            char byteRead = 0x00;
            byteBuffer.flip();
            while (byteBuffer.hasRemaining()) {
                byteRead = (char) byteBuffer.get();
                if (byteRead == 0x00) {
                    break;
                }
                message += byteRead;
            }
            if (byteRead == 0x00) {
                break;
            }
            byteBuffer.clear();
        }
        return message;
    } catch (IOException ex) {
        ex.printStackTrace();
    }
    return "";
}
```

We are now ready to demonstrate the application.

Running the chat server/client application

Start the server first. The output will appear as follows:

Chat Server started

Waiting for request ...

Next, start the client, which will result in the following output:

Connected to Chat Server

Waiting for message from the server ...

These users interchange between the server and the client is limited with the current implementation. When both applications have been started, the client will be waiting for a message from the server. This is reflected by a server window, as shown here:

Chat Server started

Waiting for request ...

Connected to Client

>

When a message is entered, it is sent to the client. Enter the message **Hello**. The client window will now display the message, as shown here:

Connected to Chat Server

Waiting for message from the server ...

Message: Hello

>

On the server side, the following output will appear:

Sent: Hello

Waiting for message from client ...

We can now send a message from the client to the server. Messages can be interchanged in this manner until the `quit` message is sent from either application.

Handling multiple clients

Handling multiple clients can be achieved using threads. In this section, we will develop a simple parts server and client applications. The server will use a separate thread to handle each client. This technique is simple to implement, but it will not always be suitable for more demanding applications. We will introduce alternate techniques to multitask in *Chapter 7, Network Scalability*.

The parts server is implemented in the `PartsServer` class, and the client is implemented in the `PartsClient` class. A new instance of a `ClientHandler` class will be created for each client. This handler will accept requests for the price of a part. The client will send the name of the part to the handler. The handler will look up the price of the part using the `getPrice` method of `PartsServer`. It will then return the price to the client.

The parts server

The parts server uses a `HashMap` variable to hold information about parts. The name of the part is used as a key, and the value is stored as a `Float` object. The `PartsServer` class is declared here:

```java
public class PartsServer {
    private static final HashMap<String,Float> parts =
            new HashMap<>();

    public PartsServer() {
        System.out.println("Part Server Started");
        ...
    }

    public static void main(String[] args) {
        new PartsServer();
    }
}
```

Once the server has started, the `initializeParts` method is called:

```java
        initializeParts();
```

This method follows:

```java
        private void initializeParts() {
            parts.put("Hammer", 12.55f);
            parts.put("Nail", 1.35f);
            parts.put("Pliers", 4.65f);
            parts.put("Saw", 8.45f);
        }
```

The handler will use the `getPrice` method to retrieve the price of a part, as shown next:

```
public static Float getPrice(String partName) {
    return parts.get(partName);
}
```

After the `initializeParts` method has been called, a try block is used to open a connection to a client as shown here:

```
try {
    ServerSocketChannel serverSocketChannel =
        ServerSocketChannel.open();
    serverSocketChannel.socket().bind(
        new InetSocketAddress(5000));
    ...
} catch (IOException ex) {
    ex.printStackTrace();
}
```

Next, an infinite loop will create a new handler for each client. While there are several ways of creating a thread in Java, the approach that is used next creates a new instance of the `ClientHandler` class, passing the client's socket to the class's constructor. This approach does not limit the number of threads created by the application, which makes it susceptible to a denial of service attack. In *Chapter 7, Network Scalability*, we will examine several alternate threading approaches.

The `ClientHandler` instance is used as the argument of the `Thread` class. The class will create a new thread that will execute the `ClientHandler` class's `run` method. However, the `run` method should not be called directly, but instead the `start` method is invoked. This method will create the program stack that is needed for the thread:

```
while (true) {
    System.out.println("Waiting for client ...");
    SocketChannel socketChannel
            = serverSocketChannel.accept();
    new Thread(
        new ClientHandler(socketChannel)).start();
}
```

When the server is started, it will display the following output:

Part Server Started

Waiting for client ...

Let's examine how the handler works.

The parts client handler

The ClientHandler class is defined in the following code. The socketChannel instance variable is used to connect to the client. In the run method, a message indicating the start of the handler will be displayed. It is not required, but it will help us look at how the server, client, and handler interact.

An infinite loop is entered where the receiveMessage method, developed in the *The HelperMethods class* section, is used to get the name of the part. A quit message will terminate the handler. Otherwise, the getPrice method is called, which is returned back to the client using the sendMessage method:

```
public class ClientHandler implements Runnable{
    private final SocketChannel socketChannel;

    public ClientHandler(SocketChannel socketChannel) {
        this.socketChannel = socketChannel;
    }

    public void run() {
        System.out.println("ClientHandler Started for "
            + this.socketChannel);
        String partName;
        while (true) {
            partName =
                HelperMethods.receiveMessage(socketChannel);
            if (partName.equalsIgnoreCase("quit")) {
                break;
            } else {
                Float price = PartsServer.getPrice(partName);
                HelperMethods.sendMessage(socketChannel, "" +
                    price);
            }
        }
        System.out.println("ClientHandler Terminated for "
            + this.socketChannel);
    }
}
```

We will observe the output of the run method when we demonstrate the client.

The parts client

The `PartsClient` class is defined in the next code sequence. A connection to the server is established. Messages are displayed indicating when the client starts, and the server connection is made. The `Scanner` class is used in the while loop to get input from the user:

```java
public class PartsClient {

    public PartsClient() {
        System.out.println("PartsClient Started");
        SocketAddress address =
            new InetSocketAddress("127.0.0.1", 5000);
        try (SocketChannel socketChannel =
                SocketChannel.open(address)) {
            System.out.println("Connected to Parts Server");
            Scanner scanner = new Scanner(System.in);
            while (true) {
                ...
            }
            System.out.println("PartsClient Terminated");
        } catch (IOException ex) {
            ex.printStackTrace();
        }
    }

    public static void main(String[] args) {
        new PartsClient();
    }
}
```

The body of the loop will prompt the user for a part name. If the name is quit, then the client will terminate. Otherwise, the `sendMessage` method will send the name to the handler for processing. The client will block at the `receiveMessage` method invocation until the server responds. The price of this part will then be displayed:

```java
System.out.print("Enter part name: ");
String partName = scanner.nextLine();
if (partName.equalsIgnoreCase("quit")) {
    HelperMethods.sendMessage(socketChannel, "quit");
    break;
} else {
    HelperMethods.sendMessage(socketChannel, partName);
    System.out.println("The price is "
        + HelperMethods.receiveMessage(socketChannel));
}
```

Now, let's see how they all work together.

Running the parts client/server

Start the server first. The server will produce the following output when it is started:

Part Server started

Waiting for client ...

Now, start the client application. You will get this output:

PartsClient Started

Connected to Parts Server

Enter part name:

Enter a part name, such as Hammer. The client output will now appear as shown next. The **Sent: Hammer** output is an artifact of the sendMessage method and can be removed by modifying the sendMessage method if desired:

PartsClient Started

Connected to Parts Server

Enter part name: Hammer

Sent: Hammer

The price is 12.55

Enter part name:

On the server side, you will get an output similar to the following one. A message displaying information about the handler is seen whenever a new client is started:

Part Server Started

Waiting for client ...

ClientHandler Started for java.nio.channels.SocketChannel[connected local=/127.0.0.1:5000 remote=/127.0.0.1:51132]

Waiting for client ...

Sent: 12.55

From the client side, we can continue checking prices until we enter the `quit` command. This command will terminate the client. One possible sequence of requests is as follows:

PartsClient Started

Connected to Parts Server

Enter part name: Hammer

Sent: Hammer

The price is 12.55

Enter part name: Pliers

Sent: Pliers

The price is 4.65

Enter part name: saw

Sent: saw

The price is null

Enter part name: Saw

Sent: Saw

The price is 8.45

Enter part name: quit

Sent: quit

PartsClient Terminated

The server will continue running as there may be other clients seeking price information. Output similar to the following one will be displayed by the server when a client handler terminates:

ClientHandler Terminated for java.nio.channels.SocketChannel[connected local=/127.0.0.1:5000 remote=/127.0.0.1: 51132]

Start up two or more clients, and watch how they interact with the server. We will investigate more sophisticated ways of scaling an application in *Chapter 7, Network Scalability*.

Asynchronous socket channels

Asynchronous communication involves making a request, and then proceeding with some other operation without having to wait for the request to be completed. This is referred to as non-blocking.

There are three classes used to support asynchronous channel operations:

- `AsynchronousSocketChannel`: This is a simple asynchronous channel to a socket

- `AsynchronousServerSocketChannel`: This is an asynchronous channel to a server socket

- `AsynchronousDatagramChannel`: This is a channel for a datagram-oriented socket

The read/write methods of the `AsynchronousSocketChannel` class are asynchronous. The `AsynchronousServerSocketChannel` class possesses an `accept` method, which returns an `AsynchronousSocketChannel` instance. This method is also asynchronous. We will discuss the `AsynchronousDatagramChannel` class in *Chapter 6, UDP and Multicasting*.

There are two ways of handling asynchronous I/O operations:

- Using the `Future` interface found in the `java.util.concurrent` package
- Using a `CompletionHandler` interface

The `Future` interface represents a pending result. This supports asynchronous operations by allowing the application to continue executing and not block. Using this object, you can use one of the following methods:

- The `isDone` method
- The `get` method, which blocks until completion

The `get` method is overloaded with one version supporting a timeout. The `CompletionHandler` instance is invoked when the operation has completed. This is essentially a callback. We will not illustrate this approach here.

We will develop an asynchronous server and client called `AsynchronousServerSocketChannelServer` and `AsynchronousSocketChannelClient`, respectively. The client/server application is limited and only allows messages to be sent from the client to the server. This will allow us to focus on the asynchronous aspects of the application.

Creating the asynchronous server socket channel server

The `AsynchronousServerSocketChannelServer` class is defined in the next code sequence. A message indicating that the server has started is displayed, and a try-with-resources block is entered where an instance of the `AsynchronousServerSocketChannel` class is created and the actual work occurs:

```
public class AsynchronousServerSocketChannelServer {

    public AsynchronousServerSocketChannelServer() {
        System.out.println("Asynchronous Server Started");
        try (AsynchronousServerSocketChannel serverChannel
                = AsynchronousServerSocketChannel.open()) {
            ...
        } catch (IOException | InterruptedException
                | ExecutionException ex) {
            ex.printStackTrace();
        }

    }

    public static void main(String[] args) {
        new AsynchronousServerSocketChannelServer();
    }

}
```

The `bind` method is used to associate the `serverChannel` variable, representing the `AsynchronousServerSocketChannel` instance, with the localhost and port `5000`:

```
InetSocketAddress hostAddress
    = new InetSocketAddress("localhost", 5000);
serverChannel.bind(hostAddress);
```

The server then waits for a client to connect. The `Future` instance is reference by the `acceptResult` variable:

```
System.out.println("Waiting for client to connect... ");
Future acceptResult = serverChannel.accept();
```

Another try block is used to handle client requests. It creates an instance of the AsynchronousSocketChannel class, which connects to the client. The get method will block until the channel is created:

```
try (AsynchronousSocketChannel clientChannel
        = (AsynchronousSocketChannel) acceptResult.get()) {
    ...
}
```

The body of the try block will allocate a buffer and then read from the channel to populate the buffer. When the buffer has been populated, the flip method is applied to the buffer and the message is processed and displayed:

```
System.out.println("Messages from client: ");
while ((clientChannel != null) && (clientChannel.isOpen())) {
    ByteBuffer buffer = ByteBuffer.allocate(32);
    Future result = clientChannel.read(buffer);
    // Wait until buffer is ready using
    // one of three techniques to be discussed
    buffer.flip();
    String message = new String(buffer.array()).trim();
    System.out.println(message);
    if (message.equals("quit")) {
        break;
    }
}
```

There are three ways of determining whether the buffer is ready. The first technique polls the Future object, represented by the result variable, using the isDone method until the buffer is ready, as shown here:

```
while (!result.isDone()) {
    // do nothing
}
```

The second technique uses the get method, which blocks until the buffer is ready:

```
result.get();
```

The third technique also uses the get method but uses a timeout to determine how long to wait. In this example, it waits 10 seconds before timing out:

```
result.get(10, TimeUnit.SECONDS);
```

When this version of the get method is used, a catch block needs to be added to the enclosing try block to handle a TimeoutException exception.

When the server is started, we get the following output:

Asynchronous Server Started

Waiting for client to connect...

Now, let's examine the client.

Creating the asynchronous socket channel client

The client is implemented using the AsynchronousSocketChannelClient class in the next code snippet. A message indicating that the client has started is displayed, followed by a try block that creates a AsynchronousSocketChannel instance:

```
public class AsynchronousSocketChannelClient {

    public static void main(String[] args) {
        System.out.println("Asynchronous Client Started");
        try (AsynchronousSocketChannel client =
                AsynchronousSocketChannel.open()) {
            ...
        } catch (IOException | InterruptedException
                            | ExecutionException ex) {
            // Handle exception
        }
    }

}
```

An InetSocketAddress instance is created specifying the address and port number used by the server. A Future object representing the connection is then created. The get method will block until the connection is made:

```
InetSocketAddress hostAddress =
        new InetSocketAddress("localhost", 5000);
Future future = client.connect(hostAddress);
future.get();
```

Once the connection is made, a message is displayed. An infinite loop is entered where the user is prompted for a message. The `wrap` method will populate the buffer with the message. The `write` method will start writing the message to the `AsynchronousSocketChannel` instance and will return a `Future` object. The `isDone` method is used to wait for the write to complete. If the message is **quit**, the client application will terminate:

```
System.out.println("Client is started: " + client.isOpen());
System.out.println("Sending messages to server: ");

Scanner scanner = new Scanner(System.in);
String message;
while (true) {
    System.out.print("> ");
    message = scanner.nextLine();
    ByteBuffer buffer = ByteBuffer.wrap(message.getBytes());
    Future result = client.write(buffer);
    while (!result.isDone()) {
        // Wait
    }
    if (message.equalsIgnoreCase("quit")) {
        break;
    }
}
```

Let's take a look at the asynchronous client/server in action.

With the server running, start the client application. This will produce the following output:

Asynchronous Client Started

Client is started: true

Sending messages to server:

>

The output for the server now appears as follows:

Asynchronous Server Started

Waiting for client to connect...

Messages from client:

Using the client, we can enter the following messages:

> Hello

> This message is from the asynchronous client and is sent to the server

> quit

These will be sent to the server one at a time. From the server, we will get the following response:

Hello

This message is from the asynchr

onous client and is sent to the

server

quit

Note that the longer message has been split across multiple lines. This is the result of using a server buffer size of only 32 bytes. A larger buffer would have avoided this issue. However, unless we know the size of the largest message that will be sent, we need to develop a way of handling long messages. This is left as an exercise for the reader.

Other buffer operations

We will wrap up by examining several other buffer operations that can be useful. These include bulk data transfers between a buffer and an array using a view, and read-only buffers.

Bulk data transfer

Bulk transfer is a way of transferring data between a buffer and an array. There are several get and put type methods that support bulk data transfers. They usually have two versions. The first version uses a single argument, which is the transfer array. The second version also uses an array, but it has two additional arguments: the starting index in the array, and the number of elements to transfer.

To demonstrate these techniques, we will use an `IntBuffer` buffer. We will use the following `displayBuffer` method to help us understand how data transfers work:

```
public void displayBuffer(IntBuffer buffer) {
    for (int i = 0; i < buffer.position(); i++) {
        System.out.print(buffer.get(i) + " ");
    }
    System.out.println();
}
```

We will start by declaring an array and transferring its contents to a buffer. The array is declared and initialized in the following statement:

```
int[] arr = {12, 51, 79, 54};
```

A buffer is allocated, which is larger than the array, as shown next. The difference between the array size and the data available in the buffer is important. If not handled properly, exceptions will be thrown:

```
IntBuffer buffer = IntBuffer.allocate(6);
```

Next, we will use the bulk `put` method to transfer the contents of the array to the buffer:

```
buffer.put(arr);
```

The buffer is then displayed using the following statements:

```
System.out.println(buffer);
displayBuffer(buffer);
```

The output is as follows. The entire array has been transferred, and the position is set to the next available index:

java.nio.HeapIntBuffer[pos=4 lim=6 cap=6]

12 51 79 54

As there is still room in the buffer, we can transfer more data into it. However, we have to be careful not to try to transfer too much, otherwise an exception will be thrown. The first step is to determine how much space is left in the buffer. As shown next, the `remaining` method does this. The bulk `put` statement then transfers the first two elements of the array to the last two positions of the buffer, as shown here:

```
int length = buffer.remaining();
buffer.put(arr, 0, length);
```

If we display the buffer and its contents again, we get the following output:

java.nio.HeapIntBuffer[pos=6 lim=6 cap=6]

12 51 79 54 12 51

The `get` method is overloaded to support bulk data transfer. We can modify the `displayBuffer` method to illustrate how this works, as shown next. An integer array is created that is the same size as the contents of the buffer. The `rewind` method will move the position of the buffer back to zero. The bulk `get` method then performs the transfer followed by a for-each loop to actually display its contents:

```
public void displayBuffer(IntBuffer buffer) {
    int arr[] = new int[buffer.position()];
    buffer.rewind();
    buffer.get(arr);
    for(int element : arr) {
        System.out.print(element + " ");
    }
}
```

Using a view

A view mirrors the data in another buffer. Modification to either buffer will affect the other buffer. However, the position and limit are independent. A view can be created with several methods, including the `duplicate` method. In the following example, a view is made of a buffer using the bulk `getBytes` method against a string. The view is then created:

```
String contents = "Book";
ByteBuffer buffer = ByteBuffer.allocate(32);
buffer.put(contents.getBytes());
ByteBuffer duplicateBuffer = buffer.duplicate();
```

To demonstrate that the modification of one buffer will affect the other buffer, the first character of the duplicate is changed to the letter 'L'. The first byte of each buffer is then displayed to confirm the change:

```
duplicateBuffer.put(0,(byte)0x4c); // 'L'
System.out.println("buffer: " + buffer.get(0));
System.out.println("duplicateBuffer: " +
    duplicateBuffer.get(0));
```

The output will show that the letter has been changed in both buffers. The `slice` method will also create a view, but it uses only a portion of the original buffer.

Using read-only buffers

A buffer, by default, is read-write. However, it can be read-only or read-write. To create a read-only buffer, use the buffer class's `asReadOnlyBuffer` method. In the next sequence, a read-only buffer is created:

```
ByteBuffer buffer = ByteBuffer.allocate(32);
ByteBuffer readOnlyBuffer = buffer.asReadOnlyBuffer();
```

The `isReadOnly` method will determine if a buffer is read-only as demonstrated here:

```
System.out.println("Read-only: " +
    readOnlyBuffer.isReadOnly());
```

The read-only buffer is a different view of the original buffer. Any modifications to a buffer is reflected in the other buffer.

Controlling socket options

The underlying socket implementation for the socket classes can be configured. The options available are dependent on the socket type. Frequently, the actual mechanism used to support an option is OS-specific. Also, sometimes the option is just a hint to the underlying implementation.

The options available for each socket class shown next is adapted from the Java API documentation:

Class	Option name	Description
SocketChannel	SO_SNDBUF	This is the size of the socket send buffer
	SO_RCVBUF	This is the size of the socket receive buffer
	SO_KEEPALIVE	This keeps the connection alive
	SO_REUSEADDR	This re-uses the address
	SO_LINGER	This lingers on close if data is present (when configured in blocking mode only)
	TCP_NODELAY	This will disable the Nagle algorithm
ServerSocketChannel	SO_RCVBUF	This is the size of the socket receive buffer
	SO_REUSEADDR	This re-uses address

Class	Option name	Description
AsynchronousSocketChannel	SO_SNDBUF	This is the size of the socket send buffer
	SO_RCVBUF	This is the size of the socket receive buffer
	SO_KEEPALIVE	This keeps the connection alive
	SO_REUSEADDR	This re-uses address
	TCP_NODELAY	This will disable the Nagle algorithm

Socket options are configured using the setOption method. The following code illustrates this method using a server socket channel used in *The parts server* section:

```
serverSocketChannel.setOption(SO_RCVBUF, 64);
```

The first argument is an instance of the SocketOption<T> interface. This interface defines the name and type methods for an option. The StandardSocketOptions class defines a series of options, which implement this interface. For example, the SO_RCVBUF instance is defined as follows:

```
public static final SocketOption<Integer> SO_RCVBUF;
```

There may be additional, implementation-specific options available.

Summary

In this chapter, we examined the use of the NIO's channel and buffer classes. A channel connects to an external source and transfers data to and from a buffer. We illustrated channel sockets, which connect to another socket across the network.

Buffers are temporary repositories for data. Using a buffer allows data to be accessed either sequentially or randomly. There are many buffer operations, which makes this a good choice for many applications.

We examined several types of channel sockets, including the SocketChannel, ServerSocketChannel, and AsynchronousSocketChannel classes. The ServerSocketChannel class supports a server and uses an accept method to block until a client requests a connection. The method will return a SocketChannel instance, which will be connected to the client's SocketChannel. The AsynchronousSocketChannel and AsynchronousSocketChannel classes support asynchronous communication enabling non-blocking communication between two applications. The DatagramChannel is also supported, which we will investigate in *Chapter 6, UDP and Multicasting*.

We explained how the buffer and channel classes work together and illustrated their use in several client/server applications. We also examined a simple approach to handle multiple clients using threads.

We demonstrated how bulk data transfers are performed between an array and a buffer. Views and the use of read-only buffers were also examined. We ended with an introduction to how the underlying OS socket support can be configured.

In the next chapter, we will use many of these classes and techniques to support other client/server applications.

4
Client/Server Development

In this chapter, we will explore the process of developing a client/server application that is primarily oriented around HTTP. This is an important protocol, and it serves as the primary communication medium for a multitude of applications. We will examine the protocol, the requirements placed on a client, and the requirements placed on a server for various versions of the protocol.

Specifically, we will:

- Examine the nature of the HTTP protocol
- Demonstrate how low-level sockets can support the protocol
- Use the `HttpURLConnect` and `HTTPServer` classes to create an HTTP server
- Examine various open source Java HTTP servers
- Investigate various configuration issues and how cookies are handled

HTTP servers are used extensively, so a good understanding of how Java supports them is important.

The HTTP protocol structure

HTTP is a network protocol that is used to deliver resources across the **World Wide Web (WWW)**. Resources are usually **HyperText Markup Language (HTML)** files, but they also include a number of other file types, such as images, audio, and video. Users often enter a URL into a browser to obtain a resource. The term **URL** stands for **Uniform Resource Locator** with the emphasis here on resource.

Most people use a browser to communicate across WWW. The browser represents a client application, while the web server responds to client requests. The default port used by these servers is port 80.

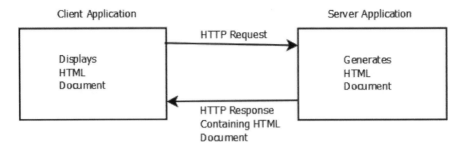

HTTP has evolved over the years. HTTP/1.0 originated in the 1980s and 1990s with the first documentation released in 1991. The latest definition of HTTP/1.1 was released as a six-part specification in June 2014. A **Request For Comments (RFC)** for HTTP 2.0 was released in May 2015. HTTP is an evolving standard.

The following links may prove useful for the interested reader:

Version	Reference
HTTP 1.0	http://www.w3.org/Protocols/HTTP/1.0/spec.html
HTTP/1.1	http://tools.ietf.org/html/rfc2616
HTTP/2	https://en.wikipedia.org/wiki/HTTP/2

HTTP servers are used in a variety of situations. The most common use is within organizations to support the dissemination of information to users. Often this is supported by production-quality servers, such as those provided by the Apache Software Foundation (http://www.apache.org/foundation/), or Gemini (http://www.eclipse.org/gemini/).

However, not all servers need to support the level of service typified by production servers. They can be quite small and even embedded in remote devices where they may affect a change in a device instead of only supplying information.

This chapter will examine the various network technologies that are supported by Java to address these types of concerns. These include the following:

- An overview of HTTP protocol syntax
- Low-level socket support for clients/servers

- Using the `URLConnection` class
- Using the `HTTPServer` class
- An overview of open source Java servers

HTTP is a complex topic, and we are only able to skim its surface.

 Robots, often called **spiders**, are applications that automatically follow links, frequently to collect web pages for use by search engines. If you desire to develop such an application, research their use and how they are built (`http://www.robotstxt.org/`). These types of applications can be disruptive if not designed carefully.

The nature of HTTP messages

Let's examine the format of an HTTP message. Messages are either a request message sent from a client to a server, or a response message sent from a server to a client. Based on an understanding of the format, we will show you how Java supports these messages. HTTP messages are, for the most part, readable by humans. Both the request and response messages use this structure:

- A line indicating the type of message
- Zero or more header lines
- A blank line
- An optional message body containing data

The following is an example of an HTTP request:

GET /index HTTP/1.0

User-Agent: Mozilla/5.0

A client request message consists of an initial request line and zero or more header lines. A response message consists of an initial response line (called the **status line**), zero or more header lines, and an optional message body.

Let's examine these elements in more detail.

Initial request line format

The formats of the request and response initial lines differ. The request line consists of three parts separated by spaces:

- Request method name
- Local path of the resource
- The HTTP version

The method names refer to the action requested by the client. The most common method used is the **GET** method, which simply requests that a specific resource be returned. The **POST** command is also common and is used to insert and update data. A list of HTTP/1.0 methods names is found at `http://www.w3.org/Protocols/HTTP/1.0/spec.html#Methods`. HTTP/1.1 method names can be found at `http://www.w3.org/Protocols/rfc2616/rfc2616-sec9.html`. Method names are always written in uppercase.

The local path typically references the resource desired. It follows the hostname in the URL request. For example, in the following URL, the local path is **/books/info/packt/faq/index.html**:

www.packtpub.com/books/info/packt/faq/index.html

The HTTP version is always in uppercase and consists of the acronym, HTTP, followed by a forward slash, and then the version number:

HTTP/x.x

The following is an example of a request initial line:

GET /index HTTP/1.0

The response initial line consists of three parts separated by spaces, as follows:

- The HTTP version
- A response status code
- A response phrase describing the code

The following line is an example of a response initial line. The response code reflects the status of the result and is easily interpreted by a computer. The reason phrase is meant to be human readable.

HTTP/1.0 404 Not Found

The HTTP version uses the same format that is used for the request line.

The following table contains a list of more commonly used codes. A complete list can be found at `https://en.wikipedia.org/wiki/List_of_HTTP_status_codes`:

Status code	Standard text	Meaning
200	**OK**	This indicates that the request was a success
301	**Moved Permanently**	This indicates that the URL has been moved permanently and the link should be updated
302	**Found**	This indicates that the resource is temporarily located somewhere else, but the URL should still be used
307	**Temporary Redirect**	This is similar to 302, but the method used should not be changed, which may happen with 302
308	**Permanent Redirect**	This is similar to 301, but the method used should not be changed, which may happen with 301
400	**Bad Request**	This indicates that request access was incorrect
401	**Unauthorized**	This indicates that the resource is restricted often because the login attempt failed
403	**Forbidden**	This indicates that access to the requested resource is forbidden
404	**Not Found**	This indicates that the resource is no longer available
500	**Internal server error**	This reflects some sort of error with the server
502	**Bad Gateway**	This indicates that the gateway server received an invalid response from another server
503	**Service Unavailable**	This indicates that the server is not available
504	**Gateway Timeout**	This indicates that the gateway server did not receive a response from another server in a timely manner

The status code is a three-digit number. The first digit of this number reflects the category of the code:

- 1xx: This represents an informational message
- 2xx: This represents a success
- 3xx: This redirects the client to another URL
- 4xx: This represents a client error
- 5xx: This represents a server error

Header lines

Headers lines provide information regarding the request or response, such as the e-mail address of the sender, and an application identifier. The header consists of a single line. The format of this line starts with the header identifier, followed by a colon, spaces, and then the value assigned to the header. The following header illustrates the `User-Agent` header that is used by Firefox 36.0. This header identifies the application as the Firefox browser running on a Windows platform:

User-Agent: Mozilla/5.0 (Windows NT 6.3; rv:36.0) Gecko/20100101 Firefox/36.0

A list of header fields and descriptions is found at `https://en.wikipedia.org/wiki/List_of_HTTP_header_fields`. A list of agent strings can be found at `http://useragentstring.com/pages/useragentstring.php`.

HTTP 1.0 defines 16 headers (`http://www.w3.org/Protocols/HTTP/1.0/spec.html#HeaderFields`), while HTTP 1.1 has 47 headers (`http://tools.ietf.org/html/rfc2616#section-14`). Its `Host` header is required.

Headers are useful in helping troubleshoot problems when they occur. It is a good idea to include the `From` and `User-Agent` headers for requests so that the server can be in a better position to respond to the request.

Message body

This is the data constituting the message. While normally a message body is included, it is optional and is not needed for some messages. When a body is included, the `Content-Type` and `Content-Length` headers are included to provide more information about the body.

For example, the following headers can be used for a message body:

Content-type: text/html

Content-length: 105

The message body may appear as follows:

**<html><h1>HTTPServer Home Page.... </h1>
Welcome to the new and improved web server!
</html>**

Client/Server interaction example

The following interaction is a simple demonstration of a client sending a request and the server responding. The client request message uses the GET method against a path of \index:

GET /index HTTP/1.0

User-Agent: Mozilla/5.0

The server will respond with the following message, assuming that it was able to process the request. The Server, Content-Type, and Content-Length headers are used. A blank line separates the headers and the HTML message body:

HTTP/1.0 200 OK

Server: WebServer

Content-Type: text/html

Content-Length: 86

**<html><h1>WebServer Home Page.... </h1>
Welcome to my web server!
</html>**

Other headers lines can be included.

Java socket support for HTTP client/server applications

An HTTP client will make a connection to an HTTP server. The client will send a request message to the server. The server will send back a response message, frequently, as an HTML document. In the early HTTP version, once the response was sent, the server would terminate the connection. This is sometimes referred to as a stateless protocol because the connection is not maintained.

With HTTP/1.1, persistent connections can be maintained. This improves the performance by eliminating the need to open and close connections when multiple pieces of data need to be transferred between the server and a client.

We will focus on creating an HTTP server and an HTTP client. While browsers typically serve as HTTP clients, other applications can also access web servers. In addition, it helps illustrate the nature of HTTP requests. Our server will support a subset of the HTTP/1.0 specification.

Building a simple HTTP server

We will use a class called WebServer to support the HTTP/1.0 protocol. The server will use a ClientHandler class to handle a client. The server will be limited to handling only GET requests. However, this will be adequate to illustrate the basic server elements needed. Support of other methods can be easily added.

The WebServer definition is shown next. The ServerSocket class is the foundation of the server. Its accept method will block until a request is made. When this happens, a new thread based on the ClientHandler class will be started:

```java
public class WebServer {

    public WebServer() {
        System.out.println("Webserver Started");
        try (ServerSocket serverSocket = new ServerSocket(80)) {
            while (true) {
                System.out.println("Waiting for client request");
                Socket remote = serverSocket.accept();
                System.out.println("Connection made");
                new Thread(new ClientHandler(remote)).start();
            }
        } catch (IOException ex) {
            ex.printStackTrace();
        }
    }

    public static void main(String args[]) {
        new WebServer();
    }
}
```

Mac users may encounter an error when using port 80. Use port 3000 or 8080 instead. Threads are concurrently executing sequences of code within a process. In Java, a thread is created using the Thread class. The constructor's argument is an object that implements the Runnable interface. This interface consists of a single method: run. When the thread is started using the start method, a separate program stack is created for the new thread, and the run method executes on this stack. When the run method terminates, the thread terminates. The ClientHandler class, shown next, implements the Runnable interface. Its constructor is passed to the socket representing the client. When the thread starts, the run method executes. The method displays, starting and terminating messages. The actual work is performed in the handleRequest method:

```java
public class ClientHandler implements Runnable {

    private final Socket socket;
```

```
public ClientHandler(Socket socket) {
    this.socket = socket;
}

@Override
public void run() {
    System.out.println("\nClientHandler Started for " +
        this.socket);
    handleRequest(this.socket);
    System.out.println("ClientHandler Terminated for "
        + this.socket + "\n");
}

}
```

The `handleRequest` method uses the input and output streams to communicate with the server. In addition, it determines what request was made and then processes that request.

In the code that follows, the input and output streams are created and the first line of the request is read. The `StringTokenizer` class is used to token this line. When the `nextToken` method is invoked, it returns the first word of the line, which should correspond to an HTTP method:

```
public void handleRequest(Socket socket) {
    try (BufferedReader in = new BufferedReader(
            new InputStreamReader(socket.getInputStream()));) {
        String headerLine = in.readLine();
        StringTokenizer tokenizer =
            new StringTokenizer(headerLine);
        String httpMethod = tokenizer.nextToken();
        ...
    } catch (Exception e) {
        e.printStackTrace();
    }
}
```

A tokenizer is a process that splits text into a series of tokens. Frequently, these tokens are simple words. The `StringTokenizer` class's constructor is passed the text to be tokenized. The `nextToken` method will return the next available token.

The next code sequence handles the GET method. A message is displayed on the server side to indicate that a GET method is being processed. This server will return a simple HTML page. The page is built using the StringBuilder class where the append methods are used in a fluent style. The sendResponse method is then invoked to actually send the response. If some other method was requested, then a 405 status code is returned:

```
if (httpMethod.equals("GET")) {
    System.out.println("Get method processed");
    String httpQueryString = tokenizer.nextToken();
    StringBuilder responseBuffer = new StringBuilder();
    responseBuffer
        .append("<html><h1>WebServer Home Page.... </h1><br>")
        .append("<b>Welcome to my web server!</b><BR>")
        .append("</html>");
    sendResponse(socket, 200, responseBuffer.toString());
} else {
    System.out.println("The HTTP method is not recognized");
    sendResponse(socket, 405, "Method Not Allowed");
}
```

If we wanted to handle other methods, then a series of else-if clauses can be added. To further process the GET method, we will need to parse the remainder of the initial request line. The following statement will give us a string that we can process:

```
String httpQueryString = tokenizer.nextToken();
```

The previous statement is not needed for this example and should not be included in the code. It simply offers one possible way of further processing HTTP queries.

Once we have created a response, we will use the sendResponse method to send it to the client as shown next. This method is passed the socket, a status code, and the response string. An output stream is then created:

```
public void sendResponse(Socket socket,
        int statusCode, String responseString) {
    String statusLine;
    String serverHeader = "Server: WebServer\r\n";
    String contentTypeHeader = "Content-Type: text/html\r\n";

    try (DataOutputStream out =
            new DataOutputStream(socket.getOutputStream());) {
        ...
        out.close();
    } catch (IOException ex) {
```

```
            // Handle exception
        }
    }
```

If the status code is `200`, then a simple HTML page is returned. If the status code is `405`, then a single status code line is returned. Otherwise, a `404` response is sent. As we used the `DataOutputStream` class to write, we use its `writeBytes` method to handle strings:

```
if (statusCode == 200) {
    statusLine = "HTTP/1.0 200 OK" + "\r\n";
    String contentLengthHeader = "Content-Length: "
        + responseString.length() + "\r\n";

    out.writeBytes(statusLine);
    out.writeBytes(serverHeader);
    out.writeBytes(contentTypeHeader);
    out.writeBytes(contentLengthHeader);
    out.writeBytes("\r\n");
    out.writeBytes(responseString);
} else if (statusCode == 405) {
    statusLine = "HTTP/1.0 405 Method Not Allowed" + "\r\n";
    out.writeBytes(statusLine);
    out.writeBytes("\r\n");
} else {
    statusLine = "HTTP/1.0 404 Not Found" + "\r\n";
    out.writeBytes(statusLine);
    out.writeBytes("\r\n");
}
```

When the server starts, it will display the following:

Connection made

Waiting for client request

When a client makes a GET request, output similar to the following one will be displayed:

ClientHandler Started for Socket[addr=/127.0.0.1,port=50573,localport=80]

Get method processed

ClientHandler Terminated for Socket[addr=/127.0.0.1,port=50573,localport=80]

With a simple server in place, let's take a look at how we can build an HTTP client application.

Building a simple HTTP client

We will use the following `HTTPClient` class to access our HTTP server. In its constructor, a socket connecting to the server is created. The `Socket` class's `getInputStream` and `getOutputStream` return input and output streams for the socket, respectively. The `sendGet` method is called, which sends a request to the server. The `getResponse` method returns the response, which is then displayed:

```java
public class HTTPClient {

    public HTTPClient() {
        System.out.println("HTTP Client Started");
        try {
            InetAddress serverInetAddress =
                InetAddress.getByName("127.0.0.1");
            Socket connection = new Socket(serverInetAddress, 80);

            try (OutputStream out = connection.getOutputStream();
                BufferedReader in =
                    new BufferedReader(new
                        InputStreamReader(
                            connection.getInputStream())))) {
                sendGet(out);
                System.out.println(getResponse(in));
            }
        } catch (IOException ex) {
            ex.printStackTrace();
        }
    }

    ...

    public static void main(String[] args) {
        new HTTPClient();
    }
}
```

The `sendGet` method follows this, which sends a `GET` method request using a simple path. This is followed by a `User-Agent` header. We used an instance of the `OutputStream` class with the `write` method. The `write` method requires an array of bytes. The `String` class's `getBytes` method returns this array of bytes:

```java
private void sendGet(OutputStream out) {
    try {
        out.write("GET /default\r\n".getBytes());
```

```
        out.write("User-Agent: Mozilla/5.0\r\n".getBytes());
    } catch (IOException ex) {
        ex.printStackTrace();
    }
}
```

The `getResponse` method is as follows and is passed a `BufferedReader` instance to get the response from the server. It returns a string created using the `StringBuilder` class:

```
private String getResponse(BufferedReader in) {
    try {
        String inputLine;
        StringBuilder response = new StringBuilder();
        while ((inputLine = in.readLine()) != null) {
            response.append(inputLine).append("\n");
        }
        return response.toString();
    } catch (IOException ex) {
        ex.printStackTrace();
    }
    return "";
}
```

When the client application executes, we get the following output reflecting the server's response:

HTTP Client Started

HTTP/1.0 200 OK

Server: WebServer

Content-Type: text/html

Content-Length: 86

**<html><h1>WebServer Home Page.... </h1>
Welcome to my web server!
</html>**

If we use the same request from a browser, we will get the following:

WebServer Home Page....

Welcome to my web server!

These client and server applications can be further enhanced. However, we can use the HttpURLConnection class to achieve similar results.

Client/server development using standard Java classes

Specifically, we will use the HttpURLConnection and HTTPServer classes to implement a client and server application. These classes support much of the functionality required for clients and servers. Using these classes will avoid writing low-level code to implement HTTP functionality. Low-level code refers to the non-specialized classes, such as the Socket class. Higher-level and more specialized classes, such as the HttpURLConnection and HTTPServer classes, supplement and provide additional support for specialized operations.

The HttpURLConnection class is derived from the HttpConnection class. This base class has a number of methods that not are directly concerned with the HTTP protocol.

Using the HttpURLConnection class

The HttpURLConnection class provides a convenient technique to access a web server. With this class, we can connect to a site, make a request, and access the respond headers and the response message.

We will use the HttpURLConnectionExample class that is defined as follows. A sendGet method supports transmitting the GET method request to the server. The HttpURLConnectionExample class supports other HTTP methods. For this example, we are only using the GET method:

```
public class HttpURLConnectionExample {

    public static void main(String[] args) throws Exception {
```

```
HttpURLConnectionExample http =
    new HttpURLConnectionExample();
http.sendGet();
    }


}
```

The `sendGet` method implementation is shown next. A Google query (`http://www.google.com/search?q=java+sdk&ie=utf-8&oe=utf-8`) is used to illustrate the process where we search for "java sdk". The latter part of the query, `&ie=utf-8&oe=utf-8`, is additional information attached to the query by the Google search engine. The `openConnection` method will connect to the Google server:

```
private void sendGet() throws Exception {
    String query =
  "http://www.google.com/search?q=java+sdk&ie=utf-8&oe=utf-8";
    URL url = new URL(query);
    HttpURLConnection connection =
        (HttpURLConnection) url.openConnection();

    ...
}
```

Using this connection, the `setRequestMethod` and `setRequestProperty` methods set the request method and user agent, respectively:

```
connection.setRequestMethod("GET");
connection.setRequestProperty("User-Agent",
    "Mozilla/5.0");
```

The response code is retrieved, and if we are successful, the `getResponse` method will retrieve the response and then display it as follows:

```
int responseCode = connection.getResponseCode();
System.out.println("Response Code: " + responseCode);
if (responseCode == 200) {
    String response = getResponse(connection);
    System.out.println("response: " +
        response.toString());
} else {
    System.out.println("Bad Response Code: " +
        responseCode);
}
```

The getResponse method is shown next. The HttpURLConnection class's getInputStream method returns an input stream, which is used to create an instance of the BufferedReader class. A StringBuilder instance is used along with this reader to create and return a string:

```
private String getResponse(HttpURLConnection connection) {
    try (BufferedReader br = new BufferedReader(
            new InputStreamReader(
                connection.getInputStream()));) {
        String inputLine;
        StringBuilder response = new StringBuilder();
        while ((inputLine = br.readLine()) != null) {
            response.append(inputLine);
        }
        br.close();
        return response.toString();
    } catch (IOException ex) {
        // Handle exceptions
    }
    return "";
}
```

When this program executes, you will get output as follows. Due to the length of the output, it has been truncated:

Sent Http GET request

Response Code: 200

response: <!doctype html><html itemscope="" ...

If we used this query in a browser, we will get output similar to the following:

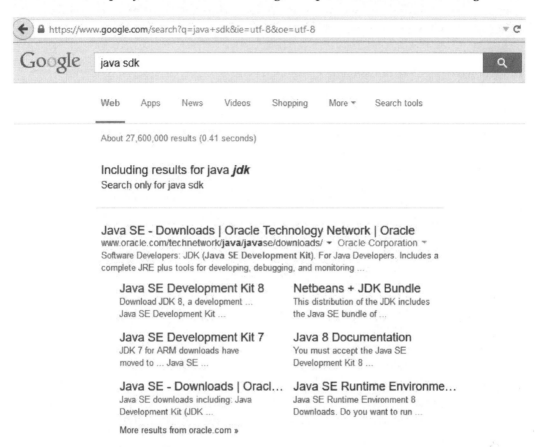

A very interesting discussion of how to use the `URLConnection` class to deal with HTTP requests can be found at `http://stackoverflow.com/questions/2793150/using-java-net-urlconnection-to-fire-and-handle-http-requests`.

URL encoding

When a URL is formed, a specific URL format needs to be used. Some of the characters of this format are reserved and others are unreserved. Reserved characters have special meaning, such as the forward slash, which is used to separate parts of a URL. Unreserved characters do not have any special meaning.

When a reserved character needs to be used in a non-reserved context, URL encoding, also known as percent-encoding, is used to represent these characters using special character sequences. More information about this process can be found at `https://en.wikipedia.org/wiki/Percent-encoding`.

In Java, we can perform URL encoding using the `URLEncoder` class. Specifically, the `URLEncoder` class has an `encode` method to convert a string that complies with the `application/x-www-form-url` encoded MIME format.

This method is overloaded. The single argument method has been deprecated. The two-argument method accepts a string to be converted and a string that specifies the character encoding scheme. For HTTP messages, use the UTF-8 format.

Previously, we used the following string to create a new URL instance:

```
String query =
   "http://www.google.com/search?q=java+sdk&ie=utf-8&oe=utf-8";
```

This string was actually formatted by the browser. Instead of using the browser, the following code illustrates how to use the `encode` method to achieve similar results:

```
String urlQuery = "http://www.google.com/search?q=";
String userQuery = "java sdk";
String urlEncoded = urlQuery + URLEncoder.encode(
    userQuery, "UTF-8");
```

This will produce the string: `http://www.google.com/search?q=java+sd`. You can see how the blanks have been converted to + symbols for this URL. The latter part of the original query, `&ie=utf-8&oe=utf-8`, is not included in our URL encoded string.

The `URLDecoder` class is available to decode URL encoded strings if necessary. For a comprehensive discussion of URL encoding, see: `http://blog.lunatech.com/2009/02/03/what-every-web-developer-must-know-about-url-encoding`.

Using the HTTPServer class

The `HTTPServer` class is found in the `com.sun.net.httpserver` package. It provides a powerful set of features to support a simple HTTP server. Many of the tasks that we had to perform manually with our previous servers are simplified with this server. The interaction between a client and server is referred to as an exchange.

This and other supporting classes and interfaces are members of the `com.sun.net.httpserver` package. They are normally included with most IDEs. The API documentation can be found at `http://docs.oracle.com/javase/8/docs/jre/api/net/httpserver/spec/index.html?com/sun/net/httpserver/package-summary.html`.

This package consists of a number of classes. The primary classes that we will use include:

Class/interface	Purpose
HttpServer	This class supports the basic functionality of an HTTP server
HttpExchange	This class encapsulates the request and response associated with a client/server exchange
HttpHandler	This class defines a handle method used to process specific exchanges
HttpContext	This class maps a URI path to an HttpHandler instance
Filter	This class supports the preprocessing and post-processing of requests

The server uses an HttpHandler derived class to process client requests. For example, one handler can process requests for basic web pages, while another handler may process service related requests.

The HttpExchange class supports the life-cycle activities of an exchange between a client and a server. It possesses a number of methods providing access to request and response information. These methods are listed in the following table in the order that they are normally used. Not all methods need to be used for all requests:

Method	Purpose
getRequestMethod	This method returns the HTTP method requested
getRequestHeaders	This method returns the request headers
getRequestBody	This method returns an InputStream instance for the request body
getResponseHeaders	This method returns the response headers except for content-length
sendResponseHeaders	This method sends the response headers
getResponseBody	This method returns an OutputStream instance used to send the response

An exchange is closed when the input and output streams are closed. The sendResponseHeaders method must be used before the getResponseBody method is invoked.

> The performance of the initial version of this class was not very good. However, newer versions have better performance. In addition, the filter facility can assist in processing exchanges.

Using the `com.sun.*` classes can be used without concerns. Problems can occur if the `sun.*` classes are used with different JREs. The `HTTPServer` class fully supports HTTP/1.0, but it only provides partial support for HTTP/1.1.

Implementing a simple HTTPServer class

The class that follows implements a simple server using the `HTTPServer` class. An instance of the `HttpServer` class is created using the localhost and port 80 (3000 or 8080 on a Mac). The `createContext` method associates the `/index` path with an instance of the `IndexHandler` class. This handler will process the request. The `start` method starts the server. The server will continue running, processing multiple requests until it is manually stopped:

```
public class MyHTTPServer {

    public static void main(String[] args) throws Exception {
        System.out.println("MyHTTPServer Started");
        HttpServer server = HttpServer.create(
            new InetSocketAddress(80), 0);
        server.createContext("/index", new IndexHandler());
        server.start();
    }

}
```

When the `createContext` method matches the path expressed as a string to a handler, it uses a specific matching process. The details of this process are explained in the *Mapping request URIs to HttpContext paths* section of the `HTTPServer` class documentation found at `http://docs.oracle.com/javase/8/docs/jre/api/net/httpserver/spec/com/sun/net/httpserver/HttpServer.html`.

The `IndexHandler` class is declared next. It implements the `HttpHandler` interface by overriding the `handle` method. The `handle` method is passed an `HttpExchange` instance, which we can use to process the request.

In this method, we perform the following actions:

* Display the address of the client
* Send back a request with a status code of 200
* Send the response to the client

The `sendResponseHeaders` method will send an initial response line for status code `200` and a header for the content length. The `getResponseBody` method returns an output stream used to send the message body. The stream is then closed terminating the exchange:

```
static class IndexHandler implements HttpHandler {

    @Override
    public void handle(HttpExchange exchange)
            throws IOException {
        System.out.println(exchange.getRemoteAddress());
        String response = getResponse();
        exchange.sendResponseHeaders(200, response.length());
        OutputStream out = exchange.getResponseBody();
        out.write(response.toString().getBytes());
        out.close();
    }
}
```

The `sendResponseHeaders` method uses two parameters. The first is the response code, and the second controls the transmission of the message body, as detailed in the next table:

Value	Meaning
Greater than zero	This is the length of the message. The server must send this number of bytes.
Zero	This is used for chunked transfer where an arbitrary number of bytes is sent.
-1	This is when no response body is sent.

The `getResponse` method uses the `StringBuilder` class to construct a string:

```
public String getResponse() {
    StringBuilder responseBuffer = new StringBuilder();
    responseBuffer
        .append(
            "<html><h1>HTTPServer Home Page.... </h1><br>")
        .append("<b>Welcome to the new and improved web "
                + "server!</b><BR>")
        .append("</html>");
    return responseBuffer.toString();
}
```

When the server is started, the following output is displayed:

MyHTTPServer Started

If we enter the URL `http://127.0.0.1/index` in a browser, the browser will display the page similar to the one in the image in the section *Building a simple HTTP client*.

The server will display the following for each request:

/127.0.0.1:50273

This class is instrumental in processing client requests. Here, we will illustrate several of this class's methods using a different handler called `DetailHandler`, as declared next:

```
static class DetailHandler implements HttpHandler {

    @Override
    public void handle(HttpExchange exchange)
            throws IOException {
        . . .
    }
}
```

To use this handler, replace the `createContext` method, and call in the `MyHTTPServer` with this statement:

```
server.createContext("/index", new DetailHandler());
```

Let's start by examining the use of the `getRequestHeaders` method, which returns an instance of the `Headers` class. This will permit us to display each request header sent by the client and perform additional processing based on the headers if needed.

Add the following code to the `handle` method. The `keyset` method returns a `Set` of key/values pairs for each header. In the for-each statement, the `Set` interface's `get` method returns a list of values for each header. This list is used to display the headers:

```
Headers requestHeaders = exchange.getRequestHeaders();
Set<String> keySet = requestHeaders.keySet();
for (String key : keySet) {
    List values = requestHeaders.get(key);
    String header = key + " = " + values.toString() + "\n";
    System.out.print(header);
}
```

Using the previous URL (`http://127.0.0.1/index`) from the Firefox browser, we get the following output:

Accept-encoding = [gzip, deflate]

Accept = [text/html,application/xhtml+xml,application/xml;q=0.9,*/*;q=0.8]

Connection = [keep-alive]

Host = [127.0.0.1]

User-agent = [Mozilla/5.0 (Windows NT 10.0; WOW64; rv:40.0) Gecko/20100101 Firefox/40.0]

Accept-language = [en-US,en;q=0.5]

Cache-control = [max-age=0]

Using a different browser may return a different set of request headers. The `getRequestMethod` method returns the name of the request method, as shown here:

```
String requestMethod = exchange.getRequestMethod();
```

We can use this to differentiate between client requests.

Some request methods will pass a message body along with the request. The `getRequestBody` method will return an `InputStream` instance to access this body.

The following code illustrates how we can obtain and display the message body:

```
InputStream in = exchange.getRequestBody();
if (in != null) {
    try (BufferedReader br = new BufferedReader(
            new InputStreamReader(in));) {
        String inputLine;
        StringBuilder response = new StringBuilder();
        while ((inputLine = br.readLine()) != null) {
            response.append(inputLine);
        }
        br.close();
        System.out.println(inputLine);
    } catch (IOException ex) {
        ex.printStackTrace();
    }
} else {
    System.out.println("Request body is empty");
}
```

As our request did not have a body, nothing is displayed.

Managing response headers

The server can send back response headers using the `sendResponseHeaders` method. However, these headers need to be created using a combination of the `getResponseHeaders` method and the `set` methods.

In the next code sequence, the `getResponseHeaders` method will return an instance of the `Header` class:

```
Headers responseHeaders = exchange.getResponseHeaders();
```

We use the `getResponse` method to get our response. We will need this to compute the content length. The `set` method is then used to create **Content-Type** and **Server** headers:

```
String responseMessage = HTTPServerHelper.getResponse();
responseHeaders.set("Content-Type", "text/html");
responseHeaders.set("Server", "MyHTTPServer/1.0");
```

The headers are sent using the `sendResponseHeaders` method described earlier, shown as follows:

```
exchange.sendResponseHeaders(200,
    responseMessage.getBytes().length);
```

These response headers can be displayed using the following code sequence. This performs the same functionality as the for-each statement that we used to display the request headers. However, this implementation uses a Java 8 Stream class and two lambda expressions instead:

```
Set<String> responseHeadersKeySet = responseHeaders.keySet();
responseHeadersKeySet
        .stream()
        .map((key) -> {
            List values = responseHeaders.get(key);
            String header = key + " = " +
                values.toString() + "\n";
            return header;
        })
        .forEach((header) -> {
            System.out.print(header);
        });
```

This implementation uses a stream. The `stream` method returns the keys found in the set. The `map` method processes each key using it to look up a list of values associated with the key. The list is converted into a string. The `forEach` method will then display each of these strings.

The HTTPServer, and its accompanying classes provide a simple, but convenient to use technique to implement an HTTP server. Support is also provided for secure communications using the HttpsServer class, which is discussed in *Chapter 8, Network Security*.

Open source Java HTTP servers

While we can develop a web server using any of the technologies discussed in this chapter, another option is to use any of a number of open source Java-based HTTP servers. Such servers frequently provide a number of features, including:

- Full compliancy with HTTP standards
- Support for logging and monitoring
- Handling of virtual hosts
- Performance tuning capability
- Scalable
- Chunked data transfer
- Configurability
- Support for NIO (Grizzly)

Leveraging these systems can save you a lot of time and effort that would otherwise be devoted to building a custom server. A partial list of a few Java-based servers include the following:

- Jakarta Tomcat (http://tomcat.apache.org/)
- Jetty (http://www.eclipse.org/jetty/)
- JLHTTP (http://www.freeutils.net/source/jlhttp/)
- GlassFish (https://glassfish.java.net/)
- Grizzly (https://grizzly.java.net/)
- Simple (http://www.simpleframework.org/)

One list of open source Java servers is found at http://java-source.net/open-source/web-servers.

At a higher level, Java EE is frequently used to support Web Servers. While this edition has evolved over the years, servlets form the basis to handle web requests. A servlet is a Java application that hides much of the detail surrounding the low-level processing of requests and responses. This permits the developer to focus on processing requests.

Servlets are held in containers that provide support for tasks, such as database access, managing performance, and providing security. A simple servlet is shown next to give you a feel as to how they are structured.

The `doGet` and `doPost` methods handle GET and POST type messages, respectively. However, as the differences between these two HTTP messages are hidden, only one is needed. The `HttpServletRequest` class represents an HTTP request and the `HttpServletResponse` class represents the response. These classes provide access to the messages. For example, the `getWriter` method returns a `PrintWriter` class instance, which allows us to write the HTML response in a clearer fashion:

```java
public class ServletExample extends HttpServlet {

    @Override
    public void doGet(HttpServletRequest request,
            HttpServletResponse response)
                throws ServletException, IOException {
        response.setContentType("text/html");
        PrintWriter out = response.getWriter();
        out.println("<h1>" + "Message to be sent" + "</h1>");
    }

    @Override
    public void doPost(HttpServletRequest request,
            HttpServletResponse response)
                throws IOException, ServletException {
        doGet(request, response);
    }

}
```

Servlets are normally developed using the Java EE SDK. The previous example will not compile correctly unless developed using this API.

Many technologies have evolved and have hidden servlets. Over the years, this has included **JavaServer Pages (JSP)** and **JavaServer Faces (JSF)**, which have largely eliminated the need to write servlets directly.

There are a number of web servers for Java. A comparison of some of these is found at `https://en.wikipedia.org/wiki/Comparison_of_application_servers#Java`.

Server configuration

The configuration of a server depends on the technology that was used to build it. Here, we will focus on the configuration of the URLConnection class. This class has a number of protected fields that control how the connection behaves. These fields are accessed using corresponding get and set methods.

One field deals with user interactions. When set to true, it allows users to engage in interactions, such as responding to an authentication dialog box. A connection can be used for input and/or output. The connection can be configured to disallow input or output.

When data is transferred between a client and a server, it may be cached. The UseCaches variable determines whether caches are ignored or not. If set to true, then caches are used as appropriate. If false, caching is not performed.

The ifModifiedSince variable controls whether the retrieval of an object occurs. It is a long value that represents time as the number of milliseconds since the epoch (January 1, 1970, GMT). If the object has been modified more recently than that time, then it is fetched.

The following table summarizes the methods that are used to configure a connection established using the URLConnection class. Each of these methods have a corresponding GET method:

Method	Default	Purpose
setAllowUserInteraction	NA	This method controls user interaction
setDoInput	true	If its argument is set to true, then input is allowed
setDoInput	true	If its argument is set to true, then output is allowed
setIfModifiedSince	NA	This sets the ifModifiedSince variable
setUseCaches	true	This sets the UseCaches variable

More sophisticated servers, such as Tomcat, have many more options to control how it is configured.

When an application is deployed, there are numerous configuration options found in the `deployment.properties` file. Many of these options are low level, and JRE related. A description of the options is found at `https://docs.oracle.com/javase/8/docs/technotes/guides/deploy/properties.html`. The *21.2.4 Networking* section discusses the network options, while the *21.2.5 Cache and Optional Package Repository* section is concerned with the configuration of caches.

An **HTTP proxy** is a server that acts as an intermediary between a client and a server. A proxy is frequently used to manage the network, monitor traffic, and improve network performance.

Generally, we are not concerned with the use or configuration of a proxy. However, if a proxy needs to be configured, we can control it either using the JVM command line or within the code using the `System` class's `getProperties` method. We can control the proxy used and specify the user and password to access it if needed. A short discussion of these capabilities is found at `http://viralpatel.net/blogs/http-proxy-setting-java-setting-proxy-java/`.

Handling cookies

A cookie is a string containing a key/value pair representing information of interest to the server such as user preferences. It is sent from a server to a browser. The browser should save the cookie to a file so that it can be used later.

A cookie is a string that consists of a name followed by an equal sign and then a value. The following is one possible cookie:

userID=Cookie Monster

A cookie can have multiple values. These values will be separated by a semicolon and white space.

We will use the `HTTPServer` class and the `HttpURLConnection` classes to demonstrate the handling of cookies. In the `MyHTTPServer` class server's handler class's `handle` method, add the following code after the other headers:

```
responseHeaders.set("Set-cookie", "userID=Cookie Monster");
```

When the server responds, it will send that cookie.

In the `HttpURLConnectionExample` class's `getResponse` method, add the following code at the beginning of its try block. A string is built containing the cookie text. Multiple `substring` and `indexOf` methods are used to extract the cookie's name and then its value:

```
Map<String, List<String>> requestHeaders =
    connection.getHeaderFields();
Set<String> keySet = requestHeaders.keySet();
for (String key : keySet) {
    if ("Set-cookie".equals(key)) {
        List values = requestHeaders.get(key);
        String cookie = key + " = " +
            values.toString() + "\n";
        String cookieName =
            cookie.substring(0, cookie.indexOf("="));
        String cookieValue = cookie.substring(
            cookie.indexOf("=")+ 1, cookie.length());
        System.out.println(cookieName + ":" + cookieValue);
    }
}
```

When the server sends a response, it will include the cookie. The client will then receive the cookie. In the server and the client, you should see the following output displaying the cookie:

Set-cookie : [userID=Cookie Monster]

The previous example handles simple single-value cookies. The code to handle multiple values is left as an exercise for the reader.

Summary

In this chapter, we examined the various Java approaches that can be used to develop HTTP client/server applications. Communication using HTTP is a common practice. Understanding how Java supports this process is a valuable skill to possess.

We started with an overview of HTTP messages. We examined the format of the initial request and response lines. Headers lines were also examined, which are used to convey information about the message. An optional message body may appear in an HTTP message. This is more common in a response where the body is often an HTML document.

We demonstrated how a client/server can be developed using simple socket. While possible, this approach requires a lot of work to develop a fully functional HTTP server. This discussion was followed by the use of the `HTTPServer` and `HttpURLConnection` classes to support a server and client, respectively. The use of these classes made the development process much easier.

There are a number of open source Java-based HTTP servers available. These may be viable candidates for some environments. The more complex web servers, typified by Apache Tomcat, were also discussed. They work with servlets and hide much of the low-level HTTP details from the developer.

We wrapped the chapter up with a brief discussion of server configuration issues and how cookies are created and consumed by servers and clients.

While the client/server architecture is very common, the peer-to-peer architecture is an alternative to share information across a network. We will delve into this topic in the next chapter.

5

Peer-to-Peer Networks

A **peer-to-peer (P2P)** computer network refers to an architecture whose nodes frequently serve as both a server and as a client. The primary objective of P2P systems is to eliminate the need for separate servers to manage the system. The configuration of the P2P network will change dynamically with nodes joining and leaving the network in an unpredictable manner. The nodes may differ in terms of factors, such as processing speed, bandwidth support, and storage capabilities. The term peer implies a level of equality between the nodes.

There are various definitions and interpretations of a P2P network. They can be characterized as a decentralized, constantly changing, and self-regulated architecture. Servers tend to provide services, while clients request them. A P2P node usually does both. A pure P2P network will not have nodes designated as a client or server. In reality, these networks are rare. Most P2P networks rely on a central facility, such as a DNS server, for support.

Certain networks may be a hybrid between the client/server architecture and a more pure P2P architecture where there is never a specific node acting as a "master" server. For example, a file sharing P2P may use the nodes of the network to download the files, while a server may provide additional supporting information.

P2P can be classified in several ways. We will use a couple of common classification categories that are useful in understanding the nature of P2P networks. One classification is based on how **indexing**, the process of finding a node, is performed:

- **Centralized**: This is when a central server keeps track of where the data is located among peers
- **Local**: This is when each peer keeps track of its own data
- **Distributed**: This is when the data references are maintained by multiple peers

Hybrid P2P networks use a centralized indexing scheme. Pure P2P networks use local or distributed indexes.

Algorithms are used to determine the location of information in a system. The system is decentralized with no overriding server executing the algorithm. The algorithm supports a self-organizing system that dynamically reconfigures itself as nodes are added and removed. In addition, these systems will ideally balance the load and resources as the network membership changes.

In this chapter, we will cover:

- The P2P concepts and terminology
- Java support for P2P networks
- The nature of distributed hash tables
- How FreePastry supports P2P applications

 P2P applications provide a flexible alternative to the traditional client/server architecture.

P2P functions/characteristics

One way of understanding a P2P network is to examine its characteristics. These include the following:

- Nodes that contribute resources to the system, including:
    - Data storage
    - Computational resources
- They provide support for a set of services
- They are very scalable and fault tolerant
- They support load balancing of resources
- They may support limited anonymity

The nature of P2P systems is that a user may not be able to access a specific node to use a service or resources. As nodes join and leave a system randomly, a specific node may not be available. The algorithm will determine how the system responds to requests.

The basics functions of a P2P system include:

- Enrollment of peers in a network
- Peer discovery — the process of determining which peer has the information of interest
- Sending messages between peers

Not all peers perform all of these functions.

The resources of a P2P system are identified using a **Globally Unique Identifier (GUID)** that is usually generated using a secure hashing function, which we will examine in DHT components. The GUID is not intended to be human readable. It is a randomly generated value providing little opportunity for conflicts.

The nodes of a P2P are organized using **routing overlays**. It is a type of **middleware** that routes requests to the appropriate node. The overlay refers to a network that is on top of the physical network as identified by resources using IP addresses. We can envision a network as composed on a series of IP-based nodes. However, an overlay is a subset of these nodes usually focusing on a single task.

The routing overlay will take into consideration factors, such as the number of nodes between a user and a resource, and the bandwidth of the connection, to determine which node should fulfill a request. Frequently, a resource may be duplicated or even split across multiple nodes. A routing overlay will attempt to provide the optimal path to a resource.

As nodes join and leave a system, the routing overlay needs to account for these changes. When a node joins a system, it may be asked to take on some responsibilities. When a node leaves, other parts of the system may need to pick up some of the departing nodes responsibilities.

In this chapter, we will explain various concepts, which are often embedded as part of a system. We will briefly overview different P2P application, which will be followed by a discussion of Java support for this architecture. The use of distributed hash tables is demonstrated, and an in-depth examination of FreePastry is presented, which will provide insight into how many of the P2P frameworks work.

When applicable, we will illustrate how some of these concepts can be implemented manually. While these implementations are not needed to use the system, they will provide a more in-depth understanding of these underlying concepts.

Applications-based P2P networks

There are many applications that are based on a P2P network. They can be used for the following:

- **Content distribution**: This is file sharing (files, music, videos, images)
- **Distributed computing**: This is when a problem is divided into smaller tasks and executed in a parallel fashion
- **Collaboration**: This is when users work together to solve a common problem
- **Platforms**: These are systems on which P2P applications are built, such as JXTA, and Pastry

Distributed computing leverages the power of larger numbers of smaller computers to perform a task. The problems amenable to this approach require that they be broken down into smaller units and then executed concurrently on multiple machines. The results of these smaller tasks then need to be combined to produce a final result.

P2P networks support a number of applications, such as the following ones:

- **Skype**: This is a video-conferencing application
- **Freecast**: This is peer-to-peer streaming audio program
- **BitTorrent**: This is a popular peer-to-peer file sharing system
- **Tor**: This program shields users' identities
- **Haihaisoft**: This is used for distribution of prerecorded TV programs
- **WoW**: This uses a P2P for game updates
- **YaCy**: This is a search engine and web crawler
- **Octoshape**: This supports live TV

A good overview of P2P applications is found at `http://p2peducation.pbworks.com/w/page/8897427/FrontPage`.

Java support for P2P applications

Java support beyond the low-level socket support that was detailed in earlier chapters consists of various frameworks. These range from well-known frameworks, such as JXTA, to small limited-capability protocols. These frameworks provide the basis for more specialized applications.

The following table lists several of these frameworks:

P2P framework	URL
TomP2P	`http://tomp2p.net/`
JXTA	`https://jxta.kenai.com/`
Hive2Hive	`https://github.com/Hive2Hive/Hive2Hive`
jnmp2p	`https://code.google.com/p/jnmp2p/`
FlexGP	`http://flexgp.github.io/flexgp/javalibrary.html`
JMaay	`http://sourceforge.net/projects/jmaay/`
P2P-MPI	`http://grid.u-strasbg.fr/p2pmpi/`
Pastry	`http://www.freepastry.org/`

These frameworks use an algorithm to route messages between peers. Hash tables frequently form the basis of these frameworks, as discussed next.

Distributed hash tables

A **Distributed Hash Table (DHT)** uses a key/value pair to locate resources in a network. This mapping function is spread across peers making it distributed. This architecture allows P2P networks to scale easily to a large number of nodes and to handle peers joining and leaving a network randomly. A DHT is the basis to support core P2P services. Many applications use DHT, including BitTorrent, Freenet, and YaCy.

The following figure illustrates mapping a key to a value. The key is frequently a string containing the identity of a resource, such as the name of a book; and the value is a number generated to represent the resource. The number can be used to locate the resource in a network and can correspond to the identifier of a node.

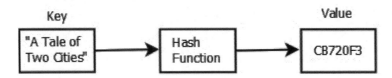

P2P networks have been in use for a while. The evolution of these networks is reflected in how resources are mapped as typified by Napster, Gnutella, and Freenet:

- Napster (`https://en.wikipedia.org/wiki/Napster`) was the first large-scale P2P content delivery system. It uses a server to keep track of the nodes in the network. The nodes held the actual data. When a client needs this data, the server will look up the current set of nodes that holds the data, and this node's location will be sent back to the client. The client will then contact the node holding the data. This made it easy for attacks to be launched against it and, eventually, led to its demise through lawsuits.

- Gnutella (`https://web.archive.org/web/20080525005017`, `http://www.gnutella.com/`) does not use a central server but broadcasts to every node in a network. This resulted in the network being flooded with messages, and the approach was modified in later versions.

- Freenet (`https://freenetproject.org/`) uses a heuristic key-based routing scheme and focuses on censorship and anonymity issues. However, DHS uses a more structured key-based routing approach resulting in the following:
    - Decentralization
    - Fault tolerance
    - Scalability
    - Efficiency

However, DHT does not support exact-match search. If this type of search is needed, then it has to be added.

DHT components

A **keyspace** is a set of 160-bit strings (keys) that is used to identify an element. **Keyspace partitioning** is the process of splitting the keyspace among the nodes of the network. An overlay network connects the nodes.

A commonly used hashing algorithm is **Secure Hash Algorithm (SHA-1)** (`https://en.wikipedia.org/wiki/SHA-1`). SHA-1 was designed by the NSA and generates a 160-bit hash value known as a message digest. Most P2Ps do not require the developer to explicitly perform the hashing function. However, it is instructive to see how it is done. The following is an example of using Java to create a digest.

The `MessageDigest` class's `getInstance` method accepts a string specifying the algorithm to use and returns a `MessageDigest` instance. Its `update` method requires an array of bytes containing the key to hash. In this example, a string is used. The `digest` method returns an array of bytes holding the hash value. The byte array is then displayed as a hexadecimal number:

```java
String message = "String to be hashed";
try {
    MessageDigest messageDigest =
        MessageDigest.getInstance("SHA-1");
    messageDigest.update(message.getBytes());
    byte[] digest = messageDigest.digest();

    StringBuffer buffer = new StringBuffer();
    for (byte element : digest) {
        buffer.append(Integer
            .toString((element & 0xff) + 0x100, 16)
            .substring(1));
    }
    System.out.println("Hex format : " +
        buffer.toString());

} catch (NoSuchAlgorithmException ex) {
    // Handle exceptions
}
```

Executing this sequence will produce the following output:

Hex format : 434d902b6098ac050e4ed79b83ad93155b161d72

To store data, such as a file, we can use the filename to create a key. A put type function is then used to store the data:

```
put(key, data)
```

To retrieve the data corresponding to a key, a get type function is used:

```
data = get(key)
```

Every node in an overlay either contains the data that is represented by the key, or it is a node closer to the node containing the data. The routing algorithm determines the next node to visit on the way to the node containing the data.

DHT implementations

There are several Java implementations of DHTs, as listed in the following table:

Implementation	URL
openkad	`https://code.google.com/p/openkad/`
Open Chord	`http://open-chord.sourceforge.net/`
TomP2P	`http://tomp2p.net/`
JDHT	`http://dks.sics.se/jdht/`

We will use the **Java Distributed Hash Table (JDHT)** to illustrate the use of a DHT.

Using JDHT

In order to use JDHT, you will need the JAR files that are listed in the following table. The `dks.jar` file is the main jar file used. However, the other two JAR files are used by JDHT. Alternate sources for the `dks.jar` file is listed as follows:

JAR	Site
`dks.jar`	• `http://dks.sics.se/jdht/` • `https://www.ac.upc.edu/projects/cms/browser/cms/trunk/lib/dks.jar?rev=2`
`xercesImpl.jar`	`http://www.java2s.com/Code/Jar/x/DownloadxercesImpljar.htm`
Apache log4j 1.2.17	`https://logging.apache.org/log4j/1.2/download.html`

The following example has been adapted from the one on the website. First, we create a `JDHT` instance. JDHT uses port `4440` as its default. With this instance, we can then use its `put` method to add a key/value pair to the table:

```
try {
    JDHT DHTExample = new JDHT();
    DHTExample.put("Java SE API",
        "http://docs.oracle.com/javase/8/docs/api/");
    ...
} catch (IOException ex) {
    // Handle exceptions
}
```

In order for a client to connect with this instance, we need to get a reference to this node. This is achieved as shown here:

```
System.out.println(((JDHT) DHTExample).getReference());
```

The following code will keep the program running until the user terminates it. The `close` method is then used to close the table:

```
Scanner scanner = new Scanner(System.in);
System.out.println("Press Enter to terminate application: ");
scanner.next();
DHTExample.close();
```

When the program is executed, you will get an output similar to the following:

dksref://192.168.1.9:4440/0/2179157225/0/1952355557247862269

Press Enter to terminate application:

The client application is described as follows. A new JDHT instance is created using a different port. The second argument is the reference to the first application. You will need to copy the reference and paste it into the client. A different reference will be generated each time the first application is executed:

```
try {
    JDHT myDHT = new JDHT(5550, "dksref://192.168.1.9:4440"
        + "/0/2179157225/0/1952355557247862269");
    ...
} catch (IOException | DKSTooManyRestartJoins |
        DKSIdentifierAlreadyTaken | DKSRefNoResponse ex) {
    // Handle exceptions
}
```

Next, we use the `get` method to retrieve the value associated with the key. The value is then displayed and the application is closed:

```
String value = (String) myDHT.get("Java SE API");
System.out.println(value);
myDHT.close();
```

The output is as follows:

http://docs.oracle.com/javase/8/docs/api/

This simple demonstration illustrates the basics of a distributed hash table.

Using FreePastry

Pastry (`http://www.freepastry.org/`) is a P2P routing overlay system. FreePastry (`http://www.freepastry.org/FreePastry/`) is an open source implementation of Pastry and is simple enough for us to use to illustrate many of the features of a P2P system. Pastry will route messages with a network of *n* nodes in *O(log n)* steps. That is, given a network of nodes, it requires, at most, log base 2 of *n* steps to reach the node. This is an efficient routing approach. However, while it may only require traversing three nodes to get to a resource, it may require a considerable number of IP hops to get to it.

Pastry uses the concept of **leaf sets** in the routing process. Each node has a leaf set. A leaf set is a collection of GUIDS and IP addresses of nodes that are numerically closest to this node. The nodes are logically arranged in a circle, as shown next.

In the following figure, each dot represents a node with an identifier. The addresses used here range from 0 to FFFFFF. The real addresses range from 0 to 2128. If a message representing a request originates at address 9341A2 and needs to be sent to address E24C12, then based on the numerical address the overlay router may route the messages through the intermediate nodes, as depicted by the arrows:

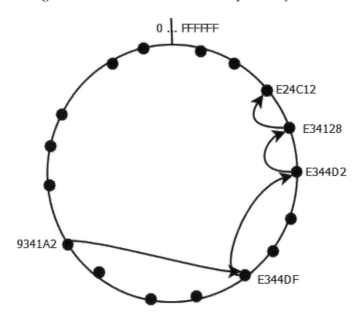

Other applications have been built on top of FreePastry, including:

- **SCRIBE**: This is a group communication and event notification system supporting the publisher/subscriber paradigm
- **PAST**: This is an archival storage utility system
- **SplitStream**: This program supports content streaming and distribution
- **Pastiche**: This is backup system

Each of these applications uses an API to support their use.

The FreePastry demonstration

To demonstrate how FreePastry supports a P2P application, we will create an application based on the FreePastry tutorials found at `https://trac.freepastry.org/wiki/FreePastryTutorial`. In this demonstration, we will create two nodes and demonstrate how they can send and receive messages. The demonstration uses three classes:

- `FreePastryExample`: This is used to bootstrap the network
- `FreePastryApplication`: This executes the functionality of the node
- `PastryMessage`: This is the message that is sent between nodes

Let's start with the bootstrap application.

Understanding the FreePastryExample class

There are several components used with FreePastry applications. These include:

- **Environment**: This class represents the application's environment
- **Bind port**: This represents the local port that the application will bind to
- **Boot port**: This is the boot port that is used for the node's `InetAddress`
- **Boot address**: This is the IP address of the boot node

The `FreePastryExample` class is defined next. It contains a main method and a constructor:

```
public class FreePastryExample {
    ...
}
```

We will start with the `main` method. An instance of the `Environment` class is created first. This class holds the parameter settings for the node. Next, the NAT search policy is set to never, which allows us to use the program in a local LAN without difficulty:

```
public static void main(String[] args) throws Exception {
    Environment environment = new Environment();
    environment.getParameters()
        .setString("nat_search_policy", "never");
    ...
}
```

The ports and `InetSocketAddress` instance are initialized. We will set both ports to the same number at this time. We used the IP address `192.168.1.14` to instantiate the `InetAddress` object. You will need to use the address of your machine instead. This is a local LAN address. Do not use `127.0.0.1` as it will not work properly. The `InetAddress` object along with the `bootPort` value are used to create the `InetSocketAddress` instance. All of this is placed in a try block to handle exceptions:

```
try {
    int bindPort = 9001;
    int bootPort = 9001;
    InetAddress bootInetAddress =
        InetAddress.getByName("192.168.1.14");
    InetSocketAddress bootAddress =
            new InetSocketAddress(bootInetAddress, bootPort);
    System.out.println("InetAddress: " + bootInetAddress);
    ...
} catch (Exception e) {
    // Handle exceptions
}
```

The last task is to create an instance of the `FreePastryExample` class by calling the constructor:

```
FreePastryExample freePastryExample =
    new FreePastryExample(bindPort, bootAddress, environment);
```

The constructor will create and launch the node's application. To accomplish this, we need to create a `PastryNode` instance and attach the application to it. To create the node, we will use a factory.

Every node needs a unique ID. The `RandomNodeIdFactory` class generates an ID based on the current environment. Using this object with the bind port and the environment, an instance of the `SocketPastryNodeFactory` is created. With this factory the `newNode` method is invoked to create our `PastryNode` instance:

```
public FreePastryExample(int bindPort,
        InetSocketAddress bootAddress,
        Environment environment) throws Exception {
    NodeIdFactory nidFactory =
        new RandomNodeIdFactory(environment);
    PastryNodeFactory factory =
        new SocketPastryNodeFactory(
            nidFactory, bindPort, environment);
    PastryNode node = factory.newNode();
    ...
}
```

Next, an instance of the `FreePastryApplication` class is created, and the node is started using the `boot` method:

```
FreePastryApplication application =
    new FreePastryApplication(node);
node.boot(bootAddress);
...
```

The node's ID is then displayed as shown in the next code sequence. As there will be multiple nodes in the network, we pause for 10 seconds to allow the other nodes to start. We used the FreePastry timer to effect this delay. A random node ID is created, and the application's `routeMessage` message is called to send a message to that node:

```
System.out.println("Node " + node.getId().toString() +
" created");
environment.getTimeSource().sleep(10000);
Id randomId = nidFactory.generateNodeId();
application.routeMessage (randomId);
```

Before we execute the program, we need to develop the application class.

Understanding the FreePastryApplication class

The `FreePastryApplication` class implements the `Application` interface and implements the functionality of the node. The constructor creates and registers an `Endpoint` instance and initializes a message. The `Endpoint` instance is used by the node to send messages. The class and constructor are shown here:

```
public class FreePastryApplication implements Application {
    protected Endpoint endpoint;
```

```
            private final String message;
            private final String instance = " Instance ID";

            public FreePastryApplication(Node node) {
                this.endpoint = node.buildEndpoint(this, instance);
                this.message = "Hello there! from Instance: "
                        + instance + " Sent at: [" + getCurrentTime()
                        + "]";
                this.endpoint.register();
            }


            ...
    }
```

You may get a "Leaking this in constructor" warning when this code is compiled. This is caused by a reference to the constructor's object being passed as an argument to the buildEndpoint method using the this keyword. This is a potentially bad practice because the object may have not been fully constructed when it was passed. Another thread may try to do something with the object before it is ready. It is not as much of a problem if it is passed to a package-private method that performs common initialization. In this situation, it is not likely to cause problems.

The Application interface requires that three methods be implemented:

- deliver: This is called when a message is received
- forward: This is used to forward a message
- update: This informs the application that a node has joined or left a set of local nodes

We are only interested in the deliver method for this application. In addition, we will add the getCurrentTime and routeMessage methods to the application. We will use the getCurrentTime methods to show the time that our messages are sent and arrive. The routeMessage method will send a message to another node.

The getCurrentTime method is as follows. It uses the EndPoint object to access the node's environment and then the time:

```
        private long getCurrentTime() {
            return this.endpoint
                    .getEnvironment()
                    .getTimeSource()
                    .currentTimeMillis();
        }
```

The `routeMessage` method is passed the identifier of the destination node. The message text is constructed adding the end point and time information. A `PastryMessage` instance is created using the end-point identifier and the message text. The `route` method is then called to send this message:

```
public void routeMessage(Id id) {
    System.out.println(
            "Message Sent\n\tCurrent Node: " +
                this.endpoint.getId()
            + "\n\tDestination: " + id
            + "\n\tTime: " + getCurrentTime());
    Message msg = new PastryMessage(endpoint.getId(),
            id, message);
    endpoint.route(id, msg, null);
}
```

When a message is received by a node, the `deliver` method is invoked. The implementation of this method is as follows. The end point identifier, the message, and the time of arrival are displayed. This will help us understand how messages are sent and received:

```
public void deliver(Id id, Message message) {
    System.out.println("Message Received\n\tCurrent Node: "
            + this.endpoint.getId() + "\n\tMessage: "
            + message + "\n\tTime: " + getCurrentTime());
}
```

The `PastryMessage` class implements the `Message` interface, as shown next. The constructor accepts the destination, source, and message:

```
public class PastryMessage implements Message {
    private final Id from;
    private final Id to;
    private final String messageBody;

    public PastryMessage(Id from, Id to, String messageBody) {
        this.from = from;
        this.to = to;
        this.messageBody = messageBody;
    }

    ...
}
```

The `Message` interface possesses a single `getPriority` method that needs to be overridden. Here, we return a low priority so that it does not interfere with underlying P2P maintenance traffic:

```
public int getPriority() {
  return Message.LOW_PRIORITY;
}
```

The `toString` method is overridden to provide a more detailed description of the message:

```
public String toString() {
  return "From: " + this.from
        + " To: " + this.to
        + " [" + this.messageBody + "]";
}
```

Now, we are ready to execute the example. Execute the `FreePastryExample` class. The initial output will consist of the following output. The abbreviated node identifier is displayed, which in this case is `<0xB36864..>`. The identifier that you get will be different:

InetAddress: /192.168.1.14 Node <0xB36864..> created

After this, a pause a message is sent and subsequently received by the current node. This message was created in the `FreePastryExample` class using the code repeated here for your convenience:

```
Id randomId = nidFactory.generateNodeId();
application.routeMessage(randomId);
```

A random identifier was used because we do not have a specific node to send the message to. When the message is sent, the following output is generated. The random identifier for this run is `<0x83C7CD..>`:

Message Sent

Current Node: <0xB36864..>

Destination: <0x83C7CD..>

Time: 1441844742906

Message Received

Current Node: <0xB36864..>

Message: From: <0xB36864..> To: <0x83C7CD..> [Hello there! from Instance: Instance ID Sent at: [1441844732905]]

Time: 1441844742915

The time between the sending and receiving of the message is minimal. If a larger set of nodes comprised the P2P network, more significant delays would show up.

In the previous output, the node addresses were truncated. We can use the `toStringFull` method, as shown here, to get the full address:

```
System.out.println("Node " + node.getId().toStringFull()
    + " created");
```

This will produce output similar to the following:

Node B36864DE0C4F9E9C1572CBCC095D585EA943B1B4 created

We did not provide a specific address for our messages. Instead, we randomly generated addresses. This application demonstrated the basic elements of a FreePastry application. Additional layers are used to facilitate communication between nodes, such as the publisher/provider paradigm support by Scribe.

We can start a second node using the same program, but we will need to use a different bind port to avoid binding conflicts. The message sent by either node will not necessarily be received by the other node. This is the result of the routes generated by FreePastry.

Sending a message to a specific node

To send a message directly to a node, we need its identifier. To get a remote node's identifier, we need to use a leaf set. This collection is not strictly a set because for small networks, such as the one we are using, the same node may appear twice.

The `LeafSet` class represents this collection and has a `get` method that will return a `NodeHandle` instance for each node. We can send messages to nodes if we have this node handle.

To demonstrate this approach, add the following method to the `FreePastryApplication` class. This is similar to the `routeMessage` method, but it uses a node handle as an argument of the `route` method:

```
public void routeMessageDirect(NodeHandle nh) {
    System.out.println("Message Sent Direct\n\tCurrent Node: "
            + this.endpoint.getId() + " Destination: " + nh
            + "\n\tTime: " + getCurrentTime());
    Message msg =
```

```
              new PastryMessage(endpoint.getId(), nh.getId(),
                  "DIRECT-" + message);
          endpoint.route(null, msg, nh);
      }
```

Add the following sequences of code to the end of the `FreePastryExample` constructor. Optionally, comment out the previous code that uses the `routeMessage` method. First, we pause for 10 seconds to allow other nodes to join the network:

```
      environment.getTimeSource().sleep(10000);
```

Next, we create an instance of the `LeafSet` class. The `getUniqueSet` method returns the leaf set, which excludes the current node. A for-each statement will then use the `routeMessageDirect` variable to send the message to the nodes of the collection:

```
      LeafSet leafSet = node.getLeafSet();
      Collection<NodeHandle> collection = leafSet.getUniqueSet();
      for (NodeHandle nodeHandle : collection) {
          application.routeMessageDirect(nodeHandle);
          environment.getTimeSource().sleep(1000);
      }
```

Start the `FreePastryExample` class using a bind port of `9001`. Then, change the bind port to `9002` and start the class a second time. After several seconds, you will see an output similar to the following one. The first set of output corresponds to the first instance of the application, while the second set corresponds to the second instance. Each instance will send one message to the other instance. Note the time stamps that are used when the messages are sent and received:

```
InetAddress: /192.168.1.9
Node <0xA5BFDA..> created
Message Sent Direct
  Current Node: <0xA5BFDA..> Destination: [SNH:
<0x2C6D18..>//192.168.1.9:9002]
  Time: 1441849240310
Message Received
  Current Node: <0xA5BFDA..>
  Message: From: <0x2C6D18..> To: <0xA5BFDA..> [DIRECT-Hello there!
from Instance: Instance ID Sent at: [1441849224879]]
  Time: 1441849245038

InetAddress: /192.168.1.9
Node <0x2C6D18..> created
Message Received
  Current Node: <0x2C6D18..>
  Message: From: <0xA5BFDA..> To: <0x2C6D18..> [DIRECT-Hello there!
from Instance: Instance ID Sent at: [1441849220308]]
```

```
    Time: 1441849240349
Message Sent Direct
    Current Node: <0x2C6D18..> Destination: [SNH:
<0xA5BFDA..>//192.168.1.9:9001]
    Time: 1441849245020
```

There is a lot more to FreePastry than we were able to illustrate here. However, the examples provide a feel for the nature of P2P application development. Other P2P frameworks work in a similar manner.

Summary

In this chapter, we explored the nature and use of P2P networks. This architecture treats all nodes as equals avoiding the use of a central server. Nodes are mapped using an overlay network, which effectively creates a subnetwork of nodes in an IP address space. These nodes will vary in their capabilities and will join and leave the network in a random manner.

We saw how a distributed hash table supports identifying and locating nodes in a network. A routing algorithm uses this table to fulfill requests by sending messages between nodes. We demonstrated the Java Distributed Hashing Table to illustrate the used of DHTs.

There are several open source Java based P2P frameworks available. We used FreePastry to demonstrate how P2P networks work. Specifically, we showed you how nodes join a network and how messages are sent between nodes. This provided a better understanding of how these frameworks function.

In the next chapter, we will examine the nature of the UDP protocol and how it supports multicasting.

6
UDP and Multicasting

User Datagram Protocol (**UDP**) sits on top of IP and provides an unreliable counterpart to TCP. UDP sends individual packets between two nodes in a network. UDP packets do not have knowledge of other packets, and there is no guarantee that a packet will actually arrive at its intended destination. When multiple packets are sent, there is no guarantee of the arrival order. UDP messages are simply sent and then forgotten as there are no acknowledgements sent from a recipient.

UDP is a connectionless protocol. There is no exchange of messages between two nodes to facilitate the packet transmission. No state information is maintained about the connection.

UDP is appropriate for services where delivery needs to be efficient, and no guarantee of delivery is needed. For example, it is used for **Domain Name System** (**DNS**) services, **Network Time Protocol** (**NTP**) services, **Voice Over IP** (**VOIP**), network communication coordination by P2P networks, and for video streaming. If a video frame is lost, then the viewer may never notice it if the loss does not occur frequently.

There are several protocols that use UDP, including:

- **Real Time Streaming Protocol (RTSP)**: This protocol is used to control the streaming of media
- **Routing Information Protocol (RIP)**: This protocol determines the route that is used to transmit packets
- **Domain Name System (DNS)**: This protocol looks up an Internet domain name and returns its IP address
- **Network Time Protocol (NTP)**: This protocol synchronizes clocks across the Internet

A UDP packet consists of an IP address and port number to identify its destination. The UDP packets have a fixed size and can be as large as 65,353 bytes. However, each packet uses a minimum of 20 bytes for an IP header and 8 bytes for a UDP header, limiting the size of a message to 65,507 bytes. If a message is larger than that, then multiple packets will need to be sent.

UDP packets can also be multicast. This means that a packet is sent to every node that belongs to a UDP group. This is an efficient way of sending information to multiple nodes without having to explicitly target each node. Instead, the packet is sent to a group whose members are responsible for capturing its group's packets.

In this chapter, we will illustrate how the UDP protocol can be used to:

- Support the traditional client/server model
- Use NIO Channels to perform UDP operations
- Multicast packets to group members
- Stream media such as audio or video to a client

We will start with an overview of Java support for UDP and provide more UDP protocol details.

Java support for UDP

Java uses the DatagramSocket class to form socket connections between nodes. The DatagramPacket class represents a packet of data. Simple send and receive methods will transmit the packets across a network.

UDP uses an IP address and a port number to identify nodes. UDP port numbers range from 0 to 65535. Port numbers are broken down into three types:

- Well-known ports (0 to 1023): These are port numbers that are used for relatively common services.
- Registered ports (1024 to 49151): These are port numbers that are assigned by IANA to a process.
- Dynamic/private ports (49152 to 65535): These are dynamically assigned to clients when a connection is initiated. These are normally temporary and cannot be assigned by IANA.

The following table is a short list of UDP specific port assignments. They illustrate how UDP is widely used to support many diverse applications and services. A more complete list of TCP/UDP port numbers is found at `https://en.wikipedia.org/wiki/List_of_TCP_and_UDP_port_numbers`:

Well-known ports (0 to 1023)	Usage
7	This is the echo protocol
9	This means wake-on-LAN
161	This is the **Simple Network Management Protocol (SNMP)**
319	These are **Precision Time Protocol (PTP)** event messages
320	These are PTP general messages
513	This indicates who the user is
514	This is the syslog — used for system logging
520	This is the **Routing Information Protocol (RIP)**
750	This is `kerberos-iv`, Kerberos version IV
944	This is the network file system service
973	This is the network file system over IPv6 service

The following table gives a list of the registered ports and their usage:

Registered ports (1024 to 49151)	Usage
1534	This is used for Eclipse **Target Communication Framework (TCF)**
1581	This is used for MIL STD 2045-47001 VMF
1589	This is used for Cisco **VLAN Query Protocol (VQP)** / VMPS
2190	This is used for TiVoConnect Beacon
2302	This is used for Halo: Combat Evolved multiplayer
3000	This is used for BitTorrent sync
4500	This is used for IPSec NAT traversal
5353	This is used for **Multicast DNS (mDNS)**
9110	This is used for SSMP message protocol
27500 to 27900	This is used for id Software's QuakeWorld
29900 to 29901	This is used for Nintendo Wi-Fi connection
36963	This is used for Unreal Software multiplayer games

TCP versus UDP

There are several differences between TCP and UDP. These differences include the following:

- **Reliability**: TCP is more reliable than UDP
- **Ordering**: TCP guarantees the order of packet transmission will be preserved
- **Header size**: The UDP header is smaller than the TCP header
- **Speed**: UDP is faster than TCP

When a packet is sent using TCP, the packet is guaranteed to arrive. If it is lost, then it is re-sent. UDP does not offer this guarantee. If the packet does not arrive, then it is not re-sent.

TCP preserves the order that packets are sent in, while UDP does not. If the TCP packets arrive at a destination in a different order than how they were sent, TCP will reassemble the packets in their original order. With UDP, this ordering is not preserved.

When a packet is created, header information is attached to assist in the delivery of the packet. With UDP the header consists of 8 bytes. The usual size of a TCP header is 32 bytes.

With a smaller header size and lack of the overhead to ensure reliability, UDP is more efficient than TCP. In addition, less effort is required to create a connection. This efficiency makes it a better choice to stream media.

Let's begin our UDP examples with how a traditional client/server architecture is supported.

UDP client/server

The UDP client/server applications are similar in structure to the structure used for TCP client/server applications. On the server side, a UDP server socket is created, which waits for client requests. The client will create a corresponding UDP socket and use it to send a message to the server. The server can then process the request and send back a response.

A UDP client/server will use the `DatagramSocket` class for the socket and a `DatagramPacket` to hold the message. There is no restriction on the message's content type. In our examples, we will be using a text message.

The UDP server application

Our server is defined next. The constructor will perform the work of the server:

```
public class UDPServer {
    public UDPServer() {
        System.out.println("UDP Server Started");
        ...
        System.out.println("UDP Server Terminating");
    }

    public static void main(String[] args) {
        new UDPServer();
    }
}
```

In the constructor's try-with-resources block, we create an instance of the `DatagramSocket` class. Several of the methods that we will be using may throw an `IOException` exception, which will be caught if necessary:

```
try (DatagramSocket serverSocket =
        new DatagramSocket(9003)) {
    ...
    }
} catch (IOException ex) {
    //Handle exceptions
}
```

An alternate way of creating the socket is to use the `bind` method, as shown next. The `DatagramSocket` instance is created using `null` as the parameter. The port is then assigned with the `bind` method:

```
DatagramSocket serverSocket = new DatagramSocket(null);
serverSocket.bind(new InetSocketAddress(9003));
```

Both approaches will create a `DatagramSocket` instance using port `9003`.

The process of sending a message consists of the following:

- Creating an array of bytes
- Creating a `DatagramPacket` instance
- Using the `DatagramSocket` instance to wait for a message to arrive

The process is enclosed in a loop, as shown next, to allow multiple requests to be handled. The message that is received is simply echoed back to the client program. The DatagramPacket instance is created using the byte array and its length. It is used as the argument of the DatagramSocket class's receive method. The packet does not hold any information at this time. This method will block until a request is made, and the packet will then be populated:

```
while (true) {
    byte[] receiveMessage = new byte[1024];
    DatagramPacket receivePacket = new DatagramPacket(
        receiveMessage, receiveMessage.length);
    serverSocket.receive(receivePacket);
    ...
}
```

When the method returns, the packet is converted into a string. If some other data type was sent, then some other conversion will be needed. The message that was sent is then displayed:

```
String message = new String(receivePacket.getData());
System.out.println("Received from client: [" + message
    + "]\nFrom: " + receivePacket.getAddress());
```

To send a response, the address and port number of the client are needed. These are obtained using the getAddress and getPort methods, respectively, against the packet, which possesses this information. We will see this when we discuss the client. Also needed is the message that is represented as an array of bytes, which the getBytes method provides:

```
InetAddress inetAddress = receivePacket.getAddress();
int port = receivePacket.getPort();
byte[] sendMessage;
sendMessage = message.getBytes();
```

A new DatagramPacket instance is created using the message, its length, and the client's address and port number. The send method sends the packet to the client:

```
DatagramPacket sendPacket =
    new DatagramPacket(sendMessage,
        sendMessage.length, inetAddress, port);
serverSocket.send(sendPacket);
```

With the server defined, let's examine the client.

The UDP client application

The client application will prompt the user for a message to send, and then it will send the message to the server. It will wait for a response and then display the response. It is declared here:

```
class UDPClient {
    public UDPClient() {
        System.out.println("UDP Client Started");
        ...
    }
        System.out.println("UDP Client Terminating ");
    }

    public static void main(String args[]) {
        new UDPClient();
    }
}
```

The `Scanner` class supports getting user input. The try-with-resources block creates a `DatagramSocket` instance and handles exceptions:

```
Scanner scanner = new Scanner(System.in);
try (DatagramSocket clientSocket = new DatagramSocket()) {
    ...
    }
    clientSocket.close();
} catch (IOException ex) {
    // Handle exceptions
}
```

The client's current address is accessed using the `getByName` method, and a reference to an array of bytes is declared. This address will be used to create a packet:

```
InetAddress inetAddress =
    InetAddress.getByName("localhost");
byte[] sendMessage;
```

An infinite loop is used to prompt the user for messages. When the user enters "quit", the application will terminate, as shown here:

```
while (true) {
    System.out.print("Enter a message: ");
    String message = scanner.nextLine();
    if ("quit".equalsIgnoreCase(message)) {
        break;
    }
    ...
}
```

To create a `DatagramPacket` instance holding the message, its constructor needs an array of bytes representing the message, its length, and the client's address and port number. In the following code, the server's port is `9003`. The `send` method will send the packet to the server:

```
sendMessage = message.getBytes();
DatagramPacket sendPacket = new DatagramPacket(
    sendMessage, sendMessage.length,
    inetAddress, 9003);
clientSocket.send(sendPacket);
```

To receive a response, a receive packet is created and used with the `receive` method in the same way that it was handled in the server. This method will block until the server responds, and then the message is displayed:

```
byte[] receiveMessage = new byte[1024];
DatagramPacket receivePacket = new DatagramPacket(
        receiveMessage, receiveMessage.length);
clientSocket.receive(receivePacket);
String receivedSentence =
    new String(receivePacket.getData());
System.out.println("Received from server ["
    + receivedSentence + "]\nfrom "
    + receivePacket.getSocketAddress());
```

Now, let's see these applications at work.

The UDP client/server in action

The server is started first. It will display the following message:

UDP Server Started

Next, start the client application. It will display the following message:

UDP Client Started

Enter a message:

Enter a message, such as the following one:

Enter a message: Top of the morning to you

The server will display that it has received the message, as shown next. You will see several empty lines of output. This is the content of the 1024-byte array that is used to hold the message. The message is then echoed back to the client:

Received from client: [Top of the morning to you

...

]

From: /127.0.0.1

On the client side, the response is displayed. In this example, the users then enter "quit" to terminate the application:

Received from server [Top of the morning to you

...

]

from /127.0.0.1:9003

Enter a message: quit

UDP Client Terminating

As we are sending and receiving test messages, we can simplify the display of the message using the `trim` method when the message is displayed, as shown next. This code can be used on both the server and the client side:

```
System.out.println("Received from client: ["
        + message.trim()
        + "]\nFrom: " + receivePacket.getAddress());
```

The output will be easier to read, as shown here:

Received from client: [Top of the morning to you]

From: /127.0.0.1

This client/server application can be enhanced in a number of ways, including the use of threads, to enable it to work better with multiple clients. This example illustrates the basics of developing a UDP client/server application in Java. In the next section, we will see how channels support UDP.

Channel support for UDP

The DatagramChannel class provides additional support for UDP. It can support nonblocking interchanges. The DatagramChannel class is derived from the SelectableChannel class that makes multithreaded application easier. We will examine its use in *Chapter 7, Network Scalability*.

The DatagramSocket class binds a channel to a port. After this class is used, it is no longer used directly. Using the DatagramChannel class means, we do not have to use datagram packets directly. Instead, data is transferred using an instance of the ByteBuffer class. This class provides several convenient methods to access its data.

To demonstrate the use of the DatagramChannel class, we will develop an echo server and client application. The server will wait for a message from a client, and then send it back to the client.

The UDP echo server application

The UDP echo server application declaration follows and uses port 9000. In the main method a try-with-resources block opens the channel and creates a socket. The DatagramChannel class does not possess public constructors. To create a channel, we use the open method, which returns an instance of the DatagramChannel class. The channel's socket method creates a DatagramSocket instance for the channel:

```
public class UDPEchoServer {

    public static void main(String[] args) {
        int port = 9000;
        System.out.println("UDP Echo Server Started");
        try (DatagramChannel channel = DatagramChannel.open();
            DatagramSocket socket = channel.socket();){
                ...
            }
        }
        catch (IOException ex) {
            // Handle exceptions
        }
        System.out.println("UDP Echo Server Terminated");
    }
}
```

Once created, we need to associate it with a port. This is done first by creating an instance of the `SocketAddress` class, which represents a socket address. The `InetSocketAddress` class is derived from the `SocketAddress` class and implements an IP address. Its use in the following code sequence will associate it with port `9000`. The `DatagramSocket` class's `bind` method ties this address to the socket:

```
SocketAddress address = new InetSocketAddress(port);
socket.bind(address);
```

The `ByteBuffer` class is central to using a datagram channel. We discussed its creation in *Chapter 3, NIO Support for Networking*. In the next statement, an instance of this class is created with the `allocateDirect` method. This method will attempt to use native OS support directly on the buffer. This can be more efficient than using the datagram packet approach. Here, we created a buffer with the maximum size possible:

```
ByteBuffer buffer = ByteBuffer.allocateDirect(65507);
```

Add the infinite loop that follows, which will receive a message from a client, display the message, and then send it back:

```
while (true) {
    // Get message
    // Display message
    // Return message
}
```

The `receive` method is applied against a channel to get a client's message. It will block until the message is received. Its single argument is the byte buffer that is used to hold the incoming data. If the message exceeds the size of the buffer, the extra bytes are silently thrown away.

The `flip` method enables the buffer to be processed. It sets the buffer's limit to the current position in the buffer and then sets the position to `0`. Subsequent get type methods will start at the beginning of the buffer:

```
SocketAddress client = channel.receive(buffer);
buffer.flip();
```

While not necessary for an echo server, the message that is received is displayed on the server. This allows us to verify that the message was received and suggests how messages can be modified to do more than simply echoing the message.

In order to display the message, we need to use the `get` method to get each byte and then convert it to the appropriate type. The echo server is intended to echo simple strings. Thus, the byte needs to be cast to a char before it is displayed.

However, the `get` method modifies the current position in the buffer. We need to restore the position to its original state before we send the message back to the client. The buffer's `mark` and `reset` method are used for this purpose.

All of this is performed in the following code sequence. The `mark` method sets the mark at the current position. A `StringBuilder` instance is used to recreate the string that was sent by the client. The buffer's `hasRemaining` method controls the while loop. The message is displayed and the `reset` method restores the position to the previously marked value:

```
buffer.mark();
System.out.print("Received: [");
StringBuilder message = new StringBuilder();
while (buffer.hasRemaining()) {
    message.append((char) buffer.get());
}
System.out.println(message + "]");
buffer.reset();
```

The last step is to send the byte buffer back to the client. The `send` method does this. A message indicating that the message has been sent is displayed, followed by the `clear` method. This method is used because we are through with the buffer. It will set the position to 0, set the limit of the buffer to its capacity, and discard the mark:

```
channel.send(buffer, client);
System.out.println("Sent: [" + message + "]");
buffer.clear();
```

When the server is started, we will see a message to this effect, as shown here:

UDP Echo Server Started

We are now ready to see how the client is implemented.

The UDP echo client application

The implementation of the UDP echo client is simple and uses these steps:

- A connection to the echo server is established
- A byte buffer is created to hold the message
- The buffer is sent to the server
- The client blocks until the message is sent back

The client's implementation details are similar to the server's. We start with the declaration of the application, as shown here:

```
public class UDPEchoClient {

    public static void main(String[] args) {
        System.out.println("UDP Echo Client Started");
        try {
            ...
        }
        catch (IOException ex) {
            // Handle exceptions
        }
        System.out.println("UDP Echo Client Terminated");
    }
}
```

In the server, the single argument `InetSocketAddress` constructor associates port `9000` with the current IP address. Within the client, we need to specify the IP address of the server along with the port. Otherwise, it will be unable to determine where to send the message. This is accomplished in the following statement using the class's two-argument constructor. We use the address, `127.0.0.1`, assuming that the client and the server are on the same machine:

```
SocketAddress remote =
    new InetSocketAddress("127.0.0.1", 9000);
```

The channel is then created with the `open` method and connected to the socket address with the `connect` method:

```
DatagramChannel channel = DatagramChannel.open();
channel.connect(remote);
```

In the next code sequence, the message string is created, and the byte buffer is allocated. The size of the buffer is set to the length of the string. The `put` method then assigns the message to the buffer. As the `put` method expects an array of bytes, we use the `String` class's `getBytes` method to obtain an array of bytes corresponding to the message's contents:

```
String message = "The message";
ByteBuffer buffer = ByteBuffer.allocate(message.length());
buffer.put(message.getBytes());
```

Before we send the buffer to the server, the `flip` method is called. It will set the limit to the current position and set the position to 0. Thus, when received by the server it can be processed:

```
buffer.flip();
```

To send the message to the server, the channel's `write` method is called, as shown next. This will send the underlying packet directly to the server. However, this method only works if the channel's socket is connected, which was achieved earlier:

```
channel.write(buffer);
System.out.println("Sent: [" + message + "]");
```

Next, the buffer is cleared, allowing us to reuse the buffer. The `read` method will receive the buffer, and the buffer will be displayed using the same process that was used in the server:

```
buffer.clear();
channel.read(buffer);
buffer.flip();
System.out.print("Received: [");
while(buffer.hasRemaining()) {
    System.out.print((char)buffer.get());
}
System.out.println("]");
```

We are now ready to use the client in conjunction with the server.

The UDP echo client/server in action

The server needs to be started first. We will see the initial server message, as shown here:

UDP Echo Server Started

Next, start the client. The following output will be displayed showing the client sending the message and then showing the returned message:

UDP Echo Client Started

Sent: [The message]

Received: [The message]

UDP Echo Client Terminated

On the server side, we will see the message being received and then being sent back to the client:

Received: [The message]

Sent: [The message]

Using the `DatagramChannel` class can make UDP communications faster.

UDP multicasting

Multicasting is the process of sending a message to multiple clients at the same time. Each client will receive the same message. In order to participate in this process, clients need to join a multicast group. When a message is sent, its destination address indicates that it is a multicast message. The multicast groups are dynamic with clients entering and leaving the group at any time.

Multicast is the old IPv4 CLASS D space and uses addresses `224.0.0.0` through `239.255.255.255`. The IPv4 Multicast Address Space Registry lists multicast address assignments and is found at `http://www.iana.org/assignments/multicast-addresses/multicast-addresses.xml`. The *Host Extensions for IP Multicasting* document is found at `http://tools.ietf.org/html/rfc1112`. It defines the implementation requirements to support multicasting.

The UDP multicast server

The server application is declared next. This server is a time server that will broadcast the current data and time every second. This is a good use for multicast messages as there may be several clients interested in the same information, and reliability is not a concern. The try block will handle exceptions as they occur:

```
public class UDPMulticastServer {

    public UDPMulticastServer() {
        System.out.println("UDP Multicast Time Server Started");
        try {
            ...
        } catch (IOException | InterruptedException ex) {
            // Handle exceptions
        }
        System.out.println(
            "UDP Multicast Time Server Terminated");
    }
```

```
     public static void main(String args[]) {
         new UDPMulticastServer();
     }
 }
```

An instance of the `MulticastSocket` class is needed along with an `InetAddress` instance holding the multicast IP address. In this example, the address, 228.5.6.7, represents the multicast group. The `joinGroup` method is used to join this multicast group, as shown here:

```
MulticastSocket multicastSocket = new MulticastSocket();
InetAddress inetAddress = InetAddress.getByName("228.5.6.7");
multicastSocket.joinGroup(inetAddress);
```

In order to send a message, we need an array of bytes to hold the message and a packet. These are declared as shown here:

```
byte[] data;
DatagramPacket packet;
```

The server application will use an infinite loop to broadcast a new date and time every second. The thread is paused for one second, and then a new date and time is created using the `Data` class. The `DatagramPacket` instance is created using this information. Port 9877 is assigned for this server and will need to be known by the client. The `send` method sends the packet to interested clients:

```
while (true) {
    Thread.sleep(1000);
    String message = (new Date()).toString();
    System.out.println("Sending: [" + message + "]");
    data = message.getBytes();
    packet = new DatagramPacket(data, message.length(),
            inetAddress, 9877);
    multicastSocket.send(packet);
}
```

The client application is discussed next.

The UDP multicast client

This application will join the multicast group as defined by the address 228.5.6.7. It will block until a message is received, and then it will display the message. The application is defined as follows:

```
public class UDPMulticastClient {

    public UDPMulticastClient() {
```

```
        System.out.println("UDP Multicast Time Client Started");
        try {
            ...
        } catch (IOException ex) {
            ex.printStackTrace();
        }

        System.out.println(
            "UDP Multicast Time Client Terminated");
    }

    public static void main(String[] args) {
        new UDPMulticastClient();
    }
}
```

An instance of the `MulticastSocket` class is created using the port number `9877`.
This is needed so that it can connect to the UDP multicast server. An `InetAddress`
instance is created using the multicast address of `228.5.6.7`. The client then joins
the multicast group using the `joinGroup` method.

```
        MulticastSocket multicastSocket = new MulticastSocket(9877);
        InetAddress inetAddress = InetAddress.getByName("228.5.6.7");
        multicastSocket.joinGroup(inetAddress);
```

A `DatagramPacket` instance is needed to receive messages that were sent to the
client. An array of bytes is created and used to instantiate this packet, as shown here:

```
        byte[] data = new byte[256];
        DatagramPacket packet = new DatagramPacket(data, data.length);
```

The client application then enters an infinite loop where it blocks at the `receive`
method until the server sends a message. Once the message has arrived, the message
is displayed:

```
        while (true) {
            multicastSocket.receive(packet);
            String message = new String(
                packet.getData(), 0, packet.getLength());
            System.out.println("Message from: " + packet.getAddress()
                + " Message: [" + message + "]");
        }
```

Next, we will demonstrate how the client and the server interact.

The UDP multicast client/server in action

Start the server. The output of the server will be similar to the following one, but the date and time will be different:

UDP Multicast Time Server Started

Sending: [Sat Sep 19 13:48:42 CDT 2015]

Sending: [Sat Sep 19 13:48:43 CDT 2015]

Sending: [Sat Sep 19 13:48:44 CDT 2015]

Sending: [Sat Sep 19 13:48:45 CDT 2015]

Sending: [Sat Sep 19 13:48:46 CDT 2015]

Sending: [Sat Sep 19 13:48:47 CDT 2015]

...

Next, start the client application. It will start receiving messages similar to the following:

UDP Multicast Time Client Started

Message from: /192.168.1.7 Message: [Sat Sep 19 13:48:44 CDT 2015]

Message from: /192.168.1.7 Message: [Sat Sep 19 13:48:45 CDT 2015]

Message from: /192.168.1.7 Message: [Sat Sep 19 13:48:46 CDT 2015]

...

> If the program is executed on a Mac, it may be through a socket exception. If this happens, use the `-Djava.net.preferIPv4Stack=true` VM option.

If you start subsequent clients, each client will receive the same series of server messages.

UDP multicasting with channels

We can also multicast with channels. We will use IPv6 to demonstrate this process. The process is similar to our previous use of the `DatagramChannel` class, except that we need to use a multicast group. To do this, we need to know which network interfaces are available. Before we get into the specifics of using channels to multicast, we will demonstrate how to obtain a list of network interfaces for a machine.

The `NetworkInterface` class represents a network interface. This class was discussed in *Chapter 2, Network Addressing*. The following is a variation of the approach demonstrated in that chapter. It has been augmented to show whether a specific interface supports multicasting, as shown next:

```
try {
    Enumeration<NetworkInterface> networkInterfaces;
    networkInterfaces =
        NetworkInterface.getNetworkInterfaces();
    for (NetworkInterface networkInterface :
            Collections.list(networkInterfaces)) {
        displayNetworkInterfaceInformation(
            networkInterface);
    }
} catch (SocketException ex) {
    // Handle exceptions
}
```

The `displayNetworkInterfaceInformation` method is shown next. This approach has been adapted from `https://docs.oracle.com/javase/tutorial/networking/nifs/listing.html`:

```
static void displayNetworkInterfaceInformation(
        NetworkInterface networkInterface) {
    try {
        System.out.printf("Display name: %s\n",
            networkInterface.getDisplayName());
        System.out.printf("Name: %s\n",
            networkInterface.getName());
        System.out.printf("Supports Multicast: %s\n",
            networkInterface.supportsMulticast());
        Enumeration<InetAddress> inetAddresses =
            networkInterface.getInetAddresses();
        for (InetAddress inetAddress :
                Collections.list(inetAddresses)) {
            System.out.printf("InetAddress: %s\n",
                inetAddress);
        }
        System.out.println();
    } catch (SocketException ex) {
        // Handle exceptions
    }
}
```

When this example is executed, you will get output similar to the following:

Display name: Software Loopback Interface 1

Name: lo

Supports Multicast: true

InetAddress: /127.0.0.1

InetAddress: /0:0:0:0:0:0:0:1

Display name: Microsoft Kernel Debug Network Adapter

Name: eth0

Supports Multicast: true

Display name: Realtek PCIe FE Family Controller

Name: eth1

Supports Multicast: true

InetAddress: /fe80:0:0:0:91d0:8e19:31f1:cb2d%eth1

Display name: Realtek RTL8188EE 802.11 b/g/n Wi-Fi Adapter

Name: wlan0

Supports Multicast: true

InetAddress: /192.168.1.7

InetAddress: /2002:42be:6659:0:0:0:0:1001

InetAddress: /fe80:0:0:0:9cdb:371f:d3e9:4e2e%wlan0

...

For our client/server, we will use the `eth0` interface. You will need to choose the one most appropriate for you platform. For example, on a Mac this may be `en0` or `awdl0`.

The UDP channel multicast server

The UDP channel multicast server will:

- Set up the channel and multicast group
- Create a buffer containing a message
- Use an infinite loop to send and display the group message

The definition of the server is as follows:

```
public class UDPDatagramMulticastServer {

    public static void main(String[] args) {
        try {
            ...
            }
        } catch (IOException | InterruptedException ex) {
            // Handle exceptions
        }
    }

}
```

The first task uses the System class's setProperty method to specify that IPv6 be used. A DatagramChannel instance is then created, and the eth0 network interface is created. The setOption method will associate the channel with the network interface that was used to identify the group. The group is represented by an InetSocketAddress instance using an IPv6 node-local scope multicast address, as shown next. More details about the *IPv6 Multicast Address Space Registry* document can be found at http://www.iana.org/assignments/ipv6-multicast-addresses/ipv6-multicast-addresses.xhtml:

```
System.setProperty(
    "java.net.preferIPv6Stack", "true");
DatagramChannel channel = DatagramChannel.open();
NetworkInterface networkInterface =
    NetworkInterface.getByName("eth0");
channel.setOption(StandardSocketOptions.
    IP_MULTICAST_IF,
    networkInterface);
InetSocketAddress group =
    new InetSocketAddress("FF01:0:0:0:0:0:0:FC",
        9003);
```

A byte buffer is then created, based on a message string. The buffer's size is set to the length of the string and is assigned using a combination of the `put` and `getBytes` methods:

```
String message = "The message";
ByteBuffer buffer =
    ByteBuffer.allocate(message.length());
buffer.put(message.getBytes());
```

Inside the while loop, the buffer is sent out to group members. To clearly see what was sent, the contents of the buffer is displayed using the same code that was used in the *The UDP echo server application* section. The buffer is reset so that it can be used again. The application pauses for one second to avoid excessive messages for this example:

```
while (true) {
    channel.send(buffer, group);
    System.out.println("Sent the multicast message: "
        + message);
    buffer.clear();

    buffer.mark();
    System.out.print("Sent: [");
    StringBuilder msg = new StringBuilder();
    while (buffer.hasRemaining()) {
        msg.append((char) buffer.get());
    }
    System.out.println(msg + "]");
    buffer.reset();

    Thread.sleep(1000);
}
```

We are now ready for the client application.

The UDP channel multicast client

The UDP channel multicast client will join the group, receive a message, display it, and then terminate. As we will see, the `MembershipKey` class represents membership to a multicast group.

The application is declared as follows. First, we specify that IPv6 is to be used. The network interface is then declared, which is the same one that was used by the server:

```
public class UDPDatagramMulticastClient {
    public static void main(String[] args) throws Exception {
```

```
        System.setProperty("java.net.preferIPv6Stack", "true");
        NetworkInterface networkInterface =
            NetworkInterface.getByName("eth0");
        ...
    }
}
```

The `DatagramChannel` instance is created next. The channel is bound to port 9003 and is associated with the network interface instance:

```
        DatagramChannel channel = DatagramChannel.open()
                .bind(new InetSocketAddress(9003))
                .setOption(StandardSocketOptions.IP_MULTICAST_IF,
                    networkInterface);
```

The group is then created based on the same IPv6 address that was used by the server, and a `MembershipKey` instance is created using the channel's `join` method, as shown next. The key and a waiting message is displayed to illustrate how the client works:

```
        InetAddress group =
            InetAddress.getByName("FF01:0:0:0:0:0:0:FC");
        MembershipKey key = channel.join(group, networkInterface);
        System.out.println("Joined Multicast Group: " + key);
        System.out.println("Waiting for a  message...");
```

A byte buffer is created with a size of 1024. This size will be sufficient for this example, The `receive` method is then called, which will block until a message is received:

```
        ByteBuffer buffer = ByteBuffer.allocate(1024);
        channel.receive(buffer);
```

To display the contents of the buffer, we need to flip it. The contents are displayed as we did previously:

```
        buffer.flip();
        System.out.print("Received: [");
        StringBuilder message = new StringBuilder();
        while (buffer.hasRemaining()) {
            message.append((char) buffer.get());
        }
        System.out.println(message + "]");
```

When we are done with a membership key, we should indicate that we are no longer interested in receiving group messages using the `drop` method:

```
key.drop();
```

Messages may still arrive if there are packets waiting to be processed by the socket.

The UDP channel multicast client/server in action

Start the server first. This server will display a series of messages every second, as shown here:

Sent the   multicast message: The message

Sent: [The message]

Sent the   multicast message: The message

Sent: [The message]

Sent the   multicast message: The message

Sent: [The message]

...

Next, start the client application. It will display the multicast group, wait for a message, and then display the message, as shown here:

Joined Multicast Group: <ff01:0:0:0:0:0:0:fc,eth1>

Waiting for a message...

Received: [The message]

The use of a channel can improve the performance of UDP multicast messages.

UDP streaming

Using UDP to stream audio or videos is common. It is efficient and any loss of packets or out-of-order packets will cause minimal problems. We will illustrate this technique by steaming live audio. A UDP server will capture the microphone's sound and send it to a client. The UDP client will receive the audio and play it on the system's speakers.

The idea of a UDP streaming server is to break up the stream into a series of packets that are sent to a UDP client. The client will then receive these packets and use them to reconstitute a stream.

In order to illustrate streaming audio, we need to know a bit about how Java handles audio streams. Audio is handled by a series of classes that are found in the `javax.sound.sampled` package. The primary classes that are used to capture and play audio include the following:

- `AudioFormat`: This class specifies the characteristics of the audio format that is used. As there are several audio formats available, the system needs to know which one is being used.

- `AudioInputStream`: This class represents the audio that is being recorded or played.

- `AudioSystem`: This class provides access to the system's audio devices and resources.

- `DataLine`: This interface controls operations applied against a stream, such as starting and stopping a stream.

- `SourceDataLine`: This represents the destination of the sound, such as a speaker.

- `TargetDataLine`: This represents the source of the sound, such as a microphone.

The terminology that is used for the `SourceDataLine` and `TargetDataLine` interfaces may be a bit confusing. The terms are from the perspective of a line and a mixer.

The UDP audio server implementation

The declaration of the `AudioUDPServer` class is as follows. It uses a `TargetDataLine` instance for the source of the audio. It is declared as an instance variable because it is used in multiple methods. The constructor uses a `setupAudio` method to initialize the audio and a `broadcastAudio` method to send this audio to a client:

```
public class AudioUDPServer {
    private final byte audioBuffer[] = new byte[10000];
    private TargetDataLine targetDataLine;

    public AudioUDPServer() {
        setupAudio();
        broadcastAudio();
    }
```

```
...
public static void main(String[] args) {
    new AudioUDPServer();
}
}
```

The following is the `getAudioFormat` method, and it is used in both the server and the client to specify the audio-stream characteristics. The analog audio signal is sampled 1,600 times a second. Each sample is a signed 16-bit number. The `channels` variable is assigned 1, meaning that the audio is mono. The order of the bytes in the sample is important and is set to big endian:

```
private AudioFormat getAudioFormat() {
    float sampleRate = 16000F;
    int sampleSizeInBits = 16;
    int channels = 1;
    boolean signed = true;
    boolean bigEndian = false;
    return new AudioFormat(sampleRate, sampleSizeInBits,
        channels, signed, bigEndian);
}
```

Big endian and little endian refers to the order of bytes. Big endian means that the most-significant byte of a word is stored at the smallest memory address and the least significant byte at the largest memory address. Little endian reverses this order. Different computer architectures use different orderings.

The `setupAudio` method initializes the audio. The `DataLine.Info` class uses the audio format information to create a line representing audio. The `AudioSystem` class's `getLine` method returns a data line that corresponds to a microphone. The line is opened and started:

```
private void setupAudio() {
    try {
        AudioFormat audioFormat = getAudioFormat();
        DataLine.Info dataLineInfo =
            new DataLine.Info(TargetDataLine.class,
                    audioFormat);
        targetDataLine =   (TargetDataLine)
            AudioSystem.getLine(dataLineInfo);
        targetDataLine.open(audioFormat);
        targetDataLine.start();
    } catch (Exception ex) {
        ex.printStackTrace();
        System.exit(0);
    }
}
}
```

The `broadcastAudio` method creates the UDP packets. A socket is created using port `8000` and an `InetAddress` instance is created for the current machine:

```java
private void broadcastAudio() {
    try {
        DatagramSocket socket = new DatagramSocket(8000);
        InetAddress inetAddress =
            InetAddress.getByName("127.0.0.1");
        ...
    } catch (Exception ex) {
        // Handle exceptions
    }
}
```

An infinite loop is entered where the `read` method fills the `audioBuffer` array and returns the number of bytes read. For counts greater than `0`, a new packet is created using the buffer and is sent to the client listening on port `9786`:

```java
while (true) {
    int count = targetDataLine.read(
        audioBuffer, 0, audioBuffer.length);
    if (count > 0) {
        DatagramPacket packet = new DatagramPacket(
        audioBuffer, audioBuffer.length, inetAddress, 9786);
        socket.send(packet);
    }
}
```

When executed, the sound from the microphone is sent to the client as a series of packets.

The UDP audio client implementation

The `AudioUDPClient` application is declared next. In the constructor, an `initiateAudio` method is called to start the process of receiving packets from the server:

```java
public class AudioUDPClient {
    AudioInputStream audioInputStream;
    SourceDataLine sourceDataLine;
    ...
    public AudioUDPClient() {
        initiateAudio();
    }
```

```
    public static void main(String[] args) {
        new AudioUDPClient();
    }
}
```

The `initiateAudio` method creates a socket that is bound to port 9786. An array of bytes is created to hold audio data contained in the UDP packet:

```
private void initiateAudio() {
    try {
        DatagramSocket socket = new DatagramSocket(9786);
        byte[] audioBuffer = new byte[10000];
        ...
    } catch (Exception e) {
        e.printStackTrace();
    }
}
```

An infinite loop will receive packets from the server, create an `AudioInputStream` instance, and then call the `playAudio` method to play the sound. The packet is created in the following code and then blocks until a packet is received:

```
while (true) {
    DatagramPacket packet
        = new DatagramPacket(audioBuffer, audioBuffer.length);
    socket.receive(packet);
    ...
}
```

Next, the audio stream is created. An array of bytes is extracted from the packet. It is used as the argument of the `ByteArrayInputStream` constructor, which is used, along with the audio format information, to create the actual audio stream. This is associated with the `SourceDataLine` instance, which is opened and started. The `playAudio` method is called to play the sound:

```
try {
    byte audioData[] = packet.getData();
    InputStream byteInputStream =
        new ByteArrayInputStream(audioData);
    AudioFormat audioFormat = getAudioFormat();
    audioInputStream =  new AudioInputStream(
        byteInputStream,
        audioFormat, audioData.length /
        audioFormat.getFrameSize());
    DataLine.Info dataLineInfo = new DataLine.Info(
        SourceDataLine.class, audioFormat);
```

```
        sourceDataLine = (SourceDataLine)
            AudioSystem.getLine(dataLineInfo);
        sourceDataLine.open(audioFormat);
        sourceDataLine.start();
        playAudio();
    } catch (Exception e) {
        // Handle exceptions
    }
```

The `getAudioFormat` method is used and is the same one that was declared in the `AudioUDPServer` application. The `playAudio` method follows. The `read` method of `AudioInputStream` populates a buffer, which is written to the source data line. This effectively plays the sound on the system's speakers:

```
private void playAudio() {
    byte[] buffer = new byte[10000];
    try {
        int count;
        while ((count = audioInputStream.read(
                buffer, 0, buffer.length)) != -1) {
            if (count > 0) {
                sourceDataLine.write(buffer, 0, count);
            }
        }
    } catch (Exception e) {
        // Handle exceptions
    }
}
```

With the server running, starting the client will play the sounds from the server. The play can be enhanced through the use of threads in the server and client to handle the recording and playback of the sound. This detail has been left out to simplify the example.

In this example, the continuous analog sound is digitized and broken into packets. These packets were then sent to a client where they were converted back into a sound and played.

There is additional support for UDP streaming found in several other frameworks. The **Java Media Framework (JMF)** (http://www.oracle.com/technetwork/articles/javase/index-jsp-140239.html) supports the processing of audio and video media. The **Real-time Transport Protocol (RTP)** (https://en.wikipedia.org/wiki/Real-time_Transport_Protocol) is used to send audio and video data across a network.

Summary

In this chapter, we examined the nature of the UDP protocol and how Java supports it. We contrasted TCP and UDP to provide some guidance in deciding which protocol was best for a given problem.

We started with a simple UDP client/server to demonstrate how the `DatagramPacket` and `DatagramSocket` classes are used. We saw how the `InetAddress` class was used to obtain addresses used by sockets and packets.

The `DatagramChannel` class supports using NIO techniques in a UDP environment, which can be more efficient than using the `DatagramPacket` and `DatagramSocket` approach. The approach used a byte buffer to hold messages that were sent between a server and a client. This example illustrated many of the techniques that were developed in *Chapter 3, NIO Support for Networking*.

This was followed by a discussion of how UDP multicasting works. This provides a simple technique to broadcast a message to members of a group. The use of the `MulticastSocket`, `DatagramChannel`, and `MembershipKey` classes were illustrated. The latter class is used to establish a group when the `DatagramChannel` class is used.

We concluded with an example of how UDP is used to support the streaming of audio. We detailed the use of several classes in the `javax.sound.sampled` package, including the `AudioFormat` and `TargetDataLine` classes to gather and play audio. We used the `DatagramSocket` and `DatagramPacket` classes to transmit the audio.

In the next chapter, we will examine the techniques that are available to improve the scalability of client/server applications.

7
Network Scalability

Network scalability is concerned with structuring an application in such a way that as more demands are placed on the application, it can adjust to handle the stress. Demands can come in the form of more users, an increased number of requests, more complicated requests, and changes in network characteristics.

There are several areas of concern listed as follows:

- Server capacity
- Multiple threads
- Network bandwidth and latency
- Execution environment

Scalability can be achieved by adding more servers, using an appropriate number of threads, improving the performance of the execution environment, and increasing the network bandwidth to eliminate bottlenecks.

Adding more servers will help by enabling load balancing between servers. However, if the network bandwidth or latency is the issue, then this will not help much. There is only so much that can be pushed through a network pipe.

Threads are frequently used to improve the performance of a system. Using an appropriate number of threads for a system allows some threads to execute while other threads are blocked. A blocked thread may be waiting for IO to occur or for a user to respond. Allowing other threads to execute while some are blocked can increase application throughput.

The execution environment includes the underlying hardware, the operating system, the JVM, and the application itself. Each of these areas is a candidate for improvement. We will not address the hardware environment as that is beyond our control. The same is true of the operating system. While some performance improvements can be achieved, we will not address these areas. JVM parameters that can affect network performance will be identified.

We will examine code improvement opportunities. Most of our discussion is concerned with the use of threads because we have more control over this architectural feature. We will illustrate several approaches to improve the scalability of an application in this chapter. These include the following:

- Multiple threaded server
- Thread pool
- Futures and callables
- Selector (TCP/UDP)

We will explore the details of using simple threads/pools because you may encounter them in your work and may not be able to use some of the newer technologies due to platform limitations. Thread pools offer the advantage of reusing threads in many situations. Futures and callables are a thread variation where data can be passed and returned from a thread. Selector allows multiple channels to be handled by a single thread.

Multithreaded server overview

The chief advantage of a multithreaded server is that long-running client requests will not block the server from accepting other client requests. If a new thread is not created, then the current request will be processed. It is only after the request has been processed that new requests can be accepted. Using a separate thread for a request means that connections and their associated requests can be processed concurrently.

When using a multithreaded server, there are several of ways of configuring the threads as follows:

- Thread-per-request
- Thread-per-connection
- Thread-per-object

In the thread-per-request model, each request that arrives at the server is assigned a new thread. While this is a simple approach, it can result in the creation of a large number of threads. In addition, each request will often mean that a new connection will be created.

This model works nicely in an environment where the previous client request does not need to be retained. For example, if the server's sole purpose is to respond to a request for a specific stock quote, then a thread does not need to be aware of any previous requests.

This approach is illustrated in the following figure. Each client request sent to the server is assigned to a new thread.

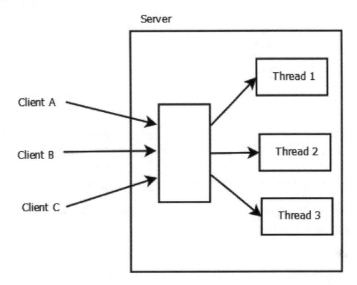

In the thread-per-connection model, a client connection is maintained for the duration of the session. A session consists of a series of requests and responses. A session is terminated either through a specific command or after a time-out period has elapsed. This approach allows state information to be maintained between requests.

This approach is illustrated in the following figure. The dash line indicates that multiple requests from the same client are handled by the same thread.

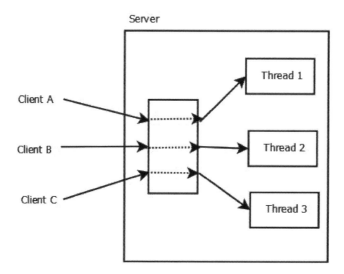

The thread-per-object approach queues associated requests with a specific object that can handle the request. The object and its methods are placed in a thread that handles requests one at a time. Requests are queued with the thread. While we will not demonstrate this approach here, it is often used with thread pools.

The process of creating and deleting connections can be expensive. If a client submits several requests, then opening and closing a connection becomes expensive and should be avoided.

To manage the problem of too many threads, a pool of threads is frequently used. When a request needs to be processed, the request is assigned to an existing unused thread to handle the request. Once the response has been sent, then the thread can be used for other requests. This assumes that state information does not need to be maintained.

The thread-per-request approach

In *Chapter 1*, *Getting Started with Network Programming*, we illustrated a simple multithreaded echo server. This approach is reintroduced here to provide a foundation for the use of threads in the remainder of the chapter.

The thread-per-request server

In this example, the server will accept requests for prices when given the name of a part. The implementation will use the ConcurrentHashMap class that supports concurrent access to the part name and price. In a multithreaded environment, concurrent data structures, such as the ConcurrentHashMap class, handle operations without the potential for data corruption. Also, this map is an example of caching, which can be useful in improving the performance of applications.

We start with the declaration of the server as follows. The map is declared as static because only one instance is needed for the server. The static initialization block initializes the map. The main method will use the ServerSocket class to accept requests from a client. They will be handled in the run method. The clientSocket variable will hold a reference to the client socket:

```
public class SimpleMultiTheadedServer implements Runnable {
    private static ConcurrentHashMap<String, Float> map;
    private Socket clientSocket;

    static {
        map = new ConcurrentHashMap<>();
        map.put("Axle", 238.50f);
        map.put("Gear", 45.55f);
        map.put("Wheel", 86.30f);
        map.put("Rotor", 8.50f);
    }

    SimpleMultiTheadedServer(Socket socket) {
        this.clientSocket = socket;
    }

    public static void main(String args[]) {
        ...
    }

    public void run() {
        ...
    }
}
```

The main method follows where the server socket waits for a client request and then creates a new thread, passing the client socket to the thread to process it. Messages are displayed showing the connection being accepted:

```
public static void main(String args[]) {
    System.out.println("Multi-Threaded Server Started");
    try {
```

```
        ServerSocket serverSocket = new ServerSocket(5000);
        while (true) {
            System.out.println(
                "Listening for a client connection");
            Socket socket = serverSocket.accept();
            System.out.println("Connected to a Client");
            new Thread(new
                SimpleMultiTheadedServer(socket)).start();
        }
    } catch (IOException ex) {
        ex.printStackTrace();
    }
    System.out.println("Multi-Threaded Server Terminated");
}
```

The `run` method processes the request, as shown next. An input stream is obtained from the client socket, and the part name is read. The map's `get` method uses this name to retrieve a price. An input stream sends the price back to the client, and the progress of the operation is displayed:

```
public void run() {
    System.out.println("Client Thread Started");
    try (BufferedReader bis = new BufferedReader(
            new InputStreamReader(
                clientSocket.getInputStream()));
        PrintStream out = new PrintStream(
            clientSocket.getOutputStream())) {

        String partName = bis.readLine();
        float price = map.get(partName);
        out.println(price);
        NumberFormat nf = NumberFormat.getCurrencyInstance();
        System.out.println("Request for " + partName
                + " and returned a price of "
                + nf.format(price));

        clientSocket.close();
        System.out.println("Client Connection Terminated");
    } catch (IOException ex) {
        ex.printStackTrace();
    }
    System.out.println("Client Thread Terminated");
}
```

Now, let's develop a client for the server.

The thread-per-request client

The client application, as shown next, will connect to the server, send a request, wait for a response, and then display the price. For this example, the client and the server reside on the same machine:

```
public class SimpleClient {

    public static void main(String args[]) {
        System.out.println("Client Started");
        try {
            Socket socket = new Socket("127.0.0.1", 5000);
            System.out.println("Connected to a Server");
            PrintStream out =
                new PrintStream(socket.getOutputStream());
            InputStreamReader isr =
                new InputStreamReader(socket.getInputStream());
            BufferedReader br = new BufferedReader(isr);

            String partName = "Axle";
            out.println(partName);
            System.out.println(partName + " request sent");
            System.out.println("Response: " + br.readLine());
                    socket.close();
        } catch (IOException ex) {
            ex.printStackTrace();
        }
        System.out.println("Client Terminated");
    }
}
```

Now, let's see how the client and the server interact.

The thread-per-request applications in action

Start the server first, which will display the following output:

Multi-Threaded Server Started

Listening for a client connection

Next, start the client application. The following output will be displayed:

Client Started

Connected to a Server

Axle request sent

Response: 238.5

Client Terminated

The server will then display the following output. You will note that the **Client Thread Started** output follows the **Listening for a client connection** output. This is because there is a slight delay before the thread starts:

Connected to a Client

Listening for a client connection

Client Thread Started

Request for Axle and returned a price of $238.50

Client Connection Terminated

Client Thread Terminated

The client thread started, processed the request, and then terminated.

Add the following code to the client application just before the close operation to send a second price request to the server:

```
partName = "Wheel";
out.println(partName);
System.out.println(partName + " request sent");
System.out.println("Response: " + br.readLine());
```

When the client is executed, you will get the following output. The response for the second string is null. This is because the server's response thread has terminated after the first request was answered:

Client Started

Connected to a Server

Axle request sent

Response: 238.5

Wheel request sent

Response: null

Client Terminated

To handle multiple requests using this approach, you will need to reopen the connection and send out separate requests. The following code illustrates this approach. Remove the code segment that sent the second request. Add the following code to the client after the socket is closed. In this sequence, the socket is reopened, the IO streams are recreated, and the message is re-sent:

```
socket = new Socket("127.0.0.1", 5000);
System.out.println("Connected to a Server");
out = new PrintStream(socket.getOutputStream());
isr = new InputStreamReader(socket.getInputStream());
br = new BufferedReader(isr);

partName = "Wheel";
out.println(partName);
System.out.println(partName + " request sent");
System.out.println("Response: " + br.readLine());
socket.close();
```

When the client is executed, it will produce the following output, which reflects the two requests and their response:

Client Started

Connected to a Server

Axle request sent

Response: 238.5

Connected to a Server

Wheel request sent

Response: 86.3

Client Terminated

On the server side, we will get the following output. Two threads were created to handle the requests:

Multi-Threaded Server Started

Listening for a client connection

Connected to a Client

Listening for a client connection

Client Thread Started

Connected to a Client

Listening for a client connection

Client Thread Started

Request for Axle and returned a price of $238.50

Client Connection Terminated

Client Thread Terminated

Request for Wheel and returned a price of $86.30

Client Connection Terminated

Client Thread Terminated

The opening and closing of the connections can be expensive. In the next section, we will address this type of problem. However, if only single requests are made, then the thread-per-request will work.

Thread-per-connection approach

In this approach, a single thread is used to handle all of the client's requests. This approach will require that the client send some sort of notification that it has no further requests. In lieu of an explicit notification, a timeout may need to be set to automatically disconnect the client after a sufficient period of time has elapsed.

The thread-per-connection server

Modify the server's `run` method by commenting out the bulk of the try block where the request is handled and the response is sent to the client. Replace it with the following code. In the infinite loop, the command request is read. If the request is `quit`, then the loop is exited. Otherwise, the request is handled in the same way as before:

```
while(true) {
    String partName = bis.readLine();
    if("quit".equalsIgnoreCase(partName)) {
        break;
    }
    float price = map.get(partName);
    out.println(price);
    NumberFormat nf =
```

```
                    NumberFormat.getCurrencyInstance();
            System.out.println("Request for " + partName
                    + " and returned a price of "
                    + nf.format(price));
        }
```

This is all that needs to be modified in the server.

The thread-per-connection client

In the client, replace the code after the buffered reader has been created with the following code. This will send three requests to the server:

```
            String partName = "Axle";
            out.println(partName);
            System.out.println(partName + " request sent");
            System.out.println("Response: " + br.readLine());

            partName = "Wheel";
            out.println(partName);
            System.out.println(partName + " request sent");
            System.out.println("Response: " + br.readLine());

            partName = "Quit";
            out.println(partName);
            socket.close();
```

Only a single connection is opened for all three requests.

The thread-per-connection applications in action

When the client is executed, you will get the following output:

Client Started

Connected to a Server

Axle request sent

Response: 238.5

Wheel request sent

Response: 86.3

Client Terminated

On the server side, the following output is generated. You will note that only one thread was created to handle the multiple requests:

Multi-Threaded Server Started

Listening for a client connection

Connected to a Client

Listening for a client connection

Client Thread Started

Request for Axle and returned a price of $238.50

Request for Wheel and returned a price of $86.30

Client Connection Terminated

Client Thread Terminated

This is a more efficient architecture for when a client makes multiple requests.

Thread pools

Thread pools are useful when the number of threads that are created need to be limited. Using a pool not only controls how many threads are created, but it can also eliminate the need to create and destroy threads repeatedly, an often expensive operation.

The following figure depicts a thread pool. Requests are assigned to threads in the pool. Some thread pools will create new threads if there are no unused threads available. Others will restrict the number of threads available. This may result in some requests being blocked.

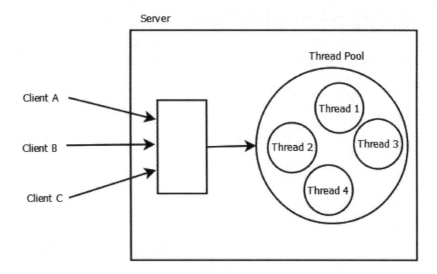

We will demonstrate thread pools using the ThreadPoolExecutor class. This class also provides methods that deliver status information regarding thread execution.

While the ThreadPoolExecutor class possesses several constructors, the Executors class provides an easy way of creating instances of the ThreadPoolExecutor class. We will demonstrate two of these methods. First, we will use the newCachedThreadPool method. The pool created by this method will reuse threads. New threads will be created when needed. However, this can result in too many threads being created. The second method, newFixedThreadPool, creates a fixed-size pool of threads.

The ThreadPoolExecutor class characteristics

When an instance of this class is created, it will accept new tasks, which are passed to the thread pool. However, the pool will not close down automatically. If idle, it will wait until new tasks are submitted. To terminate the pool, either the shutdown or shutdownNow method needs to be called. The latter method shuts down the pool immediately and will not process pending tasks.

The ThreadPoolExecutor class has a number of methods that provides additional information. For example, the getPoolSize method returns the current number of threads in the pool. The getActiveCount method returns the number of active threads. The getLargestPoolSize method returns the maximum number of threads that were in the pool at one time. There are several other methods that are available.

Simple thread pool server

The server that we will use to demonstrate a thread pool will return a price of a part when given the name of a part. Each thread will access a ConcurrentHashMap instance that holds the part information. We use the concurrent version of the hash map as it may be accessed from multiple threads.

The ThreadPool class is declared next. The main method uses a WorkerThread class to perform the actual work. In the main method, the newCachedThreadPool method is called to create a thread pool:

```java
public class ThreadPool {

    public static void main(String[] args) {
        System.out.println("Thread Pool Server Started");
        ThreadPoolExecutor executor = (ThreadPoolExecutor)
            Executors.newCachedThreadPool();
        ...
        executor.shutdown();
        System.out.println("Thread Pool Server Terminated");
    }
}
```

Next, a try block is used to catch and handle any exceptions that may occur. Within the try block, a server socket is created and its accept method blocks until a client connection is requested. When a connection is established, a WorkerThread instance is created using the client socket, as shown in the following code:

```java
try {
    ServerSocket serverSocket = new ServerSocket(5000);
    while (true) {
        System.out.println(
            "Listening for a client connection");
        Socket socket = serverSocket.accept();
        System.out.println("Connected to a Client");
        WorkerThread task = new WorkerThread(socket);
        System.out.println("Task created: " + task);
        executor.execute(task);
    }
} catch (IOException ex) {
    ex.printStackTrace();
}
```

Now, let's examine the `WorkerThread` class that is shown next. The `ConcurrentHashMap` instance is declared where a string is used as the key and the object that is stored is a float. The hash map is initialized in a static initializer block:

```
public class WorkerThread implements Runnable {
    private static final ConcurrentHashMap<String, Float> map;
    private final Socket clientSocket;

    static {
        map = new ConcurrentHashMap<>();
        map.put("Axle", 238.50f);
        map.put("Gear", 45.55f);
        map.put("Wheel", 86.30f);
        map.put("Rotor", 8.50f);
    }
    ...
}
```

The class's constructor assigns the client socket to the `clientSocket` instance variable for later use, as shown here:

```
public WorkerThread(Socket clientSocket) {
    this.clientSocket = clientSocket;
}
```

The `run` method processes the request. An input stream is obtained from the client socket and used to get the part name. This name is used as the argument of the hash map's `get` method to obtain the corresponding price. This price is sent back to the client, and a message is displayed showing the response:

```
@Override
public void run() {
    System.out.println("Worker Thread Started");
    try (BufferedReader bis = new BufferedReader(
            new InputStreamReader(
                clientSocket.getInputStream())); 
            PrintStream out = new PrintStream(
                    clientSocket.getOutputStream())) {

        String partName = bis.readLine();
        float price = map.get(partName);
        out.println(price);
        NumberFormat nf = NumberFormat.getCurrencyInstance();
        System.out.println("Request for " + partName
                + " and returned a price of "
                + nf.format(price));
```

```
            clientSocket.close();
            System.out.println("Client Connection Terminated");
        } catch (IOException ex) {
            ex.printStackTrace();
        }
        System.out.println("Worker Thread Terminated");
    }
```

We are now ready to discuss the client application.

Simple thread pool client

This application uses the `Socket` class to establish a connection to the server. Input and output streams are used to send and receive responses. This approach was discussed in *Chapter 1, Getting Started with Network Programming*. The client application follows. A connection is established with the server and a request for a part's price is sent to the server. The response is obtained and displayed.

```
public class SimpleClient {

    public static void main(String args[]) {
        System.out.println("Client Started");
        try (Socket socket = new Socket("127.0.0.1", 5000)) {
            System.out.println("Connected to a Server");
            PrintStream out =
                new PrintStream(socket.getOutputStream());
            InputStreamReader isr =
                new InputStreamReader(socket.getInputStream());
            BufferedReader br = new BufferedReader(isr);

            String partName = "Axle";
            out.println(partName);
            System.out.println(partName + " request sent");
            System.out.println("Response: " + br.readLine());
            socket.close();

        } catch (IOException ex) {
            ex.printStackTrace();
        }
        System.out.println("Client Terminated");
    }
}
```

We are now ready to see how they work together.

The thread pool client/server in action

Start the server application first. You will see the following output:

Thread Pool Server Started

Listening for a client connection

Next, start the client. It will produce the following output where a request for an axle price is sent, and then a response of 238.5 is received:

Client Started

Connected to a Server

Axle request sent

Response: 238.5

Client Terminated

On the server side, you will see output similar to the following one. The thread is created, and the request and response data is displayed. The thread then terminates. You will note that the name of the thread is preceded by the string "packt". This is the name of the package for the application:

Connected to a Client

Task created: packt.WorkerThread@33909752

Listening for a client connection

Worker Thread Started

Request for Axle and returned a price of $238.50

Client Connection Terminated

Worker Thread Terminated

If you start a second client, the server will produce output similar to the following one. You will note that a new thread is created for each request:

Thread Pool Server Started

Listening for a client connection

Connected to a Client

Task created: packt.WorkerThread@33909752

Listening for a client connection

Worker Thread Started

Request for Axle and returned a price of $238.50

Client Connection Terminated

Worker Thread Terminated

Connected to a Client

Task created: packt.WorkerThread@3d4eac69

Listening for a client connection

Worker Thread Started

Request for Axle and returned a price of $238.50

Client Connection Terminated

Worker Thread Terminated

Thread pool with Callable

Using the Callable and Future interfaces provides another approach to support multiple threads. The Callable interface supports threading where a thread needs to return a result. The Runnable interface's run method does not return a value. For some threads, this can be a problem. The Callable interface possesses a single method, call, which returns a value and can be used instead of the Runnable interface.

The Future interface is used in combination with a Callable object. The idea is that the call method is invoked and the current thread continues performing some other task. When the Callable object is complete, then a get method is used to retrieve the results. This method will block if necessary.

Using a Callable

We will use the Callable interface to supplement the WorkerThread class that we created earlier. Instead of placing the part name hash map in the WorkerThread class, we will move it to a class called WorkerCallable where we will override the call method to return the price. This is actually extra work for this application, but it illustrates one way of using the Callable interface. It demonstrates how we can return a value from the Callable object.

The `WorkerCallable` class, that is declared next, uses the same code to create and initialize the hash map:

```
public class WorkerCallable implements Callable<Float> {

    private static final ConcurrentHashMap<String, Float> map;
    private String partName;

    static {
        map = new ConcurrentHashMap<>();
        map.put("Axle", 238.50f);
        map.put("Gear", 45.55f);
        map.put("Wheel", 86.30f);
        map.put("Rotor", 8.50f);
    }
    ...
}
```

The constructor will initialize the part name, as shown here:

```
public WorkerCallable(String partName) {
    this.partName = partName;
}
```

The `call` method is shown next. The map obtains the price, which we display and then return:

```
@Override
public Float call() throws Exception {
    float price = map.get(this.partName);
    System.out.println("WorkerCallable returned " + price);
    return price;
}
```

Next, modify the `WorkerThread` class by removing the following statement:

```
float price = map.get(partName);
```

Replace it with the following code. A new `WorkerCallable` instance is created using the part name that was requested by a client. The `call` method is immediately invoked and will return the corresponding part's price:

```
float price = 0.0f;
try {
    price = new WorkerCallable(partName).call();
} catch (Exception ex) {
    ex.printStackTrace();
}
```

The application will produce the same output as before, except that you will see messages indicating that the WorkerCallable class's call method was executed. While another thread is created, we will block until the call method returns.

This example does not fully demonstrate the power of this approach. The Future interface will improve on this technique.

Using a Future

The Future interface represents the results of a completed call method. With this interface, we can invoke a Callable object and not wait for it to return. Assume that the process of computing a part price is more involved than just looking it up in a table. It is conceivable that multiple steps may be required to calculate a price, each of which may be involved and may take a bit of time to complete. Also assume that these separate steps can be performed concurrently.

Replace the previous example with the following code. We create a new ThreadPoolExecutor instance to which we will assign two Callable objects representing a two-step price determination process. This is done using the submit method, which returns a Future instance. The implementation of the call methods returns 1.0 and 2.0 respectively to keep the example simple:

```
float price = 0.0f;
ThreadPoolExecutor executor = (ThreadPoolExecutor)
    Executors.newCachedThreadPool();
Future<Float> future1 =
        executor.submit(new Callable<Float>() {
    @Override
    public Float call() {
        // Compute first part
        return 1.0f;
    }
});
Future<Float> future2 =
        executor.submit(new Callable<Float>() {
    @Override
    public Float call() {
        // Compute second part
        return 2.0f;
    }
});
```

Next, add the following try block, which uses the `get` method to obtain the two parts of the price. These are used to determine the price for the part. If the corresponding `Callable` object has not completed, then the `get` method will block:

```
try {
    Float firstPart = future1.get();
    Float secondPart = future2.get();
    price = firstPart + secondPart;
} catch (InterruptedException|ExecutionException ex) {
    ex.printStackTrace();
}
```

When this code is executed, you will get a price of 3.0 for the parts. The combination of the `Callable` and `Future` interfaces provides an easy to use this technique to handle threads that return a value.

Using the HttpServer executor

We introduced the `HTTPServer` class in *Chapter 4, Client/Server Development*. When the HTTP Server receives a request, by default, it uses the thread that was created when the `start` method is called. However, it is possible to use a different thread. The `setExecutor` method specifies how these requests are assigned to threads.

The argument of this method is an `Executor` object. We can use any of several implementations for this argument. In the following sequence, a cached thread pool is used:

```
server.setExecutor(Executors.newCachedThreadPool());
```

To control the number of threads that are used by the server, we can use a fixed thread pool of size 5, as shown here:

```
server.setExecutor(Executors.newFixedThreadPool(5));
```

This method must be called before the `start` method of `HTTPServer` is called. All requests are then submitted to the executor. The following is duplicated from the `HTTPServer` class that was developed in *Chapter 4, Client/Server Development*, and shows you the use of the `setExecutor` method:

```
public class MyHTTPServer {

    public static void main(String[] args) throws Exception {
        System.out.println("MyHTTPServer Started");
        HttpServer server = HttpServer.create(
            new InetSocketAddress(80), 0);
        server.createContext("/index", new OtherHandler());
```

```
            server.setExecutor(Executors.newCachedThreadPool());
            server.start();
        }
        ...
    }
```

The server will execute the same way as it did before, but it will use a cached thread pool instead.

Using a selector

A selector is used in an NIO application and allows one thread to handle multiple channels. The selector coordinates multiple channels and their events. It identifies those channels that are ready for processing. If we were to use a thread per channel, then we will find ourselves switching between threads frequently. This switching process can be expensive. Using a single thread to handle multiple channels avoids some of this overhead.

The following figure depicts this architecture. A thread is registered with a selector. The selector will identify the channels and events that are ready for processing.

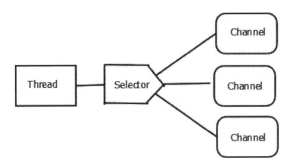

A selector is supported by two primary classes:

- Selector: This provides the primary functionality
- SelectionKey: This identifies the types of events that are ready for processing

To use a selector, perform the following actions:

- Create a selector
- Register channels with the selector
- Select a channel for use when it becomes available

Let's examine each of these steps in more detail.

Creating the selector

There are no public `Selector` constructors. To create a `Selector` object, use the static `open` method, as shown here:

```
Selector selector = Selector.open();
```

There is also an `isOpen` method to determine if a selector is open and a `close` method to close it when it is no longer needed.

Registering a channel

The `register` method registers a channel with a selector. Any channel that is registered with a selector must be in a nonblocking mode. For example, a `FileChannel` object cannot be registered because it cannot be placed in a nonblocking mode. Use the `configureBlocking` method with `false` as its argument to place the channel in a nonblocking mode, as shown here:

```
socketChannel.configureBlocking(false);
```

The `register` method is as follows. This is a method of the `ServerSocketChannel` and SocketChannel classes. In the following example, it is used with a `SocketChannel` instance:

```
socketChannel.register(selector, SelectionKey.OP_WRITE, null);
```

The `Channel` class's `register` method possesses three arguments:

- The selector to register
- The event type of interest
- Data to be associated with the channel

The event type specifies the type of channel events that an application is interested in handling. For example, we may only want to be informed of an event if the channel has data that is ready to be read.

There are four event types that are available, as listed in the following table:

Type	Event type constants	Meaning
Connect	`SelectionKey.OP_CONNECT`	This indicates that the channel has successfully connected to a server
Accept	`SelectionKey.OP_ACCEPT`	This indicates that a server socket channel is ready to accept connection requests from a client

Type	Event type constants	Meaning
Read	`SelectionKey.OP_READ`	This indicates that the channel has data ready to be read
Write	`SelectionKey.OP_WRITE`	This indicates that the channel is ready for write operations

These types are referred to as interest sets. In the following statement, the channel is associated with the read interest type. The method returns a `SelectionKey` instance, which contains a number of useful properties:

```
SelectionKey key = channel.register(selector,
    SelectionKey.OP_READ);
```

If there are multiple events of interest, then we can create a combination of these using the OR operator as shown here:

```
int interestSet = SelectionKey.OP_READ |
    SelectionKey.OP_WRITE;
SelectionKey key = channel.register(selector, interestSet);
```

The `SelectionKey` class possesses several properties that will help in working with channels. These include the following:

- **Interest set**: This contains the events of interest.
- **Ready set**: This is the set of operations that the channel is ready to handle.
- **Channel**: The `channel` method returns the channel that is associated with a selection key.
- **Selector**: The `selector` method returns the selector that is associated with the selection key.
- **Attached objects**: Further information can be attached using the `attach` method. The `attachment` method is used later to access this object.

The `interestOps` method returns an integer representing the events of interest, as shown next:

```
int interestSet = selectionKey.interestOps();
```

We will use this to process the events.

To determine which events are ready, we can use any of the following methods:

- `readOps`: This returns an integer containing the ready events
- `isAcceptable`: This indicates that the accept event is ready
- `isConnectable`: This indicates that the connection event is ready

- `isReadable`: This indicates that the read event is ready
- `isWritable`: This indicates that the write event is ready

Now, let's see these methods in action.

Using the selector to support a time client/server

We will develop a time server to illustrate the use of the `Selector` class and related classes. This server and the time client are adapted from the time server and client applications that were in *Chapter 3, NIO Support for Networking*. The focus here will be on the use of the selector. The channel and buffer operations will not be discussed here as they were covered earlier.

The channel time server

The time server will accept connections to client applications and send the current date and time to the clients every second. A client may not receive all of these messages as we will discover when we discuss the client.

The time server uses an internal static class, `SelectorHandler`, to handle the selector and send messages. This class implements the `Runnable` interface and will be the selector's thread.

In the `main` method, the server socket accepts new channel connections and registers them with the selector. The `Selector` object is declared as a static instance variable, as shown next. This allows it to be accessed from the `SelectorHandler` thread and the main application thread. Sharing this object will result in potential synchronization problems, which we will address:

```
public class ServerSocketChannelTimeServer {
    private static Selector selector;

    static class SelectorHandler implements Runnable {
        ...
    }

    public static void main(String[] args) {
        ...
    }
}
```

Let's start with the `main` method. A server socket channel is created that uses port `5000`. Exceptions are caught in a try block, as shown here:

```
public static void main(String[] args) {
    System.out.println("Time Server started");
    try {
        ServerSocketChannel serverSocketChannel =
            ServerSocketChannel.open();
        serverSocketChannel.socket().bind(
            new InetSocketAddress(5000));
        ...
    }
    } catch (ClosedChannelException ex) {
        ex.printStackTrace();
    } catch (IOException ex) {
        ex.printStackTrace();
    }
}
```

The selector is created, and a thread for the `SelectorHandler` instance is started:

```
selector = Selector.open();
new Thread(new SelectorHandler()).start();
```

An infinite loop will accept new connections. A message is displayed indicating that a connection has been made:

```
while (true) {
    SocketChannel socketChannel
            = serverSocketChannel.accept();
    System.out.println("Socket channel accepted - "
        + socketChannel);
    ...
}
```

With a good channel, the `configureBlocking` method is called, the selector is woken up, and the channel is registered with the selector. A thread may be blocked by the `select` method. Using the `wakeup` method will cause the `select` method to immediately return, which allows the `register` method to unblock:

```
if (socketChannel != null) {
    socketChannel.configureBlocking(false);
    selector.wakeup();
    socketChannel.register(selector,
        SelectionKey.OP_WRITE, null);
}
```

Once a channel has been registered with a selector, we can start processing events that are associated with that channel.

The `SelectorHandler` class will use the selector object to identify events as they occur and associate them with specific channels. Its `run` method does all of the work. As shown next, an infinite loop uses the `select` method to identify events as they occur. The `select` method uses an argument of `500`, which specifies a timeout of 500 milliseconds. It returns an integer specifying how many keys are ready to be processed:

```
static class SelectorHandler implements Runnable {

    @Override
    public void run() {
        while (true) {
            try {
                System.out.println("About to select ...");
                int readyChannels = selector.select(500);
                ...
            } catch (IOException | InterruptedException ex) {
                ex.printStackTrace();
            }
        }
    }
}
```

If the `select` method times out, it will return a value of `0`. When this happens, we display a message to that effect, as shown here:

```
if (readyChannels == 0) {
    System.out.println("No tasks available");
} else {
    ...
}
```

If there are keys ready, then the `selectedKeys` method will return this set. An iterator is then used to process each key one at a time:

```
Set<SelectionKey> keys = selector.selectedKeys();
Iterator<SelectionKey> keyIterator = keys.iterator();
while (keyIterator.hasNext()) {
    ...
}
```

Each `SelectionKey` instance is checked to see which event type has occurred. In the following implementation, only the writeable events are processed. After processing, the thread sleeps for one second. This will have the effect of delaying the sending of a date and time message by at least one second. The `remove` method is needed to remove an event for the iterator list:

```
SelectionKey key = keyIterator.next();
if (key.isAcceptable()) {
    // Connection accepted
} else if (key.isConnectable()) {
    // Connection established
} else if (key.isReadable()) {
    // Channel ready to read
} else if (key.isWritable()) {
    ...
}
Thread.sleep(1000);
keyIterator.remove();
```

If it is a writeable event, then the date and time is sent, as shown next. The `channel` method returns the channel for the event, and the message is sent to that client. A message is displayed showing that the message has been sent:

```
String message = "Date: "
    + new Date(System.currentTimeMillis());

ByteBuffer buffer = ByteBuffer.allocate(64);
buffer.put(message.getBytes());
buffer.flip();
SocketChannel socketChannel = null;
while (buffer.hasRemaining()) {
    socketChannel = (SocketChannel) key.channel();
    socketChannel.write(buffer);
}
System.out.println("Sent: " + message + " to: "
    + socketChannel);
```

With the server ready, we will develop our client application.

The date and time client application

The client application is almost identical to the one that was developed in *Chapter 3, NIO Support for Networking*. The main difference is that it will request the data and time at random intervals. This effect will be seen when we use multiple clients with our server. The application's implementation is as follows:

```
public class SocketChannelTimeClient {

    public static void main(String[] args) {
        Random random = new Random();
        SocketAddress address =
            new InetSocketAddress("127.0.0.1", 5000);
        try (SocketChannel socketChannel =
                SocketChannel.open(address)) {
            while (true) {
                ByteBuffer byteBuffer = ByteBuffer.allocate(64);
                int bytesRead = socketChannel.read(byteBuffer);
                while (bytesRead > 0) {
                    byteBuffer.flip();
                    while (byteBuffer.hasRemaining()) {
                        System.out.print((char) byteBuffer.get());
                    }
                    System.out.println();
                    bytesRead = socketChannel.read(byteBuffer);
                }
                Thread.sleep(random.nextInt(1000) + 1000);
            }
        } catch (ClosedChannelException ex) {
            // Handle exceptions
        }catch (IOException | InterruptedException ex) {
            // Handle exceptions
        }
    }
}
```

We are now ready to see how the server and client work together.

The date and time server/client in action

First, start the server. It will produce the following output:

Time Server started

About to select ...

No tasks available

About to select ...

No tasks available

About to select ...

No tasks available

...

This sequence will repeat itself until a client connects to the server.

Next, start up the client. On the client side, you will get output similar to the following one:

Date: Wed Oct 07 17:55:43 CDT 2015

Date: Wed Oct 07 17:55:45 CDT 2015

Date: Wed Oct 07 17:55:47 CDT 2015

Date: Wed Oct 07 17:55:49 CDT 2015

On the server side, you will see output reflecting the connection and then the requests, as shown next. You will note that the port number, 58907, identifies this client:

...

Sent: Date: Wed Oct 07 17:55:43 CDT 2015 to: java.nio.channels. SocketChannel[connected local=/127.0.0.1:5000 remote=/127.0.0.1:58907]

...

Sent: Date: Wed Oct 07 17:55:45 CDT 2015 to: java.nio.channels. SocketChannel[connected local=/127.0.0.1:5000 remote=/127.0.0.1:58907]

Start up a second client. You will see a similar connection message but with a different port number. One possible connection message that follows is showing a client with port number 58908:

Socket channel accepted - java.nio.channels.SocketChannel[connected local=/127.0.0.1:5000 remote=/127.0.0.1:58908]

You will then see date and time messages being sent to both clients.

Handling network timeouts

When an application is deployed in the real world, new network problems can occur that were not present when this application was developed on a LAN. Problems, such as network congestion, slow connections, and the loss of a network link can result in delays or loss of messages. It is important to detect and handle network timeouts.

There are several socket options which provide some control over socket communications. The SO_TIMEOUT option is used to set a timeout for read operations. If the specified amount of time elapses, then a SocketTimeoutException exception is thrown.

In the following statement, the socket will expire after three seconds have elapsed:

```
Socket socket = new ...
socket.setSoTimeout(3000);
```

The option must be set before a blocking read operation occurs. A timeout of zero will never time out. Handling timeouts is an important design consideration.

Summary

In this chapter, we examined several approaches to address the scalability of applications. Scalability refers to the ability of an application to compensate for increased loads placed on it. While our examples focused on applying these techniques to servers, they are equally applicable to clients.

We introduced three threading architectures, and we focused on two of them: thread-per-request and thread-per-connection. The thread-per-request model creates a new thread for each request that arrives at a server. This is suitable for situations where a client will make a single or possibly a few requests at a time.

The thread-per-connection model will create a thread to handle multiple requests from a client. This avoids having to reconnect to the client multiple times and having to incur the cost of multiple thread creations. This approach is good for clients who need to maintain a session and possibly state information.

Thread pools support an approach that avoids creating and destroying threads. A collection of threads is managed by a thread pool. Threads that are not being used can be repurposed for a different request. The size of thread pools can be controlled and, thus limited depending on the requirements of the application and the environment. The Executor class was used to create and manage thread pools.

The NIO's `Selector` class was illustrated. This class makes it easier to work with threads and NIO channels. Channels and channel-related events are registered with a selector. When an event, such as a channel becoming available for a read operation, occurs, the selector provides access to the channel and the event. This allows a single thread to manage several channels.

We briefly re-examined the `HttpServer` class that was introduced in *Chapter 4, Client/Server Development*. We demonstrated how easy it is to add a thread pool to improve the server's performance. We also examined the nature of network timeouts and how to handle them. These can occur when the network fails to support timely communication between applications.

In the next chapter, we will explore network security threats and how we can address them.

8

Network Security

In this chapter, we will explore the support that Java provides to secure communications between applications. We will examine several topics, including the following:

- The basic encryption process
- Using a keystore to store keys and certificates
- Adding encryption to a simple server/client
- Secure client/server communications using TLS\SSL
- Secure hashing

Security

There are many security related terms whose meaning and purpose can be daunting when they are first encountered. Most of these terms are applicable to network applications. We will start with a brief overview of many of these terms. In later sections of this chapter, we will go into more details about the ones that are relevant to our discussion.

Central to most security related issues is encryption. This is the process of converting information that needs to be protected to an encrypted form using a key or a set of keys. The receiver of the encrypted information can use a key or set of keys to decrypt the information and revert it to its original form. This technique will prevent unauthorized access to the information.

We will demonstrate the use of both **symmetric** and asymmetric encryption techniques. Symmetric encryption uses a single key to encrypt and decrypt messages. Asymmetric encryption uses a pair of keys. These keys are frequently stored in a file called a **keystore**, which we will demonstrate.

Symmetric encryption is usually faster but requires the sender and receiver of the encrypted data to share their keys in a safe and secure manner. For parties that are remotely dispersed, this can be a problem. Asymmetric encryption is slower, but it uses a public and private key pair that, as we will see, simplifies the sharing of keys. Asymmetric encryption is an enabling technology for digital certificates that provides a means of verifying the authenticity of documents.

Secure commerce is common and is essential for online transactions that take place globally every day. The **Transport Layer Security (TLS)** and **Secure Sockets Layer (SSL)** are protocols that allow secure and reliable communication across the Internet. It is the basis for **Hyper Text Transfer Protocol Secure (HTTPS)** that is used to conduct most transactions on the Internet. This protocol supports the following:

- Server and client authentication
- Data encryption
- Data integrity

Secure hashing is a technique that is used to create certificates. A **certificate** is used to verify the authenticity of data, and it uses a hash value. Java provides support for this process, which we will demonstrate.

Let's start with a brief introduction of common network security terms to provide a high-level perspective of the chapter. Specific terms are explored in more detail in subsequent sections.

Secure communication terminology

There are several terms that are used when working with secure communications. These include the following:

- **Authentication**: This is the process of verifying a user or system
- **Authorization**: This is the process of allowing access to protected resources
- **Encryption**: This is the process of encoding and subsequently decoding information to protect it from unauthorized individuals
- **Hashing algorithms**: These provide a way of producing a unique value for a document, and they are used in support of other security techniques
- **Digital signatures**: These provide a way of digitally authenticating a document
- **Certificates**: These are normally used as a chain, and they support the confirmation of the identity of principals and other actors

Authentication and authorization are related. Authentication is the process of determining whether a person or system is who they claim to be. This is commonly achieved using an ID and a password. However, there are other authentication techniques, such as smart cards, and biometric signatures, such as fingerprint, or iris scans.

Authorization is the process of determining what resources an individual or system has access to. It is one thing to verify that an individual is who they say they are. It is another thing to ensure that the user can only access authorized resources.

Encryption has evolved and will continue to improve. Java supports symmetric and asymmetric encryption techniques. The process starts with the generation of keys, which are normally stored in a keystore. Applications that need to encrypt or decrypt data will access a keystore to retrieve the appropriate keys. The keystore itself needs to be protected so that it cannot be tampered with or otherwise compromised.

Hashing is the process of taking data and returning a number that represents the data. A hash algorithm performs this operation, and it must be fast. However, it is extremely difficult, if not impossible, to derive the original data when given only the hash value. This is called a one-way hash function.

The advantage of this technique is that the data can be sent along with the hash value to a receiver. The data is not encrypted, but the hash value is encrypted using a set of asymmetric keys. The receiver can then use the original hash algorithm to compute a hash value for the received data. If this new hash value matches the hash value that was sent, then the receiver can be assured that the data has not been modified or corrupted in the transmission. This provides a more reliable means of transferring data that does not need to be encrypted, but where some assurance that it has not been modified can be given.

A certificate is part of the previous process and it uses a hash function and asymmetric keys. A **certificate chain** provides a means of verifying that a certificate is valid, assuming that the root of the chain can be trusted.

Encryption basics

In this section, we will examine how Java supports symmetric and asymmetric encryption. As we will see, there are various encryption algorithms that are available for both of these techniques.

Symmetric encryption techniques

Symmetric encryption uses a single key to encrypt and decrypt a message. This type of encryption is classified as either stream ciphers or block ciphers. More details about these algorithms can be found at `https://en.wikipedia.org/wiki/Symmetric-key_algorithm`. A provider provides an implementation of an encryption algorithm, and we often choose between them.

Symmetric algorithms that are supported by Java include the following ones where the key size in bits is enclosed in parentheses:

- AES (128)
- DES (56)
- DESede (168)
- HmacSHA1
- HmacSHA256

Varying lengths of data may be encrypted. Block cipher algorithms are used to handle large blocks of data. There are several block cipher modes of operations, as listed next. We will not detail how these modes work here, but additional information can be found at `https://en.wikipedia.org/wiki/Block_cipher_mode_of_operation`:

- ECB
- CBC
- CFB
- OFB
- PCBC

Before we can encrypt or decrypt data, we need a key.

Generating a key

A common way of generating a key is using the `KeyGenerator` class. There are no public constructors for the class but an overloaded `getInstance` method will return a `KeyGenerator` instance. The following example uses the AES algorithm with the default provider. Other versions of this method allow selection of the provider:

```
KeyGenerator keyGenerator = KeyGenerator.getInstance("AES");
```

The `generateKey` method returns an instance of an object that implements the `SecretKey` interface that is shown next. This is the key that is used to support symmetric encryption and decryption:

```
SecretKey secretKey = keyGenerator.generateKey();
```

With a key, we can now encrypt data.

Encrypting text using a symmetric key

We will use the following `encrypt` method in later sections. This method is passed the text to encrypt and a secret key. The term **plain text** is frequently used to refer to the unencrypted data.

The `Cipher` class provides the framework for the encryption process. The `getInstance` method returns an instance of the class where the AES algorithm is used. The `Cipher` instance is initialized for encryption using `Cipher.ENCRYPT_MODE` as the first argument, and the secret key as the second argument. The `doFinal` method encrypts the plain text byte array and returns an encrypted byte array. The `Base64` class's `getEncoder` returns an encoder that encodes the encrypted bytes:

```java
public static String encrypt(
        String plainText, SecretKey secretKey) {
    try {
        Cipher cipher = Cipher.getInstance("AES");
        byte[] plainTextBytes = plainText.getBytes();
        cipher.init(Cipher.ENCRYPT_MODE, secretKey);
        byte[] encryptedBytes =
            cipher.doFinal(plainTextBytes);
        Base64.Encoder encoder = Base64.getEncoder();
        String encryptedText =
            encoder.encodeToString(encryptedBytes);
        return encryptedText;
    } catch (NoSuchAlgorithmException|NoSuchPaddingException |
            InvalidKeyException | IllegalBlockSizeException |
            BadPaddingException ex) {
        // Handle exceptions
    }
    return null;
}
```

Encoding an encrypted byte array is used to convert it to a string so that we can use it later. Encoding strings can be a useful security technique, as explained in http://javarevisited.blogspot.sg/2012/03/why-character-array-is-better-than.html.

Decrypting text

The process of decrypting text is illustrated in the decrypt method that is shown next. It uses a reverse process where the encrypted bytes are decoded and the `Cipher` class's `init` method is initialized to decrypt the bytes using a secret key:

```
public static String decrypt(String encryptedText,
        SecretKey secretKey) {
    try {
        Cipher cipher = Cipher.getInstance("AES");
        Base64.Decoder decoder = Base64.getDecoder();
        byte[] encryptedBytes = decoder.decode(encryptedText);
        cipher.init(Cipher.DECRYPT_MODE, secretKey);
        byte[] decryptedBytes =
            cipher.doFinal(encryptedBytes);
        String decryptedText = new String(decryptedBytes);
        return decryptedText;
    } catch (NoSuchAlgorithmException|NoSuchPaddingException |
            InvalidKeyException | IllegalBlockSizeException |
            BadPaddingException ex) {
        // Handle exceptions
    }
    return null;
}
```

We will use these methods in the echo client/server applications illustrated in the *Symmetric encryption client/server* section.

Asymmetric encryption techniques

Asymmetric encryption uses a public and private key. The private key is held by one entity. The public key is made available to everyone. Data can be encrypted using either key:

- If the data is encrypted using the private key, then it can be decrypted using the public key
- If the data is encrypted using the public key, then it can be decrypted using the private key

If the owner of the private key sends out a message that is encrypted with the private key, then recipients of this message can decrypt it with the public key. They can all read the message, but they know that only the private key owner could have sent this message.

If someone else encrypts a message with the public key, then only the private key owner can read that message. However, the owner cannot be sure who actually sent the message. It could be an impostor.

However, if both the parties have their own set of public/private keys, we can guarantee that only the sender and the recipient can see its content. We can also guarantee that the sender is who they say they are.

Let's assume that Sue wants to send a message to Bob. Sue will encrypt the message, M, using her private key. Let's call this message M1. She will then encrypt M1 using Bob's public key giving us M2. The message, M2, is then sent to Bob. Now, only Bob can decrypt this message using his private key. This will return M1. Bob can now use Sue's public key to decrypt M1 to get the original message, M. He knows that this is from Sue because only Sue's public key will work.

This process to send messages requires that both participants possess their own public/private keys. In addition to this, it is not as efficient as using a symmetric key. Another approach is to use asymmetric keys to transfer a secret key to the participants. The secret key can then be used for the actual message transfer. This is the technique that is used with SSL.

There are several asymmetric algorithms. Java supports the following encryption algorithms:

- RSA
- Diffie-Hellman
- DSA

We will demonstrate asymmetric encryption/decryption using a utility class called `AsymmetricKeyUtility` that is declared next. This class encapsulates methods to create, save, load, and retrieve public and private keys. We will explain how these methods work here and use them later with the asymmetric echo client/server application:

```
public class AsymmetricKeyUtility {

    public static void savePrivateKey(PrivateKey privateKey) {
        ...
    }

    public static PrivateKey getPrivateKey() {
        ...
    }

    public static void savePublicKey(PublicKey publicKey) {
        ...
```

```
        }

        public static PublicKey getPublicKey() {
            ...
        }

        public static byte[] encrypt(PublicKey publicKey,
                String message) {
            ...
        }

        public static String decrypt(PrivateKey privateKey,
            byte[] encodedData) {
            ...
        }

        public static void main(String[] args) {
            ...
        }
    }
```

Generating and saving asymmetric keys

The main method will create the keys, save them, and then test them to see whether they work correctly. The KeyPairGenerator method will generate the keys. To use asymmetric encryption, we get an instance of the class using the RSA algorithm. The initialize method specifies that the key uses 1,024 bits. The generateKeyPair method generates the keys, and the getPrivate and getPublic methods return the private and public keys, respectively:

```
        public static void main(String[] args) {
            try {
                KeyPairGenerator keyPairGenerator =
                    KeyPairGenerator.getInstance("RSA");
                keyPairGenerator.initialize(1024);
                KeyPair keyPair = keyPairGenerator.generateKeyPair();
                PrivateKey privateKey = keyPair.getPrivate();
                PublicKey publicKey = keyPair.getPublic();
                ...
            } catch (NoSuchAlgorithmException ex) {
                // Handle exceptions
            }
```

We will use a set of methods to save and retrieve these keys to separate files. This approach is not the most secure, but it will simplify the use of the echo client/server. The next statements invoke the save methods:

```
savePrivateKey(privateKey);
savePublicKey(publicKey);
```

The methods that are used to retrieve the keys are invoked here:

```
privateKey = getPrivateKey();
publicKey = getPublicKey();
```

The next code sequence tests the encryption/decryption process. A message is created and passed to the encrypt method using the public key. The decrypt method is invoked to decrypt the message. The encodedData variable references the encrypted data:

```
String message = "The message";
System.out.println("Message: " + message);
byte[] encodedData = encrypt(publicKey,message);
System.out.println("Decrypted Message: " +
        decrypt(privateKey,encodedData));
```

The output of this example is as follows:

Message: The message

Decrypted Message: The message

Instead, we can use the private key for encryption and the public key for decryption to achieve the same results.

Encrypting/decrypting text using an asymmetric key

Now, let's examine the specifics of the encrypt and decrypt methods. The encrypt method uses getInstance to get an instance of the RSA algorithm. The init method specifies that the Cipher object will encrypt a message using a public key. The doFinal method performs the actual encryption and returns a byte array containing the encrypted message:

```
public static byte[] encrypt(PublicKey publicKey,
    String message) {
  byte[] encodedData = null;
  try {
      Cipher cipher = Cipher.getInstance("RSA ");
      cipher.init(Cipher.ENCRYPT_MODE, publicKey);
```

```
        byte[] encryptedBytes =
            cipher.doFinal(message.getBytes());
        encodedData = Base64.getEncoder().withoutPadding()
            .encode(encryptedBytes);
    } catch (NoSuchAlgorithmException|NoSuchPaddingException |
            InvalidKeyException | IllegalBlockSizeException |
            BadPaddingException ex) {
        // Handle exceptions
    }
    return encodedData;
}
```

The `decrypt` method is described next. It specifies that the `Cipher` instance will decrypt a message using the private key. The encrypted message that is passed to it must be decoded before the `doFinal` method can decrypt it. The decrypted string is then returned:

```
public static String decrypt(PrivateKey privateKey,
        byte[] encodedData) {
    String message = null;
    try {
        Cipher cipher = Cipher.getInstance("RSA ");
        cipher.init(Cipher.DECRYPT_MODE, privateKey);
        byte[] decodedData =
            Base64.getDecoder().decode(encodedData);
        byte[] decryptedBytes = cipher.doFinal(decodedData);
        message = new String(decryptedBytes);
    } catch (NoSuchAlgorithmException|NoSuchPaddingException |
            InvalidKeyException | IllegalBlockSizeException |
            BadPaddingException ex) {
        // Handle exceptions
    }
    return message;
}
```

Both of these methods catch a number of exceptions that can occur in the encryption/decryption process. We will not address these exceptions here.

Saving asymmetric keys to a file

The next two methods illustrate one technique to save and retrieve a private key. The `PKCS8EncodedKeySpec` class supports the encoding of a private key. The encoded key is saved to the `private.key` file:

```
public static void savePrivateKey(PrivateKey privateKey) {
    try {
        PKCS8EncodedKeySpec pkcs8EncodedKeySpec =
```

```
            new PKCS8EncodedKeySpec(privateKey.getEncoded());
        FileOutputStream fos =
            new FileOutputStream("private.key");
        fos.write(pkcs8EncodedKeySpec.getEncoded());
        fos.close();
    } catch (FileNotFoundException ex) {
        // Handle exceptions
    } catch (IOException ex) {
        // Handle exceptions
    }
}
```

The getPrivateKey method, that is described next, returns a private key from the file. The KeyFactory class's generatePrivate method creates the key based on the PKCS8EncodedKeySpec specification:

```
public static PrivateKey getPrivateKey() {
    try {
        File privateKeyFile = new File("private.key");
        FileInputStream fis =
            new FileInputStream("private.key");
        byte[] encodedPrivateKey =
            new byte[(int) privateKeyFile.length()];
        fis.read(encodedPrivateKey);
        fis.close();
        PKCS8EncodedKeySpec privateKeySpec =
            new PKCS8EncodedKeySpec(encodedPrivateKey);
        KeyFactory keyFactory = KeyFactory.getInstance("RSA");
        PrivateKey privateKey =
            keyFactory.generatePrivate(privateKeySpec);
        return privateKey;
    } catch (FileNotFoundException ex) {
        // Handle exceptions
    } catch (IOException | NoSuchAlgorithmException |
            InvalidKeySpecException ex) {
        // Handle exceptions
    }
    return null;
}
```

The public key's save and get methods are described next. They differ in the file that they use, and the use of the X509EncodedKeySpec class. This class represents public keys:

```
public static void savePublicKey(PublicKey publicKey) {
    try {
        X509EncodedKeySpec x509EncodedKeySpec =
            new X509EncodedKeySpec(publicKey.getEncoded());
        FileOutputStream fos =
            new FileOutputStream("public.key");
        fos.write(x509EncodedKeySpec.getEncoded());
        fos.close();
    } catch (FileNotFoundException ex) {
        // Handle exceptions
    } catch (IOException ex) {
        // Handle exceptions
    }
}

public static PublicKey getPublicKey() {
    try {
        File publicKeyFile = new File("public.key");
        FileInputStream fis =
            new FileInputStream("public.key");
        byte[] encodedPublicKey =
            new byte[(int) publicKeyFile.length()];
        fis.read(encodedPublicKey);
        fis.close();
        X509EncodedKeySpec publicKeySpec =
            new X509EncodedKeySpec(encodedPublicKey);
        KeyFactory keyFactory = KeyFactory.getInstance("RSA");
        PublicKey publicKey =
            keyFactory.generatePublic(publicKeySpec);
        return publicKey;
    } catch (FileNotFoundException ex) {
        // Handle exceptions
    } catch (IOException | NoSuchAlgorithmException |
            InvalidKeySpecException ex) {
        // Handle exceptions
    }
    return null;
}
```

The standard cryptographic algorithm names are found at https://docs.oracle.com/javase/8/docs/technotes/guides/security/StandardNames.html. A performance comparison of symmetric algorithms is available at http://www.javamex.com/tutorials/cryptography/ciphers.shtml.

Creating a keystore

A keystore stores cryptographic keys and certificates and is frequently used in conjunction with servers and clients. A keystore is usually a file, but it can be a hardware device. Java supports the following types of keystore entries:

- **PrivateKey**: This is used in asymmetric cryptography
- **Certificate**: This contains a public key
- **SecretKey**: This is used in symmetric cryptography

There are five different types of keystores that are supported by Java 8: JKS, JCEKS, PKCS12, PKCS11, and DKS:

- **JKS**: This is the **Java KeyStore (JKS)** that usually has an extension of `jks`.
- **JCEKS**: This is the **Java Cryptography Extension KeyStore (JCE)**. It can store all three keystore entity types, provides stronger protection for keys, and uses a `jceks` extension.
- **PKCS12**: In contrast to JKS and JCEKS, this keystore can be used with other languages. It can store all three keystore entity types, and it uses an extension of `p12` or `pfx`.
- **PKCS11**: This is a hardware keystore type.
- **DKS**: This is the **Domain KeyStore (DKS)** that holds a collection of other keystores.

The default keystore type in Java is JKS. Keystores can be created and maintained using the `keytool` command line tool or with Java code. We will demonstrate `keytool` first.

Creating and maintaining a keystore with keytool

The keytool is a command line program that is used to create keystores. The full documentation of its use is found at `https://docs.oracle.com/javase/8/docs/technotes/tools/unix/keytool.html`. There are several GUI tools that are used to maintain keystores that are easier to use than keytool. One of these is IKEYMAN found at `http://www-01.ibm.com/software/webservers/httpservers/doc/v1312/ibm/9atikeyu.htm`.

To use the keytool with Windows at the command prompt, you will need to configure the PATH environmental variable to locate its containing directory. Use a command similar to the following:

```
C:\Some Directory>set path=C:\Program Files\Java\jdk1.8.0_25\
bin;%path%
```

Let's use the keytool to create a keystore. At the command prompt, enter the following command. This will start the process of creating a keystore in a file named `keystore.jks`. The alias is another name that you can use to reference the keystore:

```
C:\Some Directory>keytool -genkey -alias mykeystore -keystore
keystore.jks
```

You will then be prompted for several pieces of information as follows. Respond to the prompts as appropriate. The passwords that you enter will not be displayed. For the examples in this chapter, we used a password of `password`:

```
Enter keystore password:
Re-enter new password:
What is your first and last name?
  [Unknown]:  some name
What is the name of your organizational unit?
  [Unknown]:  development
What is the name of your organization?
  [Unknown]:  mycom.com
What is the name of your City or Locality?
  [Unknown]:  some city
What is the name of your State or Province?
  [Unknown]:  some state
What is the two-letter country code for this unit?
  [Unknown]:  jv
```

You will then be prompted to confirm the input as follows. Respond with `yes` if the values are correct:

```
Is CN=some name, OU=development, O=mycom.com, L=some city, ST=some state,
C=jv correct?
  [no]:  yes
```

You can assign a separate password for the key, as shown next:

```
Enter key password for <mykeystore>
        (RETURN if same as keystore password):
```

The keystore is then created. The contents of a keystore can be displayed using the `-list` argument, as shown next. The `-v` option produces verbose output:

```
keytool -list -v -keystore keystore.jks -alias mykeystore
```

This will display the following output. The keystore password needs to be entered along with the alias name:

```
Enter keystore password:
Alias name: mykeystore
Creation date: Oct 22, 2015
Entry type: PrivateKeyEntry
Certificate chain length: 1
Certificate[1]:
Owner: CN=some name, OU=development, O=mycom.com, L=some city, ST=some
state, C=jv
Issuer: CN=some name, OU=development, O=mycom.com, L=some city, ST=some
state, C=jv
Serial number: 39f2e11e
Valid from: Thu Oct 22 18:11:21 CDT 2015 until: Wed Jan 20 17:11:21 CST
2016
Certificate fingerprints:
        MD5:   64:44:64:27:85:99:01:22:49:FC:41:DA:F7:A8:4C:35
        SHA1: 48:57:3A:DB:1B:16:92:E6:CC:90:8B:D3:A7:A3:89:B3:9C:9B:7C:
BB
        SHA256: B6:B2:22:A0:64:61:DB:53:33:04:78:77:38:AF:D2:A0:60:37:A6
:CB:3F:
3C:47:CC:30:5F:02:86:8F:68:84:7D
        Signature algorithm name: SHA1withDSA
        Version: 3


Extensions:

#1: ObjectId: 2.5.29.14 Criticality=false
SubjectKeyIdentifier [
KeyIdentifier [
0000: 07 D9 51 BE A7 48 23 34   5F 8E C6 F9 88 C0 36 CA  ..Q..H#4_.....6.
0010: 27 8E 04 22                                        '.."
]
]
```

Keytool command-line arguments

Entering the information for a keystore can be tedious. One way of simplifying this process is to use command line arguments. The following command will create the previous keystore:

```
keytool -genkeypair -alias mykeystore -keystore keystore.jks -keypass
password -storepass password -dname "cn=some name, ou=development,
o=mycom.com, l=some city, st=some state c=jv
```

You will note that there is not a matching double quote at the end of the command line. It is not needed. The command-line arguments are documented at the keytool website that was listed earlier.

This tool can create both symmetric and asymmetric keys along with certificates. The following series of commands demonstrate several of these types of operations. We will create a keystore for a pair of asymmetric keys. A pair of certificates will then be exported that can be used with a server and client application.

This command will create the serverkeystore.jck keystore file using the RSA algorithm with a key size of 1,024 bits and an expiration date of 365 days:

```
keytool -genkeypair -alias server -keyalg RSA -keysize 1024 -storetype
jceks -validity 365 -keypass password -keystore serverkeystore.jck
-storepass password -dname "cn=localhost, ou=Department, o=MyComp Inc,
l=Some City, st=JV c=US
```

This command generates a clientkeystore.jck keystore to be used by the client application:

```
keytool -genkeypair -alias client -keyalg RSA -keysize 1024 -storetype
jceks -validity 365 -keypass password -keystore clientkeystore.jck
-storepass password -dname "cn=localhost, ou=Department, o=MyComp Inc,
l=Some City, st=JV c=US
```

A certificate file for the client is created next and is placed in the client.crt file:

```
keytool -export -alias client -storetype jceks -keystore clientkeystore.
jck -storepass password -file client.crt
```

The server's certificate is exported here:

```
keytool -export -alias server -storetype jceks -keystore serverkeystore.
jck -storepass password -file server.crt
```

A trust store is a file that is used to verify credentials, while a keystore will produce credentials. Credentials usually take the form of a certificate. Trust stores typically hold certificates from a trusted third party to form a certificate chain.

The following command creates the `clienttruststore.jck` file, which is the trust store for the client:

```
keytool -importcert -alias server -file server.crt -keystore
clienttruststore.jck -keypass password -storepass storepassword
```

This command generates the following output:

```
Owner: CN=localhost, OU=Department, O=MyComp Inc, L=Some City, ST="JV
c=US"

Issuer: CN=localhost, OU=Department, O=MyComp Inc, L=Some City, ST="JV
c=US"

Serial number: 2d924315

Valid from: Tue Oct 20 19:26:00 CDT 2015 until: Wed Oct 19 19:26:00 CDT
2016

Certificate fingerprints:
        MD5:   9E:3D:0E:D7:02:7A:F5:23:95:1E:24:B0:55:A9:F7:95

        SHA1:  69:87:CE:EE:11:59:8F:40:A8:14:DA:D3:92:D0:3F:B6:A9:5A:
7B:53

        SHA256: BF:C1:7B:6D:D0:39:67:2D:1C:68:27:79:31:AA:B8:70:2B:FD:
1C:85:18:
EC:5B:D7:4A:48:03:FA:F1:B8:CD:4E

        Signature algorithm name: SHA256withRSA

        Version: 3


Extensions:

#1: ObjectId: 2.5.29.14 Criticality=false

SubjectKeyIdentifier [

KeyIdentifier [

0000: D3 63 C9 60 6D 04 49 75   FB E8 F7 90 30 1D C6 C1  .c.`m.Iu....0...
0010: 10 DF 00 CF                                        ....
]
]


Trust this certificate? [no]:  yes

Certificate was added to keystore
```

The trust store for the server is created with this command:

```
keytool -importcert -alias client -file client.crt -keystore
servertruststore.jck -keypass password -storepass password
```

Its output is as follows:

```
Owner: CN=localhost, OU=Department, O=MyComp Inc, L=Some City, ST="JV
c=US"

Issuer: CN=localhost, OU=Department, O=MyComp Inc, L=Some City, ST="JV
c=US"

Serial number: 5d5f3c40

Valid from: Tue Oct 20 19:27:31 CDT 2015 until: Wed Oct 19 19:27:31 CDT
2016

Certificate fingerprints:
        MD5:  0E:FE:B3:EB:1B:D2:AD:32:9C:BC:FB:43:40:85:C1:A7
        SHA1: 90:14:1E:17:DF:51:79:0B:1E:A3:EC:38:6B:BA:A6:F4:6F:BF:B6
:D2
        SHA256: 7B:3E:D8:2C:04:ED:E5:52:AE:B4:00:A8:63:A1:13:A7:E1:8E:59
:63:E8:
86:38:D8:09:55:EA:3A:7C:F7:EC:4B
        Signature algorithm name: SHA256withRSA
        Version: 3


Extensions:

#1: ObjectId: 2.5.29.14 Criticality=false
SubjectKeyIdentifier [
KeyIdentifier [
0000: D9 53 34 3B C0 11 F8 75   0F 18 4E 18 23 A2 47 FE  .S4;...u..N.#.G.
0010: E6 F5 C1 AF                                        ....
]
]


Trust this certificate? [no]:  yes
Certificate was added to keystore
```

We will now demonstrate how we can perform similar operations in Java.

Creating and maintaining a keystore with Java

Keystores, their keys, and certificates can be created directly with Java code. In this section, we will demonstrate how to create a keystore that contains a secret key. We will use this class in the *Symmetric encryption client/server* section.

The SymmetricKeyStoreCreation class is declared as follows. The SymmetricKeyStoreCreation method creates a keystore, while the main method generates and stores the secret key:

```
public class SymmetricKeyStoreCreation {

    private static KeyStore createKeyStore(String fileName,
            String pw) {
        ...
    }

    public static void main(String[] args) {
        ...
    }
}
```

The createKeyStore method is described next. It is passed the keystore's file name and a password. A KeyStore instance is created, which specifies a JCEKS keystore. If the keystore already exists, it will return that keystore:

```
    private static KeyStore createKeyStore(String fileName,
            String password) {
        try {
            File file = new File(fileName);

            final KeyStore keyStore =
                KeyStore.getInstance("JCEKS");
            if (file.exists()) {
                keyStore.load(new FileInputStream(file),
                    password.toCharArray());
            } else {
                keyStore.load(null, null);
                keyStore.store(new FileOutputStream(fileName),
                    password.toCharArray());
            }
            return keyStore;
        } catch (KeyStoreException | IOException |
                NoSuchAlgorithmException |
                CertificateException ex) {
```

```
            // Handle exceptions
        }
        return null;
    }
```

In the `main` method, a `KeyGenerator` instance is created using the AES algorithm. The `generateKey` method will create the `SecretKey` instance, as shown here:

```
public static void main(String[] args) {
    try {
        final String keyStoreFile = "secretkeystore.jks";
        KeyStore keyStore = createKeyStore(keyStoreFile,
            "keystorepassword");
        KeyGenerator keyGenerator =
            KeyGenerator.getInstance("AES");
        SecretKey secretKey = keyGenerator.generateKey();
        ...
    } catch (Exception ex) {
        // Handle exceptions
    }
}
```

The `KeyStore.SecretKeyEntry` class represents an entry in a keystore. We need this and an instance of the `KeyStore.PasswordProtection` class, which represents the password, to store the secret key:

```
KeyStore.SecretKeyEntry keyStoreEntry
        = new KeyStore.SecretKeyEntry(secretKey);
KeyStore.PasswordProtection keyPassword =
    new  KeyStore.PasswordProtection(
            "keypassword".toCharArray());
```

The `setEntry` method uses a string alias, the keystore entry object, and the password to store the entry, as shown here:

```
keyStore.setEntry("secretKey", keyStoreEntry,
    keyPassword);
```

This entry is then written to the keystore:

```
keyStore.store(new FileOutputStream(keyStoreFile),
        "keystorepassword".toCharArray());
```

Other keystore operations are possible using Java.

Symmetric encryption client/server

This section demonstrates how to use symmetric encryption/decryption in a client/ server application. The following example implements a simple echo client/server allowing us to focus on the basic process without digressing into specific client/ server issues. The server is implemented with the SymmetricEchoServer class and client using the SymmetricEchoClient class.

The client will encrypt a message and send it to the server. The server will then decrypt the message and send it back in plain text. The response can easily be encrypted if needed. This one-way encryption is sufficient to illustrate the basic process.

When running the applications that are discussed in this chapter in Windows, you may encounter the following dialog box. Select the **Allow access** button to allow the applications to run:

We will also use the SymmetricKeyStoreCreation class that was developed in symmetric encryption techniques.

Symmetric server application

The symmetric server is declared next. It possesses a `main`, `decrypt`, and `getSecretKey` methods. The `decrypt` method takes the encrypted message from the client and decrypts it. The `getSecretKey` method will extract the secret key from the keystore that was created in symmetric encryption techniques. The `main` method contains the basic socket and streams that are used to communicate with the client:

```java
public class SymmetricEchoServer {
    private static Cipher cipher;

    public static String decrypt(String encryptedText,
        SecretKey secretKey) {
        ...
    }

    private static SecretKey getSecretKey() {
        ...
    }

    public static void main(String[] args) {
        ...
    }
}
```

The `decrypt` method is the same one that was developed in symmetric encryption techniques, so it will not be repeated here. The `getSecretKey` method is described next. The `secretkeystore.jks` file that was created in symmetric encryption techniques holds the secret key. This method uses many of the same classes that are used in the `main` method of the `SymmetricKeyStoreCreation` class. An instance of the `KeyStore.PasswordProtection` class is used to extract the secret key from the keystore. The keystore password, `keystorepassword`, is hardcoded into the application. This is not the best practice, but it simplifies the example:

```java
private static SecretKey getSecretKey() {
    SecretKey keyFound = null;
    try {
        File file = new File("secretkeystore.jks");
        final KeyStore keyStore =
            KeyStore.getInstance("JCEKS");
        keyStore.load(new FileInputStream(file),
                "keystorepassword".toCharArray());
        KeyStore.PasswordProtection keyPassword =
            new KeyStore.PasswordProtection(
                    "keypassword".toCharArray());
```

```
      KeyStore.Entry entry =
          keyStore.getEntry("secretKey", keyPassword);
      keyFound =
          ((KeyStore.SecretKeyEntry) entry).getSecretKey();
  } catch (KeyStoreException | IOException |
        NoSuchAlgorithmException |
        CertificateException ex) {
      // Handle exceptions
  } catch (UnrecoverableEntryException ex) {
      // Handle exceptions;
  }
  return keyFound;
}
```

The main method is very similar to the server that was developed in *Chapter 1,
Getting Started with Network Programming*. The main difference is within the while
loop. Input from the client is passed to the decrypt method along with the secret
key, as shown next. The decrypted text is then displayed and returned to the client:

```
String decryptedText = decrypt(inputLine,
    getSecretKey());
```

The main method is as follows:

```
public static void main(String[] args) {
    System.out.println("Simple Echo Server");
    try (ServerSocket serverSocket = new ServerSocket(6000)) {
        System.out.println("Waiting for connection.....");

        Socket clientSocket = serverSocket.accept();
        System.out.println("Connected to client");

        try (BufferedReader br = new BufferedReader(
            new InputStreamReader(
              clientSocket.getInputStream()));
            PrintWriter out = new PrintWriter(
                clientSocket.getOutputStream(), true)) {
          String inputLine;
          while ((inputLine = br.readLine()) != null) {
            String decryptedText =
                decrypt(inputLine, getSecretKey());
            System.out.println("Client request: " +
                decryptedText);
            out.println(decryptedText;
          }

        } catch (IOException ex) {
```

```
                        // Handle exceptions
                } catch (Exception ex) {
                        // Handle exceptions
                }
        } catch (IOException ex) {
                // Handle exceptions
        }
        System.out.println("Simple Echo Server Terminating");
    }
```

Now, let's examine the client application.

Symmetric client application

The client application is described next and is very similar to the client application
that was developed in *Chapter 1, Getting Started with Network Programming*. It uses the
same getSecretKey method that is used in the server. The encrypt method that was
explained in symmetric encryption techniques is used to encrypt the user's message.
Both of these methods are not duplicated here:

```
    public class SymmetricEchoClient {
        private static Cipher cipher;

        public static String encrypt(String plainText,
                SecretKey secretKey) {
            ...
        }


            ...
        }


        public static void main(String args[]) {
            ...
        }
    }
```

The main method differs from the version in the while loop in *Chapter 1,
Getting Started with Network Programming*. The following statement encrypts
the user message:

```
            String encryptedText = encrypt(inputLine,
                getSecretKey());
```

The `main` method is as follows:

```java
public static void main(String args[]) {
    System.out.println("Simple Echo Client");

    try (Socket clientSocket
            = new Socket(InetAddress.getLocalHost(), 6000);
        PrintWriter out = new PrintWriter(
                clientSocket.getOutputStream(), true);
        BufferedReader br = new BufferedReader(
                new InputStreamReader(
                        clientSocket.getInputStream())))  {
        System.out.println("Connected to server");
        Scanner scanner = new Scanner(System.in);

        while (true) {
            System.out.print("Enter text: ");
            String inputLine = scanner.nextLine();
            if ("quit".equalsIgnoreCase(inputLine)) {
                break;
            }
            String encryptedText =
                encrypt(inputLine, getSecretKey());
            System.out.println(
                "Encrypted Text After Encryption: "
                + encryptedText);
            out.println(encryptedText);

            String response = br.readLine();
            System.out.println(
                "Server response: " + response);
        }
    } catch (IOException ex) {
        // Handle exceptions
    } catch (Exception ex) {
        // Handle exceptions
    }
}
```

We are now ready to see how the client and server interact.

Symmetric client/server in action

The applications behave the same way that they did in *Chapter 1, Getting Started with Network Programming*. The only difference is that the message sent to the server is encrypted. This encryption is not visible in the application's output other than the display of the encrypted text on the client side. One possible interaction is as follows. The server output is shown first:

Simple Echo Server

Waiting for connection.....

Connected to client

Client request: The first message

Client request: The second message

Simple Echo Server Terminating

The following is the client's application output:

Simple Echo Client

Connected to server

Enter text: The first message

Encrypted Text After Encryption: drkvP3bhnfMXrZluFiqKb0RgjoDqFIJMCo97YqqgNuM=

Server response: drkvP3bhnfMXrZluFiqKb0RgjoDqFIJMCo97YqqgNuM=

Enter text: The second message

Encrypted Text After Encryption: fp9g+AqsVqZpxKMVNx8IkNdDcr9IGHb/ qv0qrFinmYs=

Server response: fp9g+AqsVqZpxKMVNx8IkNdDcr9IGHb/qv0qrFinmYs=

Enter text: quit

We will now duplicate this functionality using asymmetric keys.

Asymmetric encryption client/server

The AsymmetricKeyUtility class developed in asymmetric encryption techniques is used to support the client and server applications. We will use it's encrypt and decrypt methods. The structure of the client and server applications is similar to what was used in previous sections. The client will send the server an encrypted message, which the server will decrypt and then respond to with plain text.

Asymmetric server application

The AsymmetricEchoServer class, as declared next, is used for the server. The main method is its only method. A server socket is created, which blocks at the accept method waiting for client request:

```java
public class AsymmetricEchoServer {

    public static void main(String[] args) {
        System.out.println("Simple Echo Server");
        try (ServerSocket serverSocket = new ServerSocket(6000)) {
            System.out.println("Waiting for connection.....");
            Socket clientSocket = serverSocket.accept();
            System.out.println("Connected to client");
            ...


        } catch (IOException | NoSuchAlgorithmException |
                NoSuchPaddingException ex) {
            // Handle exceptions
        }
        System.out.println("Simple Echo Server Terminating");
    }
}
```

Upon the acceptance of a client connection IO, streams are established and an inputLine byte array is instantiated with a size of 171. This is the size of the message that is being sent, and using this value will avoid various exceptions:

```java
        try (DataInputStream in = new DataInputStream(
                clientSocket.getInputStream());
             PrintWriter out = new PrintWriter(
                    clientSocket.getOutputStream(), true);) {
            byte[] inputLine = new byte[171];
            ...
            }
        } catch (IOException ex) {
            // Handle exceptions
```

```
        } catch (Exception ex) {
            // Handle exceptions
        }
```

To perform the decryption, we need a private key. This is obtained using the
getPrivateKey method:

```
        PrivateKey privateKey =
            AsymmetricKeyUtility.getPrivateKey();
```

A while loop will read in an encrypted message from the client. The decrypt method is
called with the message and the private key. The decrypted message is then displayed
and sent back to the client. If the message was quit, then the server terminates:

```
        while (true) {
            int length = in.read(inputLine);
            String buffer = AsymmetricKeyUtility.decrypt(
                privateKey, inputLine);
            System.out.println(
                "Client request: " + buffer);

            if ("quit".equalsIgnoreCase(buffer)) {
                break;
            }
            out.println(buffer);
```

Now, let's examine the client application.

Asymmetric client application

The client application is found in the AsymmetricEchoClient class, as shown next.
It also possesses only a single main method. Once the server connection has been
made, IO streams are established:

```
    public class AsymmetricEchoClient {

        public static void main(String args[]) {
            System.out.println("Simple Echo Client");

            try (Socket clientSocket
                    = new Socket(InetAddress.getLocalHost(), 6000);
                DataOutputStream out = new DataOutputStream(
                        clientSocket.getOutputStream());
                BufferedReader br = new BufferedReader(
                        new InputStreamReader(
                            clientSocket.getInputStream())));
```

```
                    DataInputStream in = new DataInputStream(
                            clientSocket.getInputStream()))) {
                System.out.println("Connected to server");
                ...
            }
        } catch (IOException ex) {
            // Handle exceptions
        } catch (Exception ex) {
            // Handle exceptions
        }
    }
}
```

The Scanner class is used to get user input. A public key is used to encrypt the user messages and is obtained using the AsymmetricKeyUtility class's getPublicKey method:

```
Scanner scanner = new Scanner(System.in);
PublicKey publicKey =
    AsymmetricKeyUtility.getPublicKey();
```

In the following while loop, the user is prompted for a message, which is encrypted using the encrypt method. The encrypted message is then sent to the server. If the message was quit, then the program terminates:

```
while (true) {
    System.out.print("Enter text: ");
    String inputLine = scanner.nextLine();

    byte[] encodedData =
        AsymmetricKeyUtility.encrypt(
            publicKey, inputLine);
    System.out.println(encodedData);

    out.write(encodedData);
    if ("quit".equalsIgnoreCase(inputLine)) {
        break;
    }
    String message = br.readLine();
    System.out.println("Server response: " + message);
```

Now, we can use these applications together.

Asymmetric client/server in action

Start the server and then the client. The client will prompt for a series of messages. The following shows the output of one possible interchange. The server side is shown first:

Simple Echo Server

Waiting for connection.....

Connected to client

Client request: The first message

Client request: The second message

Client request: quit

Simple Echo Server Terminating

The following shows the client interaction:

Simple Echo Client

Connected to server

Enter text: The first message

[B@6bc168e5

Server response: The first message

Enter text: The second message

[B@7b3300e5

Server response: The second message

Enter text: quit

[B@2e5c649

TLS/SSL

TLS/SSL is a set of protocols that is used to secure many servers on the Internet. SSL is the successor to TLS. However, they are not always interchangeable. SSL uses the **Message Authentication Code (MAC)** algorithm, while TLS uses the **Hashing for Message Authentication Code (HMAC)** algorithm.

SSL is often used with a number of other protocols, including **File Transfer Protocol (FTP)**, Telnet, **Net News Transfer Protocol (NNTP)**, **Lightweight Directory Access Protocol (LDAP)**, and **Interactive Message Access Protocol (IMAP)**.

TLS/SSL does incur a performance hit in providing these capabilities. However, as internet speeds increase, the hit is not usually significant.

When the HTTPS protocol is used, a user will know because the protocol is normally present in the address field of a browser. It is even used in places where you may not expect it, such as in the following Google URL:

We will not delve into the details of how the SSL protocol works. However, a brief discussion of this protocol can be found at `http://www.javacodegeeks.com/2013/04/understanding-transport-layer-security-secure-socket-layer.html`. In this section, we will illustrate how to create and use an SSL server and the Java classes that are used to support this protocol.

To simplify the applications, the client sends a message to the server, which then displays it. No response is sent back to the client. The client connects to and communicates with the server using SSL. Returning the message to the client using SSL is left as an exercise for the reader.

SSL server

The server is implemented in the following `SSLServer` class. All of the code is found in the `main` method. We will use the `keystore.jks` keystore to access a secret key that was created in symmetric encryption techniques. To provide access to the keystore, a `Provider` instance is used to specify the keystore and its password. Hardcoding the password in code is not a good idea, but it is used to simplify this example:

```
public class SSLServer {

    public static void main(String[] args) throws Exception {
        System.out.println("SSL Server Started");
```

```
        Security.addProvider(new Provider());
        System.setProperty("javax.net.ssl.keyStore",
            "keystore.jks");
        System.setProperty("javax.net.ssl.keyStorePassword",
            "password");
        ...


    }


}
```

An instance of the SSLServerSocket class is used to establish communications between a client and a server. This instance is created using the SSLServerSocketFactory class's getDefault method. Similar to previous server sockets, the accept method blocks until a client connection is established:

```
SSLServerSocketFactory sslServerSocketfactory =
    (SSLServerSocketFactory)
    SSLServerSocketFactory.getDefault();
SSLServerSocket sslServerSocket = (SSLServerSocket)
        sslServerSocketfactory.createServerSocket(5000);
System.out.println("Waiting for a connection");
SSLSocket sslSocket =
    (SSLSocket) sslServerSocket.accept();
System.out.println("Connection established");
```

A BufferedReader instance is then created from the socket's output stream:

```
PrintWriter pw =
    new PrintWriter(sslSocket.getOutputStream(), true);
BufferedReader br = new BufferedReader(
    new InputStreamReader(sslSocket.getInputStream()));
```

The following while loop reads the client request and displays it. If the message is quit, then the server terminates:

```
String inputLine;
while ((inputLine = br.readLine()) != null) {
    pw.println(inputLine);
    if ("quit".equalsIgnoreCase(inputLine)) {
        break;
    }
    System.out.println("Receiving: " + inputLine);
}
```

The SSL socket automatically handles encryption and decryption.

 On a Mac, the server may throw exceptions when executed. This can be avoided by creating a PKCS12 keystore and using the `-Djavax.net.ssl.keyStoreType=pkcs12` VM option.

SSL client

The `SSLClient` class implements the client application, as shown next. It uses essentially the same process as the server. The while loop handles user input in the same way that was performed in previous client applications:

```java
public class SSLClient {

    public static void main(String[] args) throws Exception {
        System.out.println("SSL Client Started");
        Security.addProvider(new Provider());
        System.setProperty("javax.net.ssl.trustStore",
            "keystore.jks");
        System.setProperty("javax.net.ssl.trustStorePassword",
            "password");

        SSLSocketFactory sslsocketfactory = (SSLSocketFactory)
            SSLSocketFactory.getDefault();
        SSLSocket sslSocket = (SSLSocket)
            sslsocketfactory.createSocket("localhost", 5000);
        System.out.println(
            "Connection to SSL Server Established");

        PrintWriter pw =
            new PrintWriter(sslSocket.getOutputStream(), true);
        BufferedReader in = new BufferedReader(
            new InputStreamReader(sslSocket.getInputStream()));

        Scanner scanner = new Scanner(System.in);
        while (true) {
            System.out.print("Enter a message: ");
            String message = scanner.nextLine();
            pw.println(message);
            System.out.println("Sending: " + in.readLine());
            if ("quit".equalsIgnoreCase(message)) {
                break;
```

```
                    }
                }
                pw.close();
                in.close();
                sslSocket.close();
            }
        }
```

Let's see how they interact.

SSL client/server in action

Start the server and then the client. In the following output, three messages are sent to the server and then displayed:

SSL Server Started

Waiting for a connection

Connection established

Receiving: The first message

Receiving: The second message

The client input is shown here:

SSL Client Started

Connection to SSL Server Established

Enter a message: The first message

Sending: The first message

Enter a message: The second message

Sending: The second message

Enter a message: quit

Sending: quit

The SSLServerSocket class provides a simple way of implementing SSL-enabled servers.

Secure hash functions

A secure hash function will generate a large number, called the hash value, when given a document of some sort. This document can be of almost any type. We will be using simple strings in our examples.

The function is a one-way hash function, which means that it is effectively impossible to recreate the document when given a hash value. When used in conjunction with asymmetric keys, it allows the transmission of a document with the guarantee that the document has not been altered.

The sender of a document will use a secure hash function to generate the hash value for a document. The sender will encrypt this hash value with their private key. The document and the key are then combined and sent to a receiver. The document is not encrypted.

Upon receiving the document, the receiver will use the sender's public key to decrypt the hash value. The receiver will then use the same secure hash function against the document to obtain a hash value. If this hash value matches the decrypted hash value, then the receiver is guaranteed that the document has not been modified.

The intent is not to encrypt the document. While possible, this approach is useful when it is not important to hide the document from third parties but to only provide a guarantee that the document has not been modified.

Java supports the following hashing algorithms:

- **MD5**: The default size is 64 bytes
- **SHA1**: The default size is 64 bytes

We will use the SHA hash function for our examples. This series of functions was developed by the **National Security Agency (NSA)**. There are three versions of this hash function: SHA-0, SHA-1, and SHA-2. The SHA-2 is the more secure algorithm and uses variable digest sizes: SHA-224, SHA-256, SHA-384, and SHA-512.

The `MessageDigest` class works with arbitrary-sized data producing a fixed size hash value. There are no public constructors for this class. The `getInstance` method returns an instance of the class when given the name of the algorithm. Valid names are found at http://docs.oracle.com/javase/8/docs/technotes/guides/security/StandardNames.html#MessageDigest. In this example, we use SHA-256:

```
MessageDigest messageDigest =
    MessageDigest.getInstance("SHA-256");
messageDigest.update(message.getBytes());
```

The complete example, which is adapted from `http://www.mkyong.com/java/ java-sha-hashing-example/`, is shown next. The `displayHashValue` method extracts individual hash value bytes and converts them to a printable format:

```
public class SHAHashingExample {

    public static void main(String[] args) throws Exception {
        SHAHashingExample example = new SHAHashingExample();
        String message = "This is a simple text message";
        byte hashValue[] = example.getHashValue(message);
        example.displayHashValue(hashValue);
    }

    public void displayHashValue(byte hashValue[]) {
        StringBuilder builder = new StringBuilder();
        for (int i = 0; i < hashValue.length; i++) {
            builder.append(Integer.toString((hashValue[i] & 0xff)
                + 0x100, 16).substring(1));
        }
        System.out.println("Hash Value: " + builder.toString());
    }

    public byte[] getHashValue(String message) {
        try {
            MessageDigest messageDigest =
                MessageDigest.getInstance("SHA-256");
            messageDigest.update(message.getBytes());
            return messageDigest.digest();
        } catch (NoSuchAlgorithmException ex) {
            // Handle exceptions
        }
        return null;
    }
}
```

Execute the program. This will produce the following output:

Hash Value: 83c660972991049c25e6cad7a5600fc4d7c062c097b9a75c1c4f13238375c26c

A more detailed examination of secure hashing functions that are implemented in Java can be found at `http://howtodoinjava.com/2013/07/22/how-to-generate-secure-password-hash-md5-sha-pbkdf2-bcrypt-examples/`.

Summary

In this chapter, we introduced several Java approaches to secure communications between applications. We started with a brief introduction to security-related terms and followed the introduction with a more detailed discussion later.

There are two common encryption/decryption approaches that are used today. The first is symmetric key encryption, which uses a single key that is shared between the applications. This approach requires that the key be transmitted between the applications in a secure fashion.

The second approach uses asymmetric encryption. This technique uses a private and a public key. A message encrypted with one of these keys can be decrypted with the other key. Normally, the public key is distributed using a certificate from a trusted source. The holder of the private key needs to secure it so that no one else has access to it. The public key is freely shared with anyone who needs it.

Cryptographic keys are usually stored in a keystore that permit programmatic access to the keys. The keystore is created and maintained with the keytool application. We demonstrated the creation and use of a keystore in several of our applications. In addition, we used both a symmetric key and an asymmetric key pair to support an echo client/server application.

A more common way of creating secure clients and servers uses the `SSLServerSocket` class. This performs the automatic encryption and decryption of data based on a secret key found in a keystore. We demonstrated how the class can be used in a server and client application.

We also examined the use of secure hash functions. This technique allows unencrypted data to be transferred and guarantees that it has not been modified. An asymmetric key pair is used to encrypt the hash value. We provided a simple example of this process.

In the next chapter, we will investigate the various factors that affect the interaction between distributed applications.

9
Network Interoperability

Network interoperability refers to the ability of systems that differ in implementation technology to reliably and accurately interchange information. This means that the factors, such as the underlying hardware, operating system, and implementation language, may differ between platforms, yet they will not adversely affect the ability of these systems to communicate.

There are several factors that can impact interoperability. These range from low-level issues, such as the byte order that is used by primitive data types, to higher-level technologies, such as web services that largely hide much of their implementation details. In this chapter, we will explore many of these factors.

We start with a discussion of the byte order that is used to support primitive data types. This is fundamental to the transfer of data. Different byte orders will result in significant differences in how information is interpreted.

Next, we will discuss how Java applications can interact with applications that are written in different languages. These may be JVM-based languages or languages that are radically different from Java.

The fundamental network communication construct is the socket. This entity typically functions in a TCP/IP environment. We will demonstrate how Java sockets can interact with sockets that are written in different languages, specifically C#.

The most significant support for interoperability exists in the form of communications standards that are typified by web services. These applications support communication between disparate systems using standardized middleware. Much of the details of communication are hidden by these middleware implementations.

We will investigate the following interoperability topics:

- How Java handles byte order
- Interfacing with other languages
- Communicating with sockets
- Using middleware to achieve interoperability

So, let's start with a discussion of byte order and how it can impact interoperability.

Byte order in Java

There are two types of byte order: **big endian**, and **little endian**. These terms refer to the order that a multi-byte quantity is stored in memory. To illustrate this, consider how an integer is stored in memory. As an integer consists of 4 bytes, these bytes are assigned to a 4-byte region of memory. However, these bytes can be stored in different ways. Big endian places the most significant byte first, while little endian places the least significant byte first.

Consider the following declaration and initialization of an integer:

```
int number = 0x01234567;
```

In the following example, the four bytes of memory are shown using big endian, assuming that the integer has been allocated to address 1000:

Address	Byte
1000	01
1001	23
1002	45
1003	67

The following table shows how the integer will be stored using little endian:

Address	Byte
1000	67
1001	45
1002	23
1003	01

The endianness varies by machines in the following ways:

- Intel-based processors uses little endian
- ARM processors may use little endian or big endian
- Motorola 68K processors use big endian
- Motorola PowerPC use big endian
- Sun SPARK processors use big endian

Sending data, such as ASCII strings, is not an issue because these bytes are stored in consecutive order. For other data types, such as floats, and longs, it can be an issue.

If we need to know which representation the current machine supports, the `ByteOder` class in the `java.nio` package can determine the current byte order. The following statement will display the endianness for the current platform:

```
System.out.println(ByteOrder.nativeOrder());
```

For a Windows platform, it will display the following:

LITTLE_ENDIAN

The `DataOutputStream` class's methods automatically use big endian. The `ByteBuffer` class also uses big endian by default. However, as shown next, the order can be specified:

```
ByteBuffer buffer = ByteBuffer.allocate(4096);
System.out.println(buffer.order());
buffer.order(ByteOrder.LITTLE_ENDIAN);
System.out.println(buffer.order());
```

This will display the following:

BIG_ENDIAN

LITTLE_ENDIAN

Once established, other methods, such as the `slice` method, do not change the byte order that is used, as demonstrated here:

```
buffer.order(ByteOrder.LITTLE_ENDIAN);
ByteBuffer slice = buffer.slice();
System.out.println(buffer.order());
```

The output will be as follows:

LITTLE_ENDIAN

The endianness is normally handled automatically on a machine. However, when we transfer data between machines that use different endianness, we can have a problem. It is possible that the bytes transferred will be in the wrong order at their destination.

Networks typically use big endian, which is also known as **network byte order**. Any data sent through a socket should use big endian. When sending information between Java applications, the endianness is not normally an issue. However, the endianness is more significant when interacting with non-Java technologies.

Interfacing with other languages

Sometimes, it is necessary to access libraries that are written in a different language. While this is not exclusively a network issue, Java provides support in a number of ways. Direct interface with other languages does not take place across a network, but rather occurs on the same machine. We will briefly examine some of these interface issues.

If we are using another Java library, then we simply need to load the classes. If we need to interface with non-Java languages, then we can use the **Java Native Interface (JNI)** API or some other library. However, if this language is a JVM-based language, then the process is much easier.

Interfacing with JVM based languages

The **Java Virtual Machine (JVM)** executes Java byte codes. However, this is not the only language that uses a JVM. Other languages include the following ones:

- **Nashorn**: This uses JavaScript
- **Clojure**: This is a Lisp dialect
- **Groovy**: This is a scripting language
- **Scala**: This combines the object-oriented and functional programming approaches
- **JRuby**: This is the Java implementation of Ruby
- **Jthon**: This is the Java implementation of Python
- **Jacl**: This is the Java implementation of Tcl
- **TuProlog**: This is the Java-based implementation of Prolog

A more complete list of JVM-based languages can be found at `https://en.wikipedia.org/wiki/List_of_JVM_languages`. Using the same JVM base will facilitate the sharing of code and libraries. Often, it is possible to not only use libraries that were developed in a different JVM-based language, but to also derive from classes that were developed in different languages.

Many languages have been ported to JVM because it is easier to use the JVM than create multiple compilers or interpreters for different platforms. For example, Ruby and Python have JVM implementations for this reason. These languages can take advantage of the JVM's portability and its **Just-In-Time (JIT)** compilation process. In addition to this, the JVM has a large library of well-tested code to build upon.

Nashorn is a JavaScript engine that is built on top of the JVM and was added in Java 8. This allows JavaScript code to be readily integrated into a Java application. The following code sequence illustrates this process. An instance of the JavaScript engine is obtained and then JavaScript code is executed:

```
try {
    ScriptEngine engine =
        new ScriptEngineManager().getEngineByName("nashorn");
    engine.eval("print('Executing JavaScript code');");
} catch (ScriptException ex) {
    // Handle exceptions
}
```

The output of this sequence is as follows:

Executing JavaScript code

More sophisticated JavaScript processing is possible. More details about this technology can be found at `https://docs.oracle.com/javase/8/docs/technotes/guides/scripting/nashorn/`.

Interfacing with non-JVM languages

A common technique to access code in a different language is through the JNI API. This API provides a means of accessing C/C++ code. This approach is well documented and will not be demonstrated here. However, a good introduction to this API can be found at `http://www.ibm.com/developerworks/java/tutorials/j-jni/j-jni.html`.

It is possible to access .NET code from Java. One technique uses JNI to access C#. An example of how to access C++, managed C++, and C# code is found at `http://www.codeproject.com/Articles/13093/C-method-calls-within-a-Java-program`.

Communication through simple sockets

It is possible to transfer information between applications that are written in different languages using sockets. The socket concept is not unique to Java and has been implemented in many languages. As sockets work at the TCP/IP level, they can communicate without much effort.

The primary interoperability consideration concerns the data that is transmitted. Incompatibilities can occur when the internal representation of data differs significantly between two different languages. This may be due to the use of big endian versus little endian in how a data type is represented internally, and whether a particular data type even exists in another language. For example, in C there is no distinct Boolean data type. It is represented using an integer.

In this section, we will develop a server in Java and a client in C#. To demonstrate the use sockets, a string will be transferred between these two applications. We will find that transferring even a simple data type, such as strings, can be more difficult than it seems.

The Java server

The server is declared in the `JavaSocket` class, as shown next. It looks very similar to previous versions of the echo server that was developed in this book. A server socket is created and then blocks until the `accept` method returns with a socket connected to a client:

```java
public class JavaSocket {

    public static void main(String[] args) {
        System.out.println("Server Started");
        try (ServerSocket serverSocket = new ServerSocket(5000)) {
            Socket socket = serverSocket.accept();
            System.out.println("Client connection completed");
            ...
            socket.close();
        } catch (IOException ex) {
            // Handle exceptions
        }
        System.out.println("Server Terminated");
    }
}
```

The `Scanner` class is used to read messages that are sent from a client. A `PrintWriter` instance is used to reply to the client:

```
Scanner scanner =
    new Scanner(socket.getInputStream());
PrintWriter pw = new PrintWriter(
    socket.getOutputStream(), true);
```

The `nextLine` method retrieves a message, which is displayed and sent back to the client:

```
String message = scanner.nextLine();
System.out.println("Server received: " + message);
pw.println(message);
System.out.println("Server sent: " + message);
```

The server will then terminate.

Now, let's examine the C# application.

The C# client

The `CSharpClient` class, as shown next, implements the client. C# is similar in form and syntax to Java, though the class libraries are often different. We will not provide a detailed explanation of the code, but we will cover the important features of the application.

The `using` statement corresponds to the import statement in Java. Similar to Java, the first method to execute is the `Main` method. C# typically uses a different indention style and name convention than Java:

```
using System;
using System.Net;
using System.Net.Sockets;

namespace CSharpSocket
{
    class CSharpClient
    {
        public static void Main(string[] args)
        {
            Console.WriteLine("Client Started");
            ...
        }
    }
}
```

The IPEndPoint variable represents an Internet address, and the Socket class, as you may expect, represents a socket. The Connect method connects to the server:

```
IPEndPoint serverAddress =
    new IPEndPoint(IPAddress.Parse("127.0.0.1"), 5000);
Socket clientSocket =
    new Socket(AddressFamily.InterNetwork,
        SocketType.Stream, ProtocolType.Tcp);
clientSocket.Connect(serverAddress);
```

The Console class's Write method displays information in a command window. Here, the user is prompted for a message to send to the server. The ReadLine method reads in the user input:

```
Console.Write("Enter message: ");
String message = Console.ReadLine();
```

The Send method will transmit data to the server. However, it requires the data to be placed into a byte buffer, as shown next. The message and an appended carriage return/line feed character is encoded and inserted into the buffer. The appended character is needed so that the server can read the string correctly and know when the string is terminated:

```
byte[] messageBuffer;
messageBuffer = System.Text.Encoding.ASCII.GetBytes(
    message + "\n");
clientSocket.Send(messageBuffer);
```

The Receive method reads the server's response. Similar to the Send method, it requires a byte buffer. This buffer was created with a size of 32 bytes. This limits the size of the message, but we will discuss how to overcome this limitation shortly:

```
byte[] receiveBuffer = new byte[32];
clientSocket.Receive(receiveBuffer);
```

The receiving buffer is converted into a string and displayed. The beginning and closing brackets are used to clearly delineate the buffer:

```
String recievedMessage =
    System.Text.Encoding.ASCII.GetString(
        receiveBuffer);
Console.WriteLine("Client received: [" +
    recievedMessage + "]");
```

The socket is closed and the application terminates:

```
clientSocket.Close();
Console.WriteLine("Client Terminated");
```

The client/server in action

Start the server and then the client. The client's user will be prompted for a message. Enter a message. The message will be sent and the response will be displayed in the client window.

The server output is displayed here:

Server Started

Client connection completed

Server received: The message

Server sent: The message

Server Terminated

The client side appears as follows:

Client Started

Enter message: The message

Client received: [The message

> **]**

Client Terminated

Press any key to continue . . .

You will note that the received message is larger than expected. This is because the client's receive byte buffer was 32 bytes long. This implementation used a fixed-size buffer. As the size of the response from the server may not always be known, the buffer needs to be large enough to hold responses. A size of 32 was used to limit the server's output.

This limitation can be overcome in a number of ways. One approach appends a special character at the end of the string and then uses this marker to construct the response. Another approach sends the length of the response first, followed by the response. The receiving buffer can be allocated based on the response's length.

Sending a string is useful to transmit formatted information. For example, the message that was sent could have been an XML or JSON document. This will facilitate the transmission of more sophisticated content.

Interoperability through middleware

Network technologies have evolved considerably over the last 20 years. Low-level socket support provides the foundation for most of these technologies. However, they are hidden from the user through multiple layers of software. These layers are referred to as **middleware**.

Interoperability is achieved through middleware, such as JMI, SOAP, and JAX-WS—to mention a few. The Java EE edition is aimed primarily at supporting these middleware-type technologies. Java EE started with **servlets**, a Java application that was used to support web pages. It has evolved to include **Java Server Pages (JSP)** and eventually to **Faclets** both of which hide underlying Servlets.

These technologies are concerned with providing services to users whether they are a human at a browser or another application. The users are not necessarily aware of how the service is implemented. Communication is achieved through a number of different standards and data is frequently encapsulated in language neutral XML documents. Thus, a server and a client can be written in different languages and run in different execution environments promoting interoperability.

While there are a number of technologies that are available, there are two common approaches that are used: RESTful Web Services, and SOAP-based Web Services. **REpresentational State Transfer Web Services (RESTful Web Services)** use HTTP and the standard commands (PUT, POST, GET, DELETE) to support the distribution of web pages and other resources. Its intent is to simplify how these types of services can be created. The interaction between the client and the server is stateless. That is, what was previously processed will not affect how the current request will be handled.

SOAP-based Web Services uses the **Simple Object Access Protocol (SOAP)** to exchange structured information. It uses application layer protocols, such as HTTP, and SMTP, and communicates using XML. We will focus on JAX-RS.

The **Java API for RESTful Web Services (JAX-RS)** is an API supporting the development of RESTful services. It uses a series of annotations to map resources to Java implementations. To demonstrate how this technology works, we will create a simple RESTful application using NetBeans.

Creating a RESTful service

We will create the server first and then a simple console-based application to access the server. We will use NetBeans IDE 8.0.2 to develop this service. NetBeans can be downloaded from `https://netbeans.org/downloads/`. Choose the Java EE Edition.

Once NetBeans has been installed, start it and then create a new project from the **File | New Project...** menu item. This will bring up the **New Project** dialog box, as shown next. Select the **Java Web** category and the **Web Application** project. Then, select the **Next** button:

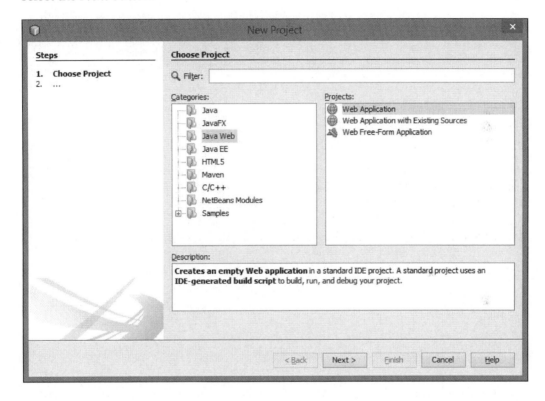

Give the project a name. In the following figure, we used `SimpleRestfulService` as its name. Choose an appropriate location to save the project and then select **Next**:

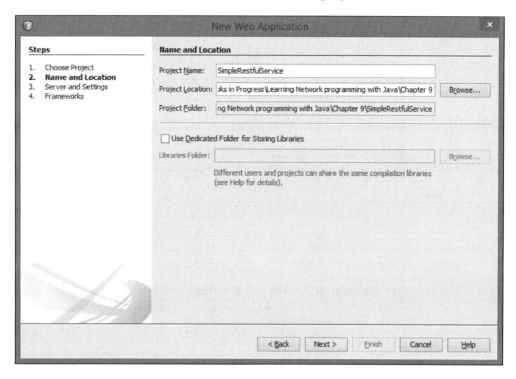

In the **Server and Settings** step, choose the GlassFish server and Java EE7 Web. GlassFish is a web server that we will use to host the service. The **Context Path** field will become part of the URL passed to the server. Click on **Next** again:

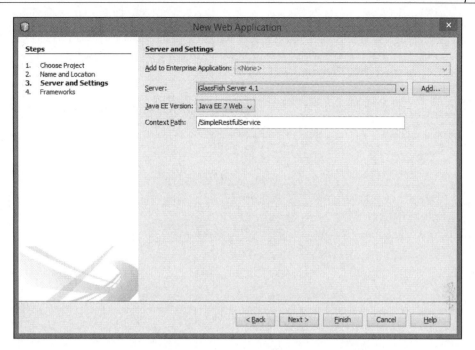

We can choose from one of three design patterns to create our RESTful service. For this example, choose the first one, **Simple Root Resource**, and then click on **Next**:

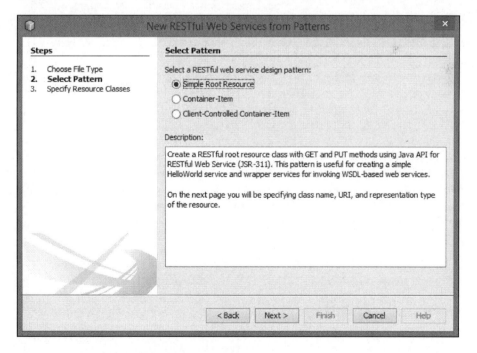

In the **Specify Resource Classes** step, complete the dialog box, as shown next. The resource package is where the Java classes will be placed. The path is used to identify the resource to the user. The class name field will be the name of the Java class supporting the resource. When done, click on **Finish**:

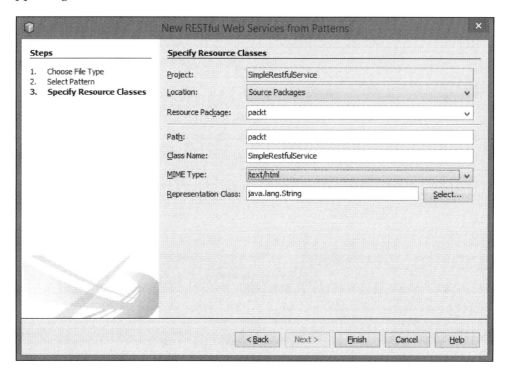

The IDE will then generate the files, including the ApplicationConfig.java and SimpleRestfulService.java files. The ApplicationConfig.java file is used to configure the service. Our main interest is the SimpleRestfulService.java file.

In the SimpleRestfulService class is the getHtml method, as duplicated next. Its purpose is to generate a response to the GET command. The first annotation designates this method as the method to call when the HTTP GET command is used. The second annotation specifies that the intended output of this method is HTML text. The return statement that is generated by the IDE has been replaced with a simple HTML response:

```
@GET
@Produces("text/html")
public String getHtml() {
    return
        "<html><body><h1>Hello, World!!</body></h1></html>";
}
```

When the service is requested with a GET command, the HTML text will be returned. All of the intermediate steps, including the use of sockets, are hidden, simplifying the development process.

Testing the RESTful service

We will develop a client application to access this resource. However, we can test the resource using built-in facilities. To test the service, right-click on the project's name in the **Project Explorer** window and select the **Test RESTful Web Services** menu item. This will bring up the following window. Click on **OK**:

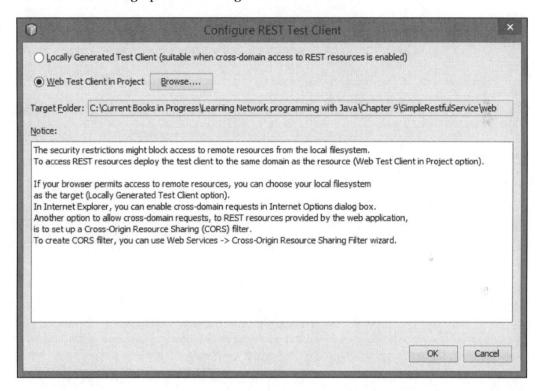

You may receive a security alert on Windows as follows. Select the **Allow access** button if this occurs:

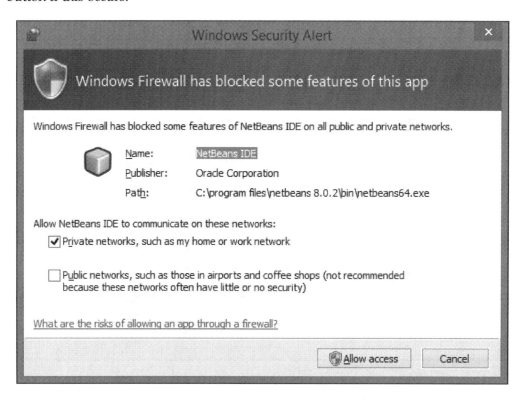

Your default browser will display the test page, as shown next. Select the **packt** node:

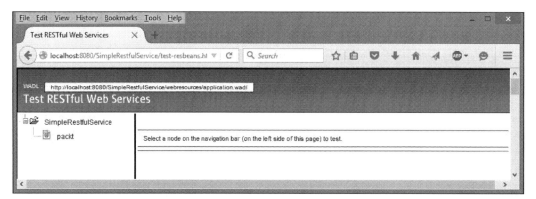

The resource will then appear on the right-hand side, as shown next. This allows us to select the test method. As the GET command has been chosen by default, click on the **Test** button:

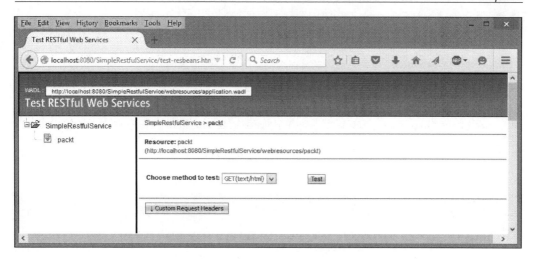

The GET command is then sent to the server and the response is displayed, as shown next.

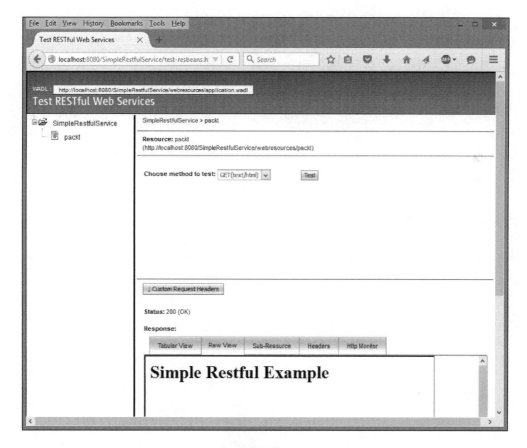

More sophisticated processing can be performed using JAX_RS. However, this illustrates the basic approach.

Creating a RESTful client

The RESTful service can be called by any number of applications that are written in various languages. Here, we will create a simple Java client to access this service.

Create a new project and select the **RESTful Java Client** option from the **Web Services** category, as shown next. Then click on **Next**:

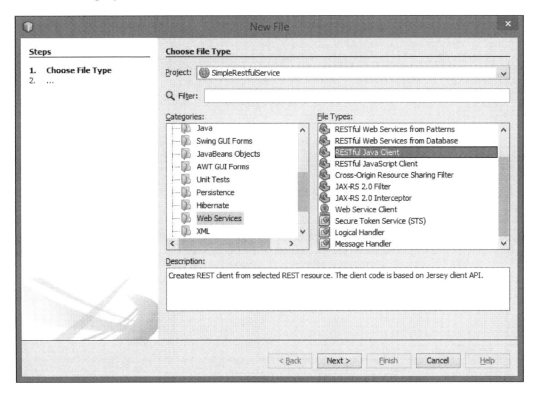

The **Name and Location** step dialog box will appear, as shown in the following screenshot. We need to select the RESTful resource. We can perform this by clicking on the **Browse...** button:

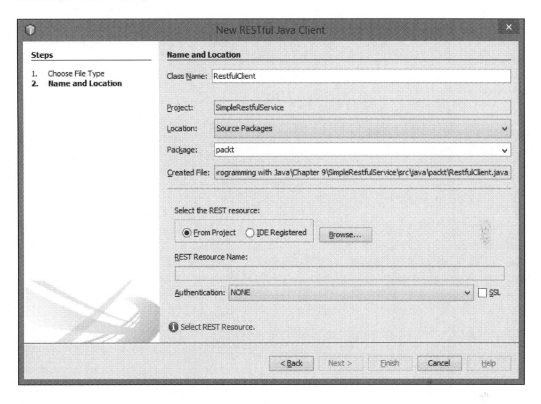

The **Available REST Resources** dialog will appear, as shown next. Expand our RESTful project and select the resource, as shown in the next screenshot, and then click on **OK**:

The completed dialog box should appear as follows. Click on **Finish**:

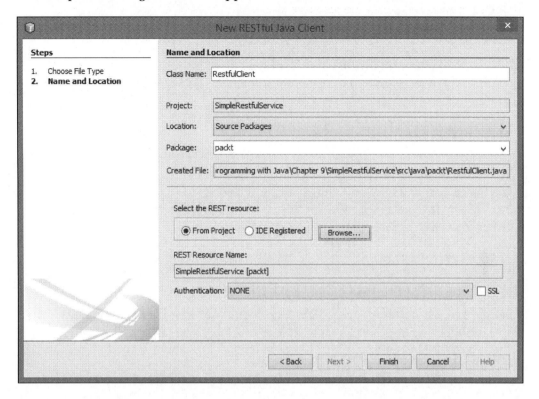

The RestfulClient class is then generated. We are interested in the getHtml method, as shown next. This will return the HTML text from the service:

```
public String getHtml() throws ClientErrorException {
    WebTarget resource = webTarget;
    return resource.
        request(javax.ws.rs.core.MediaType.TEXT_HTML).
        get(String.class);
}
```

To test the application, add the following main met`hod, which invokes the getHtml method:

```
public static void main(String[] args) {
    RestfulClient restfulClient = new RestfulClient();
    System.out.println(restfulClient.getHtml());
}
```

Make sure that the GlassFish server is running, and execute the program. The output will be as follows:

<html><body><h1>Simple Restful Example</body></h1></html>

While we will not normally display HTML text in a console, this illustrated the process that we use to obtain information from a RESTful service.

Summary

In this chapter, we explored many of the factors that impact network interoperability. At a low-level, the byte order becomes important. We learned that systems either use a big endian or a little endian byte order. The order can be determined and controlled by Java applications. Network communication normally uses big endian when transferring data.

If we need to communicate with other languages, we found that JVM-based languages are easier to work with because they share the same byte code base. If we need to work with other languages, then JNI is commonly used.

A socket is not a Java-unique concept. It normally is used in a TCP/IP environment, which implies that a socket that is written in one language can easily communicate with a socket that is written in a different language. We demonstrated this ability using a Java server and a C# client.

We also explored how middleware can support interoperability by abstracting much of the low-level communication detail. Using concepts, such as web services, we learned that the details of low-level socket interactions are hidden. We demonstrated this using JAX-RS, which supports a RESTful approach where HTTP commands, such as GET, and POST, are mapped to specific Java functionality.

Network interoperability is an important consideration in enterprise-level applications where the enterprise's functionality is distributed using various technologies. This interoperability is possible through the use of standard middleware protocols and products.

Index

H

hashing algorithms
about 202, 203
MD5 235
SHA1 235
Hashing for Message Authentication
Code (HMAC) 230
HelperMethods class
about 68
used, for handling variable length
messages 69, 70
host 29
HTTP client/server applications
HTTP client, building 100-102
HTTP server, building 96-99
with Java socket support 95
HttpExchange class
getRequestBody method 107
getRequestHeaders method 107
getRequestMethod method 107
getResponseBody method 107
getResponseHeaders method 107
sendResponseHeaders method 107
HTTP messages
client/server interaction example 95
format 91
headers lines 94
initial request line format 92, 93
message body 94
status code 93
URL, for methods 92
HTTP protocol
structure 89-91
HTTP proxy 116
HTTPServer class
implementing 108-111
response headers, managing 112, 113
URL 108
using 106-108
HttpServer executor
using 189, 190
HttpURLConnection class
URL, encoding 105, 106
using 102-105

HyperText Markup Language (HTML) 89
Hypertext Transfer Protocol (HTTP) 7

I

Inet4Address
about 49
IPv4, address types 50
IPv4, private addresses 50
Inet6Address class
about 52, 53
IPv6, private addresses 52
InetAddress class
and IP Addresses 45
isAnyLocalAddress method 47
isLinkLocalAddress method 47
isLoopbackAddress method 47
isMCGlobal method 48
isMCLinkLocal method 48
isMCNodeLocal method 48
isMCOrgLocal method 48
isMCSiteLocal method 48
isMulticastAddress method 48
isSiteLocalAddress method 48
used, for network addressing 3, 4
Interactive Message Access Protocol
(IMAP) 231
interfacing
with JVM based languages 243
with non-JVM languages 243
with other languages 242
Internet Assigned Numbers Authority
(IANA) 28
Internet of Things (IoT) 1
Internet Protocol (IP) address
about 2
and InetAddress class 45
information, obtaining 45, 46
IPv4-compatible IPv6 addresses,
using 54, 55
reachability, testing 48, 49
scoping issues 47
testing 53
Internet Service Providers (ISP) 28

V

view
  about 60
  using 85
VLAN Query Protocol (VQP) 141
Voice Over IP (VOIP) 32, 139

W

Wide Area Network (WAN) 37
World Wide Web (WWW) 89

Thank you for buying
Learning Network Programming with Java

About Packt Publishing

Packt, pronounced 'packed', published its first book, *Mastering phpMyAdmin for Effective MySQL Management*, in April 2004, and subsequently continued to specialize in publishing highly focused books on specific technologies and solutions.

Our books and publications share the experiences of your fellow IT professionals in adapting and customizing today's systems, applications, and frameworks. Our solution-based books give you the knowledge and power to customize the software and technologies you're using to get the job done. Packt books are more specific and less general than the IT books you have seen in the past. Our unique business model allows us to bring you more focused information, giving you more of what you need to know, and less of what you don't.

Packt is a modern yet unique publishing company that focuses on producing quality, cutting-edge books for communities of developers, administrators, and newbies alike. For more information, please visit our website at www.packtpub.com.

About Packt Open Source

In 2010, Packt launched two new brands, Packt Open Source and Packt Enterprise, in order to continue its focus on specialization. This book is part of the Packt Open Source brand, home to books published on software built around open source licenses, and offering information to anybody from advanced developers to budding web designers. The Open Source brand also runs Packt's Open Source Royalty Scheme, by which Packt gives a royalty to each open source project about whose software a book is sold.

Writing for Packt

We welcome all inquiries from people who are interested in authoring. Book proposals should be sent to author@packtpub.com. If your book idea is still at an early stage and you would like to discuss it first before writing a formal book proposal, then please contact us; one of our commissioning editors will get in touch with you.

We're not just looking for published authors; if you have strong technical skills but no writing experience, our experienced editors can help you develop a writing career, or simply get some additional reward for your expertise.

Boost.Asio C++ Network Programming

ISBN: 978-1-78216-326-8   Paperback: 156 pages

Enhance your skills with practical examples for C++ network programming

1. Augment your C++ network programming using Boost.Asio.

2. Discover how Boost.Asio handles synchronous and asynchronous programming models.

3. Practical examples of client/server applications.

4. Learn how to deal with threading when writing network applications.

Learning Python Network Programming

ISBN: 978-1-78439-600-8   Paperback: 320 pages

Utilize Python 3 to get network applications up and running quickly and easily

1. Leverage your Python programming skills to build powerful network applications.

2. Explore steps to interact with a wide range of network services.

3. Design multithreaded and event-driven architectures for echo and chat servers.

Please check **www.PacktPub.com** for information on our titles

iOS and OS X Network Programming Cookbook

ISBN: 978-1-84969-808-5   Paperback: 300 pages

Over 50 recipes to develop network applications in both the iOS and OS X environment

1. Use several Apple and third-party APIs to develop both server and client networked applications.

2. Shows you how to integrate all of the third-party libraries and APIs with your applications.

3. Includes sample projects for both iOS and OS X environments.

Boost.Asio C++ Network Programming

Second Edition

ISBN: 978-1-78528-307-9   Paperback: 200 pages

Learn effective C++ network programming with Boost.Asio and become a proficient C++ network programmer

1. Learn efficient C++ network programming with minimum coding using Boost.Asio.

2. Your one-stop destination to everything related to the Boost.Asio library.

3. Explore the fundamentals of networking to choose designs with more examples, and learn the basics of Boost.Asio.

Please check **www.PacktPub.com** for information on our titles

Made in the USA
San Bernardino, CA
07 January 2020